THE VAN SLYKE FAMILY IN AMERICA:
A Genealogy of Cornelis Antonissen Van Slyke 1604-1676
and his Mohawk wife Ots-Toch,
including the story of Jacques Hertel, 1603-1651,
Father of Ots-Toch and Interpreter to Samuel de Champlain.

Available from:

*Olive Tree Enterprises*
4931 Elliott Side Rd.
R.R.1
Midland ON
Canada
L4R 4K3
FAX: 705/534-2816
Internet: ote@rootsweb.com
Internet: lschulze@bconnex.net

ISBN: 0-9680-744-0-5

First Printing May 1996
Second Printing February 1997
Third Printing November 1997

## DEDICATION

To the memory of my father Cecil Norman McGinnis who, in his curiousity about his origins, inspired me to begin researching at an early age, and for my sons Sean Wilde and Tyler Schulze. This is the story of their ancestors, the people whose lives made it possible for them to exist. Without the past there is no present, nor can we build a future.

# PART ONE

## ANECDOTAL CHAPTERS

Pages 1 to 100

# CONTENTS

# INTRODUCTION

Several years ago, I discovered that one of my ninth great-grandmothers was Ots-Toch, or Alstock, a Mohawk woman born in the early 1600s in the Mohawk Valley of New York State. Ots-Toch had been born circa 1622 and later married Cornelis Van Slyke, a Dutch settler who was probably seventeen years her senior.

There were two accounts of Ots-Toch's heritage. One, that she was a full-blooded Mohawk and daughter of a sachem, or chief. The second story was that she was the daughter of a French trapper from Montreal named Jacques Hartell or Hertel. Both accounts were written of in various books, but which was correct? I immediately became intrigued and fascinated by Ots-Toch and her life, and decided to research further.

I found many references to both Ots-Toch and her husband Cornelis and her children. Cornelis himself was a well-known and respected interpreter for the tribes, even being chosen in 1650, as one of two ambassadors to the Mohawks. Cornelis also worked for Kilean Van Rensellaer, which meant that he was well-documented in court proceedings of the Rensellaerswyck area. I even found Cornelis buying children's mittens at an auction in Rensellaerswyck in 1658, a tiny tidbit of information which gave me a sense of him as a father for the first time.

After searching for more details regarding Ots-Toch and her heritage for two years, I finally, to my satisfaction, resolved the contradicting stories of her parentage. This book follows the line of descent from Ots-Toch's paternal grandfather down to her children, including my eighth great-grandfather, Jacques Cornelise Van Slyke, who was born and raised in the Mohawk castle (village) of Canajoharie and whose Mohawk name was It-sy-cho-sa-quash-ka. In later years, he became known as Akes Gautsch.

I found Ots-Toch and her children so fascinating, and discovered such a wealth of information about them, that I decided to write a book. It is my hope that Ots-Toch and her family will live again through our knowing them as people instead of merely names and dates of births and deaths.

In order to write this book, many people helped - either in words of encouragement, in sending me photocopies of primary source records, or in proofreading the chapters as I finished them. While I thank everyone who helped, I must thank some of them individually - Sandy Christie, Paddy Chitty and Tyler Schulze for proof-reading and offering suggestions for improvement; Sean Wilde for taking an active interest and helping to research Ots-Toch at the very beginning of my search; and Bryan Brown for his knowledge of and generousity in sharing Mohawk cultural traditions.

# Author's Direct Lineage from Antonis (Teunis) Van Slicht

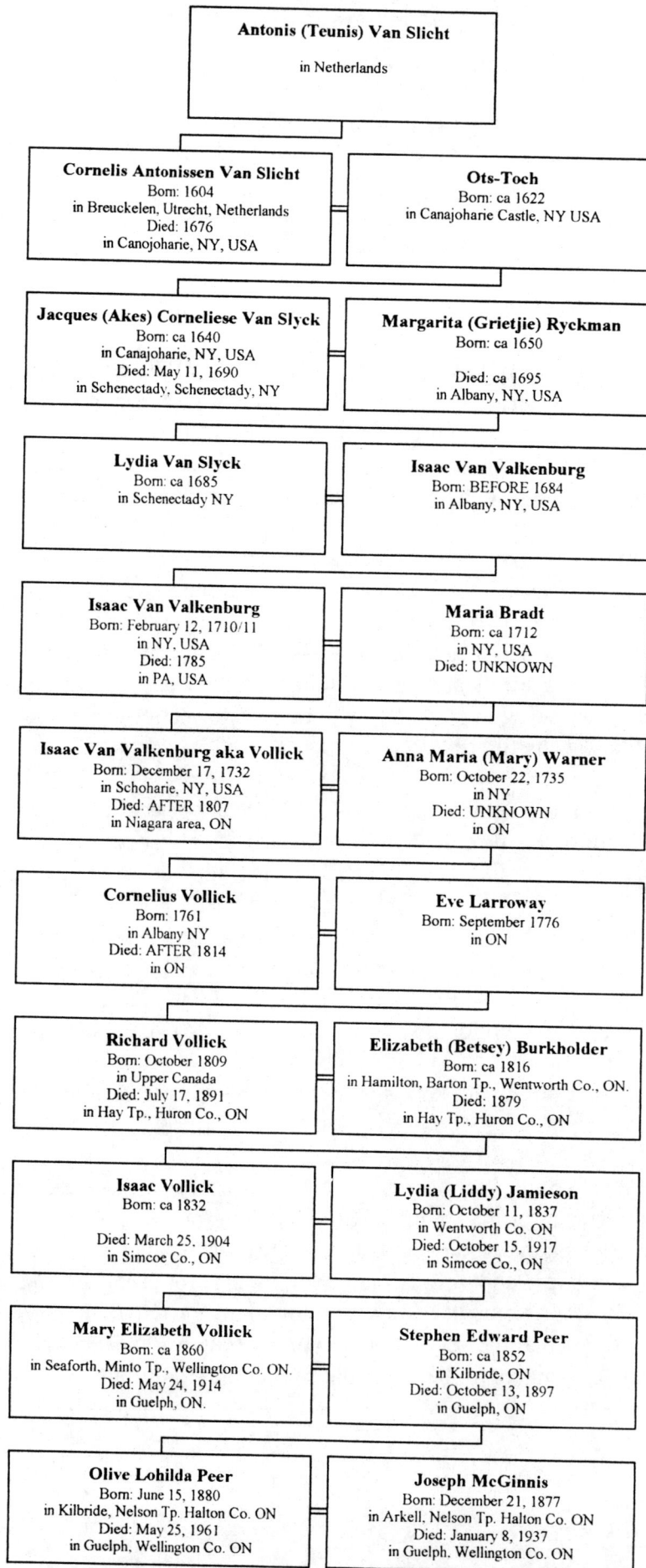

**Antonis (Teunis) Van Slicht**

in Netherlands

---

**Cornelis Antonissen Van Slicht**
Born: 1604
in Breuckelen, Utrecht, Netherlands
Died: 1676
in Canojoharie, NY, USA

**Ots-Toch**
Born: ca 1622
in Canajoharie Castle, NY USA

---

**Jacques (Akes) Corneliese Van Slyck**
Born: ca 1640
in Canajoharie, NY, USA
Died: May 11, 1690
in Schenectady, Schenectady, NY

**Margarita (Grietjie) Ryckman**
Born: ca 1650

Died: ca 1695
in Albany, NY, USA

---

**Lydia Van Slyck**
Born: ca 1685
in Schenectady NY

**Isaac Van Valkenburg**
Born: BEFORE 1684
in Albany, NY, USA

---

**Isaac Van Valkenburg**
Born: February 12, 1710/11
in NY, USA
Died: 1785
in PA, USA

**Maria Bradt**
Born: ca 1712
in NY, USA
Died: UNKNOWN

---

**Isaac Van Valkenburg aka Vollick**
Born: December 17, 1732
in Schoharie, NY, USA
Died: AFTER 1807
in Niagara area, ON

**Anna Maria (Mary) Warner**
Born: October 22, 1735
in NY
Died: UNKNOWN
in ON

---

**Cornelius Vollick**
Born: 1761
in Albany NY
Died: AFTER 1814
in ON

**Eve Larroway**
Born: September 1776
in ON

---

**Richard Vollick**
Born: October 1809
in Upper Canada
Died: July 17, 1891
in Hay Tp., Huron Co., ON

**Elizabeth (Betsey) Burkholder**
Born: ca 1816
in Hamilton, Barton Tp., Wentworth Co., ON.
Died: 1879
in Hay Tp., Huron Co., ON

---

**Isaac Vollick**
Born: ca 1832

Died: March 25, 1904
in Simcoe Co., ON

**Lydia (Liddy) Jamieson**
Born: October 11, 1837
in Wentworth Co. ON
Died: October 15, 1917
in Simcoe Co., ON

---

**Mary Elizabeth Vollick**
Born: ca 1860
in Seaforth, Minto Tp., Wellington Co. ON.
Died: May 24, 1914
in Guelph, ON.

**Stephen Edward Peer**
Born: ca 1852
in Kilbride, ON
Died: October 13, 1897
in Guelph, ON

---

**Olive Lohilda Peer**
Born: June 15, 1880
in Kilbride, Nelson Tp. Halton Co. ON
Died: May 25, 1961
in Guelph, Wellington Co. ON

**Joseph McGinnis**
Born: December 21, 1877
in Arkell, Nelson Tp. Halton Co. ON
Died: January 8, 1937
in Guelph, Wellington Co. ON

# GLOSSARY

Arquebus: a primitive rifle

Authorized Names: those names bestowed on the women of the forty-eight original Royaneh or noble families of the Iroquois League

Aum: An old Dutch and German unit of liquid capacity (as for wine) varying from 36 to 42 gallons.

Beverwyck: present-day Albany, New York First known as Fuyck.

Boslooper: woods runner, a person licensed to trade in the wilderness

Castle: Term used by the Dutch to refer to Mohawk settlements which were fortified. Castles were larger than villages, fortified with a palisade and located on hills above the Mohawk River. The Mohawk tribes had five original castles in the Mohawk Valley in 1630.

Donne: An unpaid, voluntary assistant to the Jesuits whose only remuneration was food and clothing, care during illness and support in old age

Duffel: a coarse woolen cloth with a thick nap, used as a trade item

Esopus: present-day Kingston, New York

Florin: a British coin, originally of silver, worth two shillings. The term can also refer to the Dutch coin called a guilder.

Galloon: thin braided silk ribbons used for edgings on dresses

Guilder: Abbreviation: gl. Dutch coin (now called a gulden) used in 17th century Dutch colonies of the New World. Six guilders equaled one English pound sterling. One day's work for a common labourer in New Netherland would earn one guilder.

Kill: Dutch word meaning stream or brook

Landgenoot: countryman or compatriot

Les Cents-Associes: The Company of One Hundred Associates, a fur trading company formed in the early 1620s by Cardinal Richelieu in France. This company was given control of New France, including all of North America from Spanish Florida to the Arctic. Its job was to bring settlers to New France (4000 over 15 years)

iii

Middle Traders: The Native tribes who were in the enviable position of trading furs with other tribes and the Europeans

Morgen: Dutch unit for an area of land equal to 2.1 acres by Rhineland measure and 2.06 acres by Amsterdam measure

Patronymic: System of identification of an individual using the father's first name and the predominant system used by the Dutch in the New World. The patronymic ending varies greatly, ranging from -sz, -szen, -sen, -se, all meaning "son of". A man who was the son of a man named Cornelis might use the patronymic Cornelisz, Corneliszen, Cornelisen, or Cornelise. Daughters might use the endings -x or -dr. (abreviation for *dochter* meaning daughter)

Patroon: A title used for individuals authorized to establish plantations or colonies in Dutch New Netherlands. The patroon system of ownership was equivalent to a landowner being a feudal lord over his tenants

Polder: an area of land reclaimed from the sea, and usually protected by dikes

Royaneh Families: Those families of the Iroquois nation considered noble. These were the female heirs of the Confederacy Lord titles

Sachem: A chief of a clan in a tribe. The Iroquois League had 50 life-appointed male sachems who were nominated by the headwoman of the sachem-producing lineages in each clan. A sachem could be deposed through impeachment proceedings initiated by his lineage's headwoman.

Scheppen: a magistrate who with others, heard all criminal and civil suits under the Dutch system

Schout: a sheriff. A schout investigated crimes and arrested individuals.

Seawan: form of currency used in the early colonies of North America where coinage was rare. Sometimes called wampum. In the early part of the 17th century there were two types of seawan - black and white, with white having more value. In 1661 one bunch of black seawan was valued at 42 - 9 florins (42 guilders 9 stivers) and one bunch of white at 67-9 florins.

Seigneury: system of landholding in New France where large parcels of land were given to seigneurs by Les Cents-Associes. In return for this land, the seigneurs were required to bring out settlers to farm it. Les Cents-Associes to encourage the growth of the colony.

Shallop: A common name applied to various sailing vessels.

Syndic: municipal officer appointed to conserve the rights of a community in New France.

Ville-Marie: Present day Montreal, Quebec, founded as a missionary outpost in 1642 by the Jesuits

Voorspraecke: representative

Wampum: See Seawan. Originally wampum referred to shell strings or belts which were used as tokens of leadership or nobility in the Iroquois Confederacy. By 1618 wampum was being used as an exchange medium.

Wiltwyck: present-day Kingston, New York. Also called Esopus prior to 1660.

# CHAPTER 1

## THE DUTCH IN THE NEW WORLD

Henry Hudson sailed on the *Halve Maen* and entered New York Bay in September 1609. Hudson traded for beaver and other pelts with the Natives he met near present-day Albany. With this opportunity for tax-free furs in the New World, Dutch merchants began to develop the fur trade in New Netherland, sending ships at the rate of one or more per year to trade on the Hudson River. In 1614, Fort Nassau, a fortified trading post, was built on an island near Albany. In 1621 the West India Company was chartered and given a monopoly of the fur trade in New Netherland. In 1624 three trading posts were established on the three rivers leading into the interior. One of these was Fort Orange (present-day Albany) constructed on the west bank of the Hudson River.

The Dutch at Fort Orange were in contact with local Algonquian-speaking tribes with whom they traded for furs. The Iroquois, especially the Mohawk tribe, were constantly disrupting that trade. Although instructed to avoid any involvement with native disputes, in 1626 the Dutch at Fort Orange sided with the Mahican against the Mohawk which led to the death of the Dutch commander and several soldiers at Fort Orange. After that the Dutch at Fort Orange refused to take sides and they soon found they could trade with both Algonquins and Iroquois tribes. During the 1620s and 1630s, the Dutch West India Company tried to control the fur trade in New Netherland and stop all private fur traders at Fort Orange and elsewhere in the colony. Kiliaen van Rensselaer instructed his settlers at the colony of Rensselaerswyck not to barter with the natives but official prohibitions were useless. By 1626 settlers at Fort Orange tried to outbid each other, and the Dutch West India Company, for furs.

In 1627 the New World was a wilderness in the developing stages of settlement. New France had only one hundred and seven people, Acadia had twenty, Virginia had two thousand, the Hudson River valley had about two hundred (mostly Dutch), New England's colonies of Plymouth and Salem had slightly over three hundred people and Newfoundland had one hundred. This was the world that awaited Cornelis Van Slyke, a carpenter and mason from Breuckelen Netherlands, on his arrival in New Netherland in 1634.

# CHAPTER 2

## CORNELIS ANTONISSEN VAN SLICHT, ALSO KNOWN AS BROER CORNELIS

In the early 1630s, a Dutchman named Van Rensselaer began to advertise for people to colonize his New World venture. Van Rensselaer envisioned the Patroon system of ownership with the landowner a feudal lord over his tenants. A tenant would be required to contract himself to the Patroon for a specified time, after which he could become an independent settler.

The colony of Rensselaerswyck was thus formed. By 1634, there were only twenty-six settlers living there. Rensselaerswyck lay in a wilderness surrounded by Mahicans on the east and Mohawks on the west.

Cornelis Antonissen Van Slijk from Breuckelen, [1] Netherlands, left the Netherlands in May 1634 from the Texel on board *De Endracht* and sailed to the New World. [2] He was a thirty year old carpenter and mason, and his skills were desirable in a new colony.

Cornelis had a brother, Pieterse Teunise, who does not appear to have come to the New World, although his brother's son, Willem Pieterse, did arrive in 1660 on *De Trouw*, being listed as Willem Pieterse from Amersfoort. Cornelis and his nephew Willem, also called Willem Neef, [3] were the two immigrant ancestors of the Van Slykes in North America. Willem's descendants settled below present-day Albany in Columbia County, while Cornelis settled first at Beverwyck, then Schenectady. [4] We also find an Elizabeth Van Slyke born circa 1640 married to Hendrick Cornelissen Van Buren, [5] who was born on 30 June 1637 on board the ship *Rensselaerswyck* as it sailed to the New World.[6] It is likely that Elizabeth Van Slyke was a sister to Willem Pieterse Neef, and therefore a

---

[1] Breuckelen lay 14 miles SSE of Amsterdam and 6 miles NW of Utrecht
[2] NWI: Settlers In Rensselaerswyck, 1630 to 1646: pp 28, 48 "Cornelis Antonissen Van Slyck, alias Broer Cornelissen, was the first patentee of Katskill, anno 1646. Van Slyck's island, opposite Schenectada [sic], was so called after one of his sons, Jacques, to whom it was granted 13th. Nov. 1662 by Director Stuyvesant
[3] Neef is the Dutch word for nephew
[4] GDS by Jonathan Pearson
[5] RRYJV: The Van Buren Lineage: 45
[6] Hendrick Cornelissen Van Buren was the son of Cornelis Maessen aka Cornelis Maessen van Buyrmalsen and his wife Catalyntje Martense, who was the sister of Jan Martense de Wever, aka Van Alsteyn. Jan Martense de Wever was the immigrant ancestor of the Van Alsteyn/Van Alstyne family in America.

niece to Cornelis Antonissen Van Slyke, but further research of this theory is left to others to pursue.

The Dutch patronymic system of naming indicates that Cornelis and his brother Pieter were the sons of a man named Antonis or Teunis. These sons would use the patronymic of Antonissen, Antonisz or Antonise. Teunissen, Teunisz or Teunise are the diminutive forms of Antonis with the patronymic ending applied, indicating "son of". Surnames were not commonly used before 1660, and individuals were distinguished from others of the same first name by their place of origin, their father's name, a physical characteristic, their occupation or a nickname.

The name Van Slijk means "coming from the village of Slijk". In old Dutch, the letters "y" and "ij" were used interchangeably and Slijk could be written as Slyk or Slyck. The earliest record found of the place name Slijck is from 25 March 1424 when Heer Wouter van Mijnden and van Ruwiel conveyed land "on Slijck in Maerssen" to two Utrecht convents. [7] It also emerged early as a last name when Splinter Egbertsz. van den Sliick placed his seal as a "landgenoot" of Galecop in 1441. [8]

The fact that Cornelis was using the surname Van Slicht in 1637 would indicate an established family name rather than a place of origin. In other words, if his family had lived near Slijk for centuries, the name may have been so firmly attached to his family that it became a family name early on.

Maerssen, now written as Maarssen is a town 13 km north of Utrecht, 2 km south of Breukelen (between Utrecht and Breukelen) and 20 km south from Amsterdam. It is the first place on the way from Utrecht to Amsterdam and is situated on the river De Vecht. One translation for the word "slijk" is muddy or dirty, and usually refers to water. The River Vecht, running through Breuckelen and Maarssen, is a muddy river which gives support to this area as the original homeland of the Van Slykes. Galecop is a polder just southwest of Utrecht not far from Maarssen. It is now part of the new city of Nieuwegein, which is situated just south of Utrecht.

The importance of Breukelen from a strategic point of view is shown by a number of castles along the river Vecht. Castles Gunterstein, Nijenrode and Oudaen offered the villagers of Breukelen protection but also attracted the tumult of war more than once. [9] Castle Nijenrode, the most important one, lies on the left bank of the river Vecht, just south of Breukelen. Nijenrode to Breukelen is a 10 to 15 minute walk. Cornelis must have visited this castle many times as a boy, perhaps even working on it as an adult.

[7] Rijks Archief Utrecht, KKK 1099 as found in NYG&BR April 1996
[8] 55 Gemeente Archief Utrecht, Bewaarde Archieven I, 1147 nr. 4 as found in NYG&BR April 1996
[9] Nijenrode University, Breukelen, Netherlands

# Breukelen in 1630

Brueckelen, the town Cornelis Van Slyke gave as his place of origin in the Netherlands, is the old spelling of a village now written as Breukelen. In 1139 it was known as Broclede, on a 1420 copy of a 12th century document the name was written Bruklede and in 1307 Broicleede. These names mean a 'lede' which is a dug watercourse, through or near a 'broek' or swampy lowland.

The resort area of the village of Breukelen in Utrecht extends back before the 1600s. In 838 Count Rothar gave the town of Breukelen to the Church of St. Pieter, Utrecht. From that moment, Breukelen belonged to the Church authorities of Utrecht.

It is situated in the Dutch province of Utrecht, between the towns of Utrecht and Amsterdam, 15 km from Utrecht. The village lies between the river Vecht and the Amsterdam-Rhine canal. The river was used by the Romans for shipping goods to the sea. West of the village is Kockengen, and Nieuwer Ter Aa; two quiet villages that also belong to the municipality of Breukelen. It is presently a beautiful sleepy tourist town of 13000 people.

Reproductions with permission of H. W. Kroodsma of Nijenrode University

The first Lord of Nijenrode was Splinter (1277), the third son of Gijsbrcht van Ruele, Lord of castle Ruwiel (situated between Breukelen and Nieuwer-ter-Aa). Is there a relationship between Splinter Egbertsz. van den Sliick of Galecop in 1441 and Splinter Gijsbrchtsz van Ruele? Splinter is not a common name in the Netherlands, leading to the intriguing notion that there may indeed be a relationship to be found in this family from the 13th. century, but this remains for others to research.

It is known that Breukelen was completely destroyed in 1488 during a war between Maximilian and Austria and the City of Utrecht. Castle Nijenrode itself was rebuilt several times, including 1632. We can imagine Cornelis, with his carpentry and masonry skills, involved in this rebuilding.

There is also a town called Slikkendam halfway between Breukelen and Leiden. Slikkendam is on the eastern end of a group of lakes with the collective name of Nieuwkoopse Plassen. There is also a town in the Netherlands called Slijk-Ewijk, south of Arnhem on the River Waal in the province of Gelderland, near the town of Nijmegen. In Zeeland (another province of The Netherlands) Slijk is a type of grass, and a common expression in Zeeland is "Geld is het slijk der aarde" (money is the Slijk of the earth). I offer these names as ideas for research for those who wish to pursue other avenues regarding the Van Slyke origins in Netherlands.

Although Cornelis used various names in official contracts and his name was often phonetically spelled by court officials, for the sake of clarity I have opted to use the name Cornelis Antonissen Van Slyke in the body of this book. However, it is important for researchers to be familiar with the variety of names used by Cornelis during his lifetime.

In his contract with Kiliaen van Rensselaer dated 2 April 1634, Cornelis signed his name Cornelis Antonissen van Slicht. Van Rensselaer, the patroon of the colony at Rensselaerswyck in New York, usually referred to Cornelis as Cornelis van Breuckelen, [10] meaning Cornelis from Breuckelen. He was often called Cornelis Teunissen, by his patronymic, and beginning in 1640, he began to be known by the name given him by the Mohawks - Broer (Brother) Cornelis. In some records he is found as Brodeur, which is Dutch for brother.

Eventually Cornelis' descendants took the surname Van Slyke, with the spelling variation of Slyck. Such an early official family name suggests a family of some position, and it is written that the Van Slyke silver with a crest of the rising sun is still in the Bastedo family, who married into the Van Slyke line. [11] The Van Slyke name is not a common one in present-day Netherlands, and a check of the Netherlands phone book

[10] BF
[11] Sketch of Bastedo Family by Laurabelle Lamb. 10 July 1947

reveals less than two dozen with the following spelling variations: Slijk, Van Slyke, Van Slijk, Van Slyken and Van Slijcken. .

Cornelis Van Slyke contracted to Kilean van Rensselaer as a carpenter and mason, but agreed to do farm work when necessary, for the fee of 180 florins a year. In the contract he signed on April 5, 1634 he stated he was 30 years of age. Contracts were usually drawn up for a two to six year period, with three years being the most common. The employer would pay passage money and provide bed and board in New Netherland. Farmhands received 100 to 150 gl. per year so we can see that Cornelis' skills were highly valued. But what did that 180 florins per year buy, remembering that one florin equaled one guilder? In 1639 a mare was sold for 200 gl., a shirt for 3 gl., a pair of farmer's shoes for 4 gl. and a pound of butter or pork 6 stuivers, with 20 stuivers equal to one guilder.

By August 12 1634 Cornelis was in the colony of Rensselaerswyck, and was working on a farm. The first settlers to Rensselaerswyck would have encountered vast forests in an undeveloped wilderness. The land they cleared was only a small break in the wilderness - there were no roads, few paths and no other nearby communities. However the soil was good for farming, wild berries, nuts, plums and grapes were plentiful, and game such as deer, turkey, swans, pigeons, partridge, pheasants, ducks and geese could be hunted for food. There were also fish to add variety to the early settler's diet. While the men hunted the women of the colony gathered berries, fruit and nuts and started small vegetable gardens. Sawmills were quickly started and pine was made available for the settler's houses.

Cornelis must have done a good job of farming because by 1636 he was plantation manager of a farm near Schuyler Flatts, where he worked until 1648. In one of the Patroon's letters, he mentions "the place of Broer Cornelis and the Great Flats together contain about 140 morgens according to the survey". The Great Flats was just north of Albany, New York. [12]

1639 saw several changes in the colony. Tobacco was grown and sold and the active but illegal fur trade was made less restrictive when Van Rensellaer allowed the settlers to trade if they sold all beaver furs to him and no one else. Before this he controlled the fur trade and collected all profits. A model for a church was proposed by Van Rensellaer, and he encouraged his settlers to cluster on the East banks of the river for safety.

From 1639 until 1641 Cornelis was one of three men appointed to manage the colony's affairs. Cornelis was appointed Voorspraecke or representative, in charge of keeping track of the goods received by the colony. By 1640 there was tremendous tension with other towns and the native tribes. Willem Kieft, the Director-General of New Netherland, attacked the Raritan tribe and although an uneasy peace was established, in 1642 the Raritans attacked Staten Island and war started. The Rensselaerswyck settlers

[12] F&FMC: p. 79

managed to maintain good terms with their Mohawk neighbours but natives on the outskirts of the colony were at war with each other.

By 1640 the Mohawks had depleted the beaver supply in their hunting areas, and failing to arrive at a peaceful trade agreement with the Hurons and other tribes to the north, they began sending out raiding parties north from the Mohawk River to take furs from anyone they encountered. It was during this unsettled period that Cornelis met and married his Mohawk wife, Ots-Toch.

In 1642 the colony was sent its first doctor - Abraham Staats who was an apprentice surgeon and not a graduate of the lengthy medical courses offered in the Netherlands. A minister, Dominie Megaplonsis arrived and preached the first sermon in Rensselaerswyck on August 17 in front of 100 settlers. A schoolmaster was appointed in 1648 and both girls and boys attended daily classes. The colony by this time had increased from 4 farms in 1632 to 18.

In 1643 Father Isaac Joques, a Jesuit, estimated the size of Rensselaerswyck as 100 people with 25 to 30 homes. Between 1643 and 1648 Cornelis spent much of his time at Manhattan, as interpreter and negotiator with the natives. His absence did not always sit well with the authorities, and the Secretary of Rensselaerswyck, Antony de Hooges, wrote to him in 1646 urging him to
"...come up the river to see how the harvest proceeds"
and hinted that he might at least come to the Colony once a year to look after his farm. [13]

Van Rensselaer was not happy with Cornelis by this time, and complained about his personal accounts and his service as representative, threatening to end their association if matters did not improve. He accused Cornelis of not writing often enough, not letting van Rensselaer know what the state of the finances was in the colony, and siding with the farmers instead of with the colony administrators, in disputes over fees and rents, . [14]

In 1644 Cornelis was given power of attorney from Jan Jansen Schepmoes in a legal case to collect Aeltje Claes' portion of her father's estate. Jan Jansen Schepmoes appeared as the guardian of Aelgjen Claes, surviving minor daughter of Marritjen Pieters, to appoint

"Cornelis Antonisz [15] residing in the colony of Renselaers Wyck [sic] to demand, collect and receive in his, the principal's, name from the heirs of the late Marritjen

[13] The Van Slyck Family in the New World by Ouida Nuhn Blanthorn, 1973
[14] BF by Peter R. Christoph 1994
[15] NYHMD:V 2:224,225: Cornelis Antonissen van Schlick, from Breuckelen. See Van Rensselaer Bowier Mss pp255-56, 809

Pieters [16] residing in the colony aforesaid, all such portion of the estate of the deceased Brant Pelen as is due to the above mentioned Aeltjen Claes."

In 1646 Cornelis was given a patent for a large tract of land in the Catskills by Director Kieft as part of his services in bringing about peace with the native tribes. This land became the town of Katskill (present-day Catskill).

".....On the East side of the North River, above Manhattan Island, in the summer of 1646, Adriaen Vander Donck established a patroonship, which is now represented by the town of Yonkers; and shortly after, Antonissen Van Slyke, of Breuckelen, received from Governor William Kieft as a reward for services rendered in concluding peace between the Dutch and the Native tribes, a patent for the land of Kaatskill on the North River, where he established a colony."[17]

Cornelis also owned land at Cohoes near the old Mohawk castle near the mouth of the Mohawk River, which had been granted to him by the Mohawks. [18] Cornelis was said to be a man of

"excellent character and unbending integrity"[19]

In 1647 Cornelis bought a partnership in the frigate *La Garce* with Harman Meyndersen van den Bogaert [20]. This ship was a privateer used to sail to the West Indies for the purpose of taking Spanish prizes.

"Transfer from Christiaen Pietersen Rams to Harmen Meyndertsen van den Bogaert and Cornelis Antonissen of his share in the frigate *La Garce*: This day, the 22nd of July [1647], before me, Cornelis van Tienhoven, secretary of New Netherland, appeared Christian Pitersen Rams, who in the presence of the undersigned witnesses convey and transfers as he does hereby, to and for the joint behoof of Harman Meyndersen van den Bogaert, commissary of Fort Orange, and Cornelis Antonisz, all his, the appearer's, rights and interest which he as a partner holds in the frigate *La Garce*. The sum paid in amounting to fourteen hundred guilders net. The aforesaid Christian Rams declares that he relinquishes his said interest henceforth and forever and therefore vests his title and interest as to the aforesaid share in the ship in the above mentioned Harmanus Bogardus and Cornelis Teunisz, who also accept the

[16] NYHMD:V2:224:Brant Pellen, from Nykerck on of the first settlers of Rensselaerswyck. See VRBMssL806
[17] A History of the City of Brooklyn, including the Old Town and Village of Brooklyn, the Town of Bushwick and the Village and City of Williamsburgh. Vol I by Henry R. STiles, 1867:p44; UCR
[18] ibid
[19] ibid:22
[20] Harmen Myndertsen Van den Bogaert was born in 1612, arriving in New Netherland on De Eendracht on May 24 1630. He was a barber-surgeon who in 1634 led a three man expedition into Mohawk Country. His journal of that trip is published under the title "A Journey Into Mohawk and Oneida Country 1634-1635"Harmen married Jelisje Claesen in 1640 and had four children before his death in 1647.

same and who shall bear the risk and enjoy the profit. Without fraud or deceit this is signed by Cristiaen Rams and the subscribing witnesses the day and year above written, in Fort Amsterdam in New Netherland. Signed Cristiaen Pietersen Rams. Witness Jacob H. Kip." [21]

On July 25 1647, Cornelis appears as a witness along with Jacob Kip, on a document called a power of attorney from Nicolaes Coorn to Claes Jansen Calff to collect money and an inheritance in Holland. The document was witnessed in Fort Amsterdam and Cornelis signed his name as Cornelis Anthonnisen van Schlick. [22]

In September 1650 tensions increased with the natives and rumours of an impending attack on Fort Orange by the Mohawks were rampant. The settlers at Rensselaerswyck were anxious so they decided to send Arent Van Curlar and four other trusted representatives into Mohawk country to renew old friendships and ensure peace.

On 23 September, 1650 Cornelis was one of four chosen with Arent van Curlar, to act as an ambassador to the Mohawks. He and Arent went on this important mission into what was called Maquas country. Their mission was successful and the colony could relax.

By this date, Cornelis had already formed his liaison with Ots-Toch, a Mohawk woman, [23] which produced at least four but possibly five children: Jacques, Marten, Hilletie and Lea, and Cornelis. If Cornelis was indeed a son, he may have died young, or remained among the Mohawk tribes, for nothing further is known of him. Marten predeceased his father, dying in 1662, leaving it is said, a Native wife and at least one child. This child could have been Wouter, the "full-blooded Mohawk" nephew living with Jacques Cornelise at Schenectady in the 1660s. Hilletie joined Jacques at Schenectady, and married another proprietor, Pieter Danielsen van Olinda, a former tailor turned farmer. Jacques and Hilletie occupied a very strategic position among the Dutch, English and Iroquois and became trusted interpreters for the province. Another sister, Lea, also an interpreter, married twice, to Claes Willemse van Coppernol and then to Jonathan Stevens.

In 1651 two farms, inventoried along with several others at Rensselaerswyck, were listed as used by Cornelis van Breuckelen and Cornelis Teunesse [sic] van Breuckelen. The first farm was 27 morgens, or 54 acres in size, with a value of 360 guilders, 7 horses and 11 cows and the comment "a fine farm". The second was 25.5 morgens, or 51 acres, valued at 600 guilders, with 10 horses and 9 cows.[24] Cornelis was charged rent on this farm until 1661, but did not always pay, claiming that he owned the

---

[21] NYHMD: V.II:437
[22] NYHMD: V.II:442
[23] GFSS: According to Pearson, her name was Alstock
[24] Van Rensselaer Bowier Manuscripts ed. by A.J.F. van Laer 1908, in MF:DCSNY

farm. When he left Rensselaerswyck in May 1661 he was charged back rent of over 4000 florin but he refused to pay.

A deposition made by Jean Labate to the Albany courts on 2 July 1688, stated that he and
"one Brier Cornelise who had an Indian Squae [sic] to his wife"
were sent by Governor Nicholls in 1665 to take possession of the Five-Nations territory for the English, which the Dutch had previously claimed.

Many settlers were not happy with the patroon system and in 1652 Beverwyck was formed from a portion of Rensselaerswyck. In the same year, a group of settlers left for the Esopus lands and formed the colony of Esopus. By 1655 tensions were once more high and the entire Hudson Valley south of Esopus was in danger of attack from the Hackensacks, Esopus and Tappan natives who were at war with settlements at Esopus. By now Cornelis' children are young teenagers, living in the Mohawk village but with their father in.Rensselaerswyck - caught between two worlds - white and native.

Cornelis Van Slyke is next heard of in November 1657 standing as a surety for Jan Janse Van Otterspoor in his offer to buy land from Johanna De Hulter. The contract is as follows:

"Madame Johanna de Hulter proposes to sell, at public sale, her pasture, as it stands in fence, except the garden stuff, which is thereon, and it shall be delivered on the 8th of November free and clear, the payment as before. After many offers, Jan Janse Van Otterspoor [25] remained the last bidder, for the pasture of Madam Johanna De Hulter, for the sum of eight hundred and eighty guilders, according to the aforesaid conditions, and Cornelis Teunisse [Antonisse] Van Slyke and Jurian Teunisse [Glazenmecker] stood as sureties, for the aforesaid sum, on pledge of their persons and estates, personal and real. Done in Beverwyck, the 7th. of November, A.D. 1657 in presence of Lowies Cobussen and Johannes Provoost. Signed Jan Jannsen, Cornelis Anthonissen [Van Slyke],[26] Jurryan Tunissen."

These various court documents give us a sense of Cornelis the man, active and involved in the affairs of Rensellaerswyck. However, we have no sense of him as Cornelis the husband and father, until in 1658 we find Cornelis with his neighbours in Rensellaerswyck, at an auction of Bastiaen de Winter's effects. [27] Here we have our first

[25] ERAR: V.1:58: There was a place at Manhattens on the est river called the Otterspoor, or The Otter Run
[26] ERAR: V.1:57,58. The footnote states that Cornelis Antonisse Van Slyck arrived in Albany in 16412, and was the first patentee of Catskill in 1645, given to him for emiment service rendered in bringing about a general peace and in ransoming prisoners in the hands of the Indians - O'Callaghan's History of New Netherland V.1:381. He had an Indian wife, by whom he had at least three childrenL Jacques, Marten and Hilletie. The former settled in Schenectady and left a large family ; the latter married Pieter Van Olinda and left descendants. Cornelis Antonissen Van Slyck was sometimes called Broer Cornelis.
[27] ERAR: Vol. 4 pp 78, 79

hint of Cornelis the family man, for he is buying a parcel of mittens at a cost of 5 florins. His youngest child, Lea, would have been about eleven or twelve years old.

This auction list gives us a tremendous insight into the harshness of life at that time - the things the settlers bought, such as used sheets or personal items that had been of course used by others, makes you realize how precious these items were, how luxurious to some, and how everything was recycled until it fell apart.

The list of those who bid successfully for items reads like a Who's Who of early Rensellaerswyck. We can imagine Cornelis at the auction, which was held on September 23, amidst a throng of friends and neighbours. Reading the list of purchases gives us an understanding of how valuable these commodities must have been in 1658, for many were obviously recycled. The entire list including purchases is presented below:

Volckert Janssen, candlestick, tongs, 2 pewter plates, 2 unbleached bed sheets, christening robe, a cloak, 2 fur caps, 10 Indian coats at various prices, a parcel of unfinished fur caps; Tryn Jochimsen, tongs and chain; Teeuwes Abrahamsen, pothook and pan; Claes Bever, 18 wooden plates and a kettle; Jan Tomassen, an iron pot; Jan van Eeckelen, [28] a salt cellar and pewter bowl, a parcel of laces, a parcel of mittens; Carsten Fredericksen, 4 pewter plates, two napkins, a piece of woolen cloth, a parcel of books; Barent the miller [29], a small copper pan, a dark lantern; Tomas Pouwell [30], a small copper pan and skimmer, 2 napkins, a chimney cloth and valance, 2 small Indian coats, 12 pairs of children's stockings; Abram Vosburgh [31], a parcel of earthen dinner plates; Jurriaen Teunissen, [32] a copper kettle, 2 handkerchiefs; Barent the smith [33], 2 napkins, a pillowcase; Willem Janssen Schutt, 2 napkins; Jan Harmsen Backer, a pillowcase, 3 Indian children's coats, a Bible; Caspar Jacobsen, 2 handkerchiefs; Poulus Dircksen, 3 unbleached bed sheets; Jacob Loockermans [34], 2 unbleached bed sheets; Jan van Aecken, 3 Indian children's coats, 5 fur caps, a pair of cloth stockings, an Indian coat, 6 pairs of mittens, a leather coat, and miscellany; Jacob Schermerhorn, curtains and sundries; Jan Tomassen, a Bible; Eldert Gerbertsen, some old silk stockings; Geertie Bouts, 3 pairs of Faroe stockings, 6 pairs of children's stockings, a child's shirt with two false sleeves; Mattheeus Abrahamsen, 3 cravets; Henderick Jochimsen, a sanitary girdle, a parcel of galloons and a cravat; Broer Cornelissen, a parcel of mittens; Mother Schaets, 12 pairs of children's stockings; la Montagne, 6 pairs of children's stockings.

[28] Jan Jansen van Eeckelen, a merchant in Beverwyck, married Gisseltie Albertse Bradt prior to May 1659. He died befoe March 23, 1668. His widow married Hendrick Willemsen. More information may be found in BF.
[29] Barent Pietersen Coeymans, the miller
[30] Thomas Powell
[31] Abraham Vosburgh born ca 1620 who was in Rensselaerswyck as early as 1649. He was killed by Esopus Indians in September 1659. His wife was Geertury Pieterse Cooeymans, who later married Albert Andriessen Bradt as his third wife. RRYJV: The Vosburg Lineage
[32] Jurriane Teunissen Tappan, a tavernkeeper
[33] Barent Reyndertsen, the smith
[34] Jacob Loockermans

Cornelis appears on a list of payments drawn up in August of 1659 for Dirck Dircksee Keyser:

"appeared before me Johannes La Montagen in the service of ... etc., in presence of the afternamed witnesses, Philip Pieterse Schuyler who declares that he has received of Dirck Dirckse Keyser, and taken for safe keeping, the following obligations for all which he is attorney.

Rutger Jacobsen, one of 33, and another of 32 beavers
Jurrian Teunisse [Glassmaker] an obligation of 22 beavers
Jan Verbeeck one ditto of 27 beavers
Pieter Adriaensen Soogemackelyck [35] one ditto amounting to 7 beavers
Anderien Herbertsen, an obligation of 28 beavers
Jacob Tyssen vander Heyder, one ditto of 16 1/2 beavers
Broer Cornelise [Antonissen Van Slyke] one ditto of 33 1/2 beavers
Henderick Bierman, one of 12 beavers
Geurt Hendrickse [Van Schoonhoven] one ditto of 3 beavers

Which foregoing obligations said Philip Pieterse, the subscriber, promises to restore again to the aforesaid Dirck Dirckse Keyser, or a settlement thereof to make as soon as he [Keyser] returns from the fatherland, for which he binds his persons and estate movable and immovable, present and future, putting the same in subjection to all laws and judges.

Done in Fort Orange, the 29th. of August A.D. 1659, in presence of Jan Barensen [Wemp] and Johannes Provoost, as witnesses hereto invited on this 29th. of August, A.D. 1659.
Signed Philip Pieterse Schuyler
Witnesses:
Jan Barensen
Johannes Provoost [36]"

We next have record of Cornelis in a bond of Isbrant Eldertsen to Adriaen Jansen Croon dated 17 August 1660:

"On this day, the 17th of August 1660, appeared before me, Dirck van Schelluyne, notary public, and before the hereinafter named witnesses, Isbrant Eldertsz, dwelling in the colony of Rensselaerswyck, who acknowledged that he was well and truly indebted to Adriaen Jansz Croon in the sum of thirty-two guilders of four good beavers reckoned at eight guilders apiece, growing out of the matter of wages earned of the subscriber to his satisfaction, which said four good beavers, he the subscriber,

[35] aka Pieter Adriaensen van Woggelum DSFN:21
[36] ERAR : V. 1 p. 33

13

promises to tender and pay to said Adriaen Jans Croon or order punctually in or before the month of July 1661, binding therefor his person and property, nothing excepted, subjecting the same to all courts and judges. Thus done and executed in the colony of Rensselaerswyck, in the presence of Mr. Cornelis van Breuckelen [Cornelis Van Slyke] and Claes Jacobsz, master carpenter, called as witnesses hereto. Signed Conre. van Schlick, Claes Jacobse [Claes Jacobsen Groesbeek, alias van Rotterdam]. This mark X was made by Isbrant Eldertsz aforenamed. Signed D. V. Schelluyne, Not. Pub. 1660" [37]

Cornelis appears to have been active and involved in the affairs of the colony, and on September 12, 1661 we find him on a list of obligations and accounts delivered by Jan Bastiaensz to Jeremias van Renselaer at Fort Orange. [38]

| | |
|---|---|
| Sander Leendertsz Glen | fl 9753-12-8 [39] |
| Eldert Gerbertsz Cruyff | fl 182-2 |
| Gerret Swart | fl 1470 |
| Willem Bout | fl 800 |
| Cornelise Cornelisz van Voorhout | fl 411-12 |
| Jan Thomasz | fl 712-2-4 |
| Anneke Bogardus | fl 391-1 [40] |
| Jacob Janse Flodder | fl 211-17 [41] |
| Henderick Reur | fl 280 |
| Teunis Dircksz van Vechten | fl 125-9 [42] |
| Henderick Jochgemsz | fl 138-6 |
| Claas van Rotterdam | fl 390 |
| Cornelis Teunisz van Slyck | fl 193-8 |
| Geertruy Andriesz | fl 213 [43] |
| Tomas Poulusz | fl 136 [44] |
| Philip de Brouwer | fl 416-18 [45] |

[37] ERAR V.3:29. A footnote to the bond states that the signature Corne. van Schlick refers to Cornelis Anthonissen Schlick, from Breuckelen and refers the reader to Van Renesselaer Bouvier Mss p. 255-56, 809
[38] ERAR: V. 3:pp 111, 112
[39] The Scotsman Alexander Glen, son of Leonard. He emigrated in 1639 as Sander Leeaerts and was married to Catalyn Donchessen, the sister of Margaret Donchessen who was the wife of Willem Teller. DSFM:19
[40] The famous Anneke Jans aka Webber, who married Roeloff Jans, then Everardus Bogardus. There is disagreement over whether or not Anneke is descended from royalty through William the Silent of the Netherlands
[41] aka Jacob Janse Gardenier. He came to the New World on *den Harinck* in 1638. His second wife was Barentie Straatsman, widow of Hans Coenraatse. SPL:53
[42] Teunis Dircksz aka Poentie emigrated in *Arms of Norway* in 1638 and settled at Greenbush, near Albany. EGNJ:548
[43] Geertruy Andriesen van Doesburch, widow of Jacob Jansen. Her first husband was Harry Albertsen from London.
[44] Thomas Powell
[45] Philip Hendricksen, the brewer

| | |
|---|---|
| Jan de Wever | fl 916-15-8 [46] |
| Thomas Clabbort | fl 289-4 [47] |
| Cornelis Teunisz Bos | fl 240 [48] |
| Meyndert de smit | fl 92 [49] |
| Jan Labatie | fl 210-1-8 [50] |
| Cornelis van Es | fl 144 [51] |
| Jan Roelofsz | fl 550-4 |
| Rutger Jacobsz | fl 835-12 [52] |
| Henderick Hierman, [53] Evert Noldingh | fl 1272 |
| Henderick Rooseboom | fl 644 |
| Meuwes Pietersz Hoochboom | fl 59-10 |
| Gerret van Slechtenhorst | fl 67-14 |
| Uldrick Cleyn | fl 78 |
| Evert Pels | fl 144 [54] |
| Hans de Nooreman | fl 40 [55] |
| Lodovicus Cobesz | fl 61 [56] |
| Lammert van Valckenburch | fl 41 [57] |
| Thomas Jans de Boer | fl 40 [58] |

[46] Jan Martensen, de Wever aka Van Alsteyn who was married to Dirckien Hermanse Boertgens. He is the author's 9th. great grandfather

[47] Thomas Chambers, aka Clabbort which was a corruption of the term clapboard. He was a carpenter and may have introduced the English method of weatherboarding houses with clapboards, hence the nickname. Thomas Chambers engaged 8 Esopus Indians on his farm in Sept. 1659. He gave them brandy as a reward for good service, the Indians became noisy and quarrelsome, and soldiers from the Fort were called. Thinking they were in danger, the soldiers fired and one Indian was killed. The Esopus Indians took revenge on the settlers and captured a party of 13 men. Thomas Chambers was one of them, as was Abraham Vosburg, Jacob Jansen Stoll aka Hab, Pieter Dircks, Evert Pel's son, and Lewies the Frenchman. Chambers was released and one soldier escaped. Six including Abraham Vosburg were killed. Pieter Lamertzen, a soldier, and Pieter Hillebrantzen a settler were freed by the efforts of Mahican Indians. Tradition states that Evert Pel's son refused to be exchanged or ransomed, and he married an Indian. RRYJV;

[48] aka Cornelis Theunissen Schoester or Kees Schoester from Westbroeck. He was in Rensellaerswyck in 1637. His trade may have been that of shoemaker. (schoester=shoemaker) SPL:52

[49] Myndert Fredericksen Van Iveren, the smith. This family took the surname Van Every

[50] aka Johan Labatie Fransman (Frenchman). He was a carpenter his first years in the colony and then an interpeter. SPL:51

[51] Cornelis Hendricksen Van Nes emigrated in 1641. He m1 Mayken Hendricks Van Der Burgh m2 Maritie Damen aka Maerrien Daeman. DSFN; NWI:29

[52] aka Rutger Jacobsz van Schoonderwoert. He m Tryntie Jans van Breestede. His children took the surname Rutgers and Rutsen. His brother Tuenes was the ancestor of the Van Woert family. SPL:51; DSFN

[53] Also referred to as Hendrick Biermans.

[54] from Steltyn. He was a brewer. NWI:28

[55] Hans Carelsen, Noorman (the Norwegian)

[56] Ludovicus Cobes married Alida aka Aetje Pieters, the illegitimate daughter of Maria De Trieux aka Truax, and Pieter Wolphersen. Maria De Trieux was a colourful figure in New Netherlands and those interested in her story will find a great deal written about her. *The House of Truax: Descendants of Philippe du Trieux, 1586-1653* edited by Howard S. F. Randolph, in NYGBR: Vol LVII 1926, Vol. LVIII 1927

[57] Lambert Jochemse Van Valkenburg, the author's 9th. great grandfather. He married Annetie Jacobs.

[58] This may be Thomas Jansen Mingael

| | |
|---|---|
| Harmen Bamboes | fl 56 [59] |
| Jaques [sic] Tyseñ | fl 20 |
| Harmen Bastejaensz | fl 32 |
| Jan van Hoesen | fl 53-18 [60] |
| Frans Jacobsz | fl 35-17 |
| Harmen Ryckman metselaer | fl 24 [61] |
| Sacharias Sickels | fl 48 [62] |
| Lucyas Pietersz Hout sager | fl 27 [63] |
| de maile Vries | fl 20 [64] |
| Willem Brouwer | fl 36-10 |
| Pieter Loockermans | fl 24 [65] |
| Teunis Jacobez Rierdrager | fl 10-5 [66] |
| Pieter Jacobsz Clacklayer | fl 16 [67] |
| Cornelis Segertsz | fl 21 [68] |
| Diederick van Hamel | fl 157-2 |
| Ariaen Appel | fl 310-19 |
| Thys de Goyer | fl 15 |
| Jannetie Hendericx | fl 10 [69] |
| Evert Wendel | fl 16 |
| Jacob Jansz van Nortstrant | fl 8 |
| Ysbrant Eldertsz | fl 75-2 |
| Willem Teller | fl 373-7 [70] |
| Domine Schaats | fl 116 [71] |
| Jan Helmsz | fl 58 |

We hear of Cornelis again in court on September 14, 1661. The deposition of Cornelis Gerritsen Graef relating to this follows:

"I, the undersigned, Cornelis de Graeff, declare at the request of Cornelis Theunisz van Breuckelen [Cornelis Van Slyke] that to my certain knowledge it is true that in

[59] Harmen Jacobsen Bamboes

[60] Jan Franse Van Hoesen died in 1703. He married Volkie Juriaansen. BF

[61] Harmen Jansen Ryckman, mason. He is the author's 9th. great grandfather. His wife's name is unknown

[62] Zacharias Sickels van Weenan . He married Anna Lambertse Van Valkenburg, the daughter of Lambert Jochemse Van Valkenburg and Annetie Jacobs. VVF

[63] Lucas Pietersen Coeymans, sawyer

[64] Literally means "the crazy Vries" and may refer to Adriaen Dircksen de Vries

[65] He married Marie Teller, sister of Willem Teller

[66] Teunis Jacobsen, beer carrier

[67] Pieter Jacobsen, bell ringer

[68] Cornelis Segers aka Van Egmond aka Van Voorhout. He married Bregie Jacobs. Cornelis was often in the courts of Rensellaerswyck. NWI:30; NFNY. There is a great deal of information about him in ERAR.

[69] Marten Hendricksen

[70] 1610-1701. He married Margaret Donchessen. VAF

[71] Gideon Schaats

the spring of the year 1659, the requirer [Van Breuckelen] granted to Andries Herbertsz (at his request) five acres of land to sow the same together with Philip Hendricxsz Brouwer and to enjoy the fruits thereof; for which Andries Herbertsz promised to pay the requirer for his part a half aum of brandy; all of which I am ready to confirm by oath if need be. In witness of the truth this is subscribed by me in Beverwyck in New Netherland, this 14th. of September 1661. Signed Cornelis Gerritsen Graef. In my presence, D. V. Schelluyne, Not. Pub. 1661"

It would appear that Cornelis' half aum of brandy had not been handed over as promised by Andries Herbertsz!

Valentine's Day of 1662 reveals the following bond of Cornelis to Carsten Claessen:

"On this day the 14th. of February, 1662, Cornelis Theunissz van Breuckele [sic] acknowledges that he is well and truly indebted to Carsten Claesz, master carpenter, in the quantity of ninety good, whole beavers in good friendship loaned and by him to his satisfaction received; which said ninety good, whole beavers he, van Breuckele, promises to pay to said Carsten Claesz or his [unreadable] in the month of July next, punctually, without longer delay, therefore binding his person and estate, nothing excepted, subject to all courts and judges. Done in the colony of Rensellaerswyck in New Netherlands, dated as above.

Signed C. T. v. Slicht"[72]

Although Cornelis was still at Rensellaerswyck, he and fourteen other men applied to Governor General Peter Stuyvesant for permission to purchase the Native lands at Schenectady on 18 July 1661. One of those men applying was Cornelis' son Jacques Cornelisse. On July 27 1661 a deed was drawn up between the Mohawks and Arent Van Curlar as representative of the settlers. These 15 men became the first permanent settlers at Schenectady and were known as the first fifteen proprietors.

At the time Schenectady was purchased, there was nothing between Canada and the site of Schenectady but forest, game and native tribes. It is believed that Jacques Cornelise Van Slyke, Alexander Lindsey Glen and John Teller were established there as early as 1658 with the blessings of the Mohawks. Once the land was deeded in 1661 the fifteen proprietors laid out the streets for their new village.

Cornelis was the seventh proprietor of Schenectady, and an early settler at Beverwyck. His original home was at Beverwyck but he spent most of his time with the Mohawks at their Upper castle at Canajoharie. [73] It was most likely here that he met Ots-Toch, the Mohawk woman with whom he formed a life-long liaison. Ots-Toch's

---

[72] ERAR: Vol. 3, p. 144
[73] HSCNY by Austin Yates, 1902

parentage has been the subject of two different stories, and she will be discussed in a chapter of her own. She was the mother of several children by Cornelis, and because of his relationship with Ots-Toch, he was adopted into the Mohawk tribe. [74] Yates states that Cornelis was one of two great interpreters of the Native language, the second being Arent Cornelise Viele. It was said that Cornelis Van Slyke could live anywhere among the Mohawks, whose loyalty and devotion followed the family for generations, with deeds of land to his sons Marten and Jacques Cornelise. [75]

The Mohawks had five castles or villages: Caughnawaga, Canajoharie situated near present-day Fonda, New York; Kanagaro, Monemias and Tionnongtoguen which was their principal village in terms of population and influence. The Dutch at Rensselaerswyck, Beverwyck and Schenectady were involved with three of these main villages.

The village of Schaenhechtede or Schenectady was first proposed by Arent van Curlar in the 1640s, but did not become a reality until the 1660s, when the Mohawk tribes consented to the founding of this new Dutch village.[76] The first settlers of Schenectady had, prior to its existence, been citizens of Beverwyck. In the spring of 1661 a small band of pioneers settled there. On 23 June 1662 van Curlar met with three Mohawk sachems, Cautugua from the Bear clan, Aladane from the Turtle clan and Sonareelsie who gave the village its name: Scounowee. In 1663 the lands were surveyed and then patented to fifteen people, one of whom was Cornelis Antonissen Van Slyke. [77] Yates tells us that the Mohawks began to have second thoughts about selling the land on the Groote Vlachte, which is where Schenectady was being built. They were devoted to Jacques Cornelissen Van Slyke and claimed that he owned the first flat and that much of what van Curlar had purchased belonged to Hilletie and Lea, sisters of Jacques Van Slyke. They further stated that van Curlar had bought only the grassy areas and not the land, and

"that is may be some drunken fellow may have made some writings without their knowledge" [78]

Schenectady's location was ideal for the fur trade. The deed signed by Arent van Curlar and the Mohawk sachems was the first acquisition of land by the Dutch from the Iroquois. Prior to this, the Dutch had only purchased land from the Mahican and other River Tribes, with the Mohawks consistently blocking all attempts by the Dutch to expand westward. [79] As a site for fur trade, Schenectady would benefit the Mohawks by providing easy water access to and from the their own villages, located only a day's journey away.

[74] ibid
[75] ibid
[76] MF
[77] GDS
[78] HSCNY:9
[79] MF

In 1650 Cornelis van Tienhoven reported that the first settlers of a community would dig a square pit in the ground, like a cellar, then raise a roof of spars and cover the spars with bark, "so that they can live dry and warm in these houses with their entire families for two, three or four years." Whether or not this is how Schenectady inhabitants built their first homes is not known, but it is noted that by 1663 dwelling houses and barns had been raised, lands planted, and farms stocked with animals. The lifeline for Schenectady was its cart road to and from Beverwyck.

Schenectady was a fortified village, protected by stockades. The stockade was a series of posts or logs, 15 to 18 feet long and one foot thick, sharpened at one end. After the line of the stockade was marked out, a trench three feet deep was dug. Then the poles were set in place and held fast by earth. At the angles, gates and other important points in the stockade, blockhouses for the garrison and the guards were built. Within the stockade was a free space called the rondweg, where the garrison marched. [80]

It is noted that the Dutch in Schenectady abused the Native tribes with whom they traded, and also directed hostility against any individuals of mixed blood, such as the Van Slykes, who lived among them. [81] Yet two of Cornelis and Ots-Toch's children, Hilliete and Jacques Cornelise, married within the Dutch community, and lived in Schenectady in 1680. They both held strategic positions among the Dutch, English and Iroquois and became trusted interpreters for the province. Although Cornelis and Ots-Toch did not have a formal marriage by a Christian minister, two of their children, who converted to Christianity, were able to live among and marry within the Dutch community. Tradition states that Cornelis and Ots-Toch were married in a Mohawk ceremony at Canajoharie, and it is known that Ots-Toch lived there with their children, as was in keeping with Mohawk custom, where a wife stayed with her family after marriage, bringing her husband to live with her.

Kilean van Rensselaer had warned his settlers not to mix with the Native tribes for fear of losing their Christian souls, and Jeremias van Rensselaer renewed this ban in 1652, nevertheless these prohibitions did not prevent many settlers, Cornelis among them, from forming liaisons with Mohawk women. Cornelis Van Slyke took no other woman as his wife, and remained faithful to his Mohawk wife, Ots-Toch, until he died in December 1676. [82]

Cornelis was extremely well respected and admired by both whites and natives and apparently had no enemies or anyone saying anything negative about him. He is written of as honest and admirable, upright and well respected. But then he was a white man living in a white man's world while his son Jacques was attempting to bridge a gap

[80]HSCNY
[81]ibid
[82]Deacons' Account Book of Dtuch Reformed Church of Albany

19

between white and native - one that was not always receptive to being bridged! That is likely the reason Jacques and his two sisters chose Schenectady to settle. If you look at the list of settlers, many of them had native ties or were men who lived by the land - trading and trapping, or those who simply were known to be rather eccentric. Schenectady was not as purely middle class as Albany - it was freer and more tolerant of those who were 'different'. But more on Jacques later.

# CHAPTER 3

## OTS-TOCH, THE MOHAWK WIFE OF CORNELIS ANTONISSEN VAN SLYKE

Little is known of the wife of Cornelis Van Slyke. Even her name, Ots-Toch, is clouded in controversy, with some writing it as Alstock. One word in the Mohawk language which may provide a clue to her name is "Otsihsto" meaning "the stars". "Otsihsto" is pronounced so that the sound is similar to "Asistock". It must be remembered that her name was recorded phonetically from verbal accounts and it is quite possible that Otsihsto is the correct interpretation of Ots-Toch's name. Her date of birth is unknown, although it is estimated as circa 1622. There is argument over her heritage and her parents.

There are two prevalent theories of Ots-Toch's heritage, one that she was a full-blooded Mohawk of the Turtle Clan, the daughter of a Mohawk chief or Sachem. [83] The second theory is that Ots-Toch was the daughter of a French trapper, Jacques Hertel and a full-blooded Mohawk Princess. [84] The use of the word "Princess" would imply that Ots-Toch's mother was the daughter of the Sachem or chief of her tribe.

According to Nelson Greene and other sources, Ots-Toch was "wild and savage like her mother". [85] Ouida Blanthorn, in her genealogy of Cornelis Van Slyck and his descendants written 1973, states that Ots-Toch was a "half-French, half-Indian maiden of compelling grace and beauty, whose mother was a Mohawk princess and whose father, Jacques Hartell [sic] was a French trader."

What was Ots-Toch's ancestry? Daughter of a French trapper or a Mohawk Sachem? Why not both? About the year 1622, a party of Frenchmen arrive at Canajoharie from New France. Perhaps they are on a diplomatic mission. Among them is a young interpreter, Jacques Hertel, who is about 19 years old. Jacques has apparently lived among another Iroquoian tribe (Huron possibly - a close linguistic cousin to the Iroquois) for several years, so he speaks the language and no doubt is familiar with the culture.

---

[83] National Association of the Van Valkenburg Family
[84] HSP; MV
[85] Vol. II:p.334

Jacques takes full advantage of the situation. Perhaps he is provided with a young Mohawk girl as a show of hospitality. Perhaps he merely takes advantage of the permissive Iroquoian sexual mores to have a more informal relationship with a Mohawk girl (or girls).    Anyway, it is doubtful that he stays long in the Mohawk village. His diplomatic mission completed, Jacques and his French party return to New France.

Nine months later, a Mohawk girl gives birth to a child with lighter skin tone and Caucasian features. She names her daughter Ots-Toch. Considering Jacques' probable age, it is likely that the mother is herself only in her teens, possibly 16 to 18 years old when Ots-Toch is born. There was apparently no particular stigma among the Iroquois for either the mother of an illegitimate child, or for the child herself. If she was herself merely a teenager, Ots-Toch's mother would soon seek a full time husband and a father for Ots-Toch. She may have married a promising young warrior, from a prominent family. Over a period of time, through a combination of war exploits, family connections, and wisdom in council, he gradually rises in prominence among the Mohawks. Eventually, he becomes a sachem. Now Ots-Toch has a step-father who is a Sachem of her tribe.

The troubled state of affairs between the Mohawks and the French would have prevented Jacques from visiting his Mohawk daughter, perhaps for years at a time. We do not  even have proof that he knew he had a daughter. He had probably returned to New France before Ots-Toch's mother realized she was pregnant. Perhaps he did not learn for years that he had a daughter at Canajoharie. As an interpreter/fur trader he probably led a semi-nomadic life, which (coupled with periods of hostility between the French and Iroquois) would mean that he might go years without seeing Ots-Toch.

Ots-Toch might then have a biological father (Jacques) but be raised by a Mohawk stepfather.  She might thus be described in some sources as being the daughter of Jacques, and by other writers as the daughter of a Mohawk sachem.

At this point an explanation of the Mohawks as members of the Iroquois Confederacy is in order. The Iroquois nation was a generic term applied to five (now six) closely related and politically unified tribes in central New York State. These tribes were organized into a league which they themselves referred to as Kayanerenth-Kowa, The Great Peace. The tribes, from east to west, were the Mohawks, Oneidas, Onondagas, Cayugas and Senecas. The name Iroquois comes from the Algonkian word Irinakhoiw, meaning Rattlesnakes. Some Algonkian tribes referred to them as Mingwes, Mingos, Nadowas, Maquas and Massawomekes. [86]

The original tribes of the Five Nations were :

Mohawk: People of the Flint
Onondaga: People on the Hills

[86] DCB: V. II p. xxxi

Seneca: Great Hill People
Oneida: Granite People
Cayuga: People of the Mucky Land

There were fourteen clans of the original Five Nations. The Turtle Clan was one of three within the Mohawk community, the other two being Bear and Wolf. Clan members were considered to be related and individuals were forbidden to marry within their own clan. Three chiefs represented each of the three Mohawk clans (Bear, Turtle and Wolf) The nine main Mohawk sachems were Dekarihokenh, Ayonhwathah (Hiawatha) and Shadekariwadeh of the Turtle Clan, Sharenhowaneh, Deyoenhegwenh and Orenregowah of the Wolf clan, and Dehennakarineh, Rastawenseronthah and Shoskoarowaneh who were Bear chiefs. The names of Mohawk sachems were traditional, and were passed down from generation to generation within the same matrilineal family.

Mohawk means "man-eater" and this name was given to the tribe by their Algonquian neighbours. The Mohawks called themselves Ganinengehaga or Kahniakehaka, meaning "people of the flint". The council of the Mohawk was divided into three parties, each consisting of three sachems. The duty of the sachems of the third party was simply to listen to the discussions of the first and second, in order to point out any errors. The Mohawks were appointed by Dekanawidah, the founder of the Confederacy, [87] as the heads and leaders of the Five Nations. Any question put to the Grand Council was first discussed by the Mohawks and Senecas, then by the Oneida and Cayuga Lords. [88] Their decisions were then turned over to the Onondaga Lords for final discussion and judgment. Being a Lord of the Confederacy was an honour, for these Lords or sachems were considered mentors of all their people for all time.

Mohawks in the early 1600's lived in five large villages called castles clustered on the banks of the Mohawk River within a small area just west of modern-day Albany, New York. The first castle was Monemias on an island at the mouth of the Mohawk River. The next was at Schenectady, the third at the outlet of Schoharie Creek (present-day Fort Hunter). Their fourth castle was Caughnawaga and their last was their upper and great castle called Canajoharie now in the town of Danube, Herkimer County, New York. [89]

Iroquoian villages were large (1500 -2000 people) and were surrounded by a log wall. Within the village, rows of longhouses stood in neat lines, far enough apart to prevent fire in one longhouse from spreading to another. Longhouses were about 25-30 feet wide (archeologists suspect that the building materials and techniques available put a practical limit on width) but could be 100 to 200 feet long. Anywhere from 30 to 100 people might live in a longhouse. All of them were related through the mothers. When a

[87] Dekanawidah was born near the Bay of Quinte in what is now southeastern Ontario, Canada. He established the Iroquois Confederacy prior to 1500.
[88] Shell or wampum beads two spans in length were given to each of the female familes in which Lordhsip titles were vested. The right of title was hereditary in those families owning the wampum strings.
[89] EHS

23

man married, he went to live with his wife's family. The women of the longhouse were either sisters or else cousins through a female ancestor.

The Iroquois considered the longhouse an important social institution, and a group home. The organization of the community into longhouses based on matrilineal descent is reflected in Iroquoian kinship terminology. A child addressed his mother's sisters (who lived in the same longhouse) as mother but father's sisters (who lived in another longhouse) were aunts. First cousins through the female line (who lived in the same longhouse) were brothers and sisters while those through a male ancestor were cousins.

Mohawk clothing styles underwent great changes in the late 1600's and early 1700's, with the availability of beads and trade cloth from European sources. In summer, children of both sexes who were less than three years old went naked. Older boys and men wore a loincloth. Women and older girls wore a wrap around knee-length skirt which extended to the knees and nothing above the waist. Around the village, everyone went barefoot in warm weather sincedeer skin moccasin soles wear out through heavy use. Away from the village, moccasins would be worn. A man or a boy would sometimes were leggings when away from the village, which were two tubes of deerskin that covered the ankles to the hips on each leg, worn to protect the legs from thorns, poison ivy, and other dangers. Women and girls also wore leggings, but since their skirts protected the upper legs, their leggings just extended to the knee, and tied off above the knee.

We know relatively little about their winter attire. The Jesuits mentioned mittens of fur, fur-lined moccasins insulated with dried grass, and fur caps. Both sexes were fur lined, full length robes.

Girls wore their hair long and loose. Women favoured long hair worn loose. When a boy was about 15, he began to pluck his hair except for a strip down the middle, which was greased to stick up. This is the famous Mohawk hairdo. An older boy or adult male wore his hair in a Mohawk until he was past the age for participation in warfare. Men plucked their beard. Both sexes removed any hair on their bodies below the neck.

Both sexes had their ears pierced in infancy or early childhood. Small beads of clay, copper or bone were used as ear ornaments. Other ornaments (necklaces, armbands etc.) seem primarily to have been worn for formal occasions. Paint was worn on such occassions.

The Mohawk were primarily agricultural peoples. They planted extensive gardens around their villages. The three main crops (corn, beans, and squash) were called the "three sisters" due to their important role in sustaining the life of the Iroquois. Other crops included artichokes, pumpkins, sunflowers (for the seeds and the oil) tobacco, and various herbal plants grown in small quantities for teas or medicines. Growing crops was almost exclusively the work of women and girls.

Wild plants contributed only a small percentage of the diet, but the Iroquois were familiar with a number of edible nuts, tubers and berries which added variety to the diet. Men and boys, finding berries in the woods, would eat their fill but would not collect plant foods for others. This was women's work. Women and girls would take baskets and collect the berries to take back to the village for all to share. Most cooking seems to have consisted of soups or stews containing whatever happened to be available which was cooked and served on wooden plates with wooden spoons. Their food sources led to a definite annual cycle to the Iroquois.

From November to February everyone was cooped up in the village. This was the season for merrymaking, games, storytelling and conversation. Those natives wanting to make new tools/weapons may put the materials aside in summer to have something to do in winter.

March was spawning season. Most of the Indians (except the young, sick or old) would leave the village and break up into smaller fishing camps of 100-200 people. Everyone filled themselves on fish at the fishing camp. Besides the actual work of fishing, thousands of fish had to be cleaned, then smoked. Wood had to be gathered for the smoking. Small groups of people would leave the fishing camps with baskets of smoked fish, trot back to the village (20 miles or so carrying 40-50 pounds), spend the night at home, then come back to the fishing area. When the fishing camp broke up around the first of April they often had to make several round trips to take all the smoked fish home.

April to September was the time for planting and tending the crops and this kept the women and girls close to home. Men and boys bring in a trickle of fresh fish or fresh meat from brief hunting and fishing expeditions. This was also the season for commerce with any other tribes with which the Mohawks were at peace, and for war with their enemies. Hunting took place in small groups who stalked deer, rabbit, squirrel, or other small game (occasionally, men went after moose or bear). Fishing involved hooks and lines or wading into the river and spearing the fish.

October was the month to hunt the deer which had grown fat, making their fur best before winter. This was the main hunting season. Most of the population left the main village to go to temporary hunting camps. Deer would be herded toward waiting archers by lines of women and children beating the brush with sticks. The rest of the time was spent dressing the deer, gathering wood, and smoking the meat. By the first of November everyone had returned to the village before the real cold weather set in. This is the life that Ots-Toch and her children lived.

The most important (and longest) ritual was the Mid-Winter Ceremony. It was held in mid-January, and apparently was a major relief for people who had been cooped up in their longhouses for days. The ceremony lasted less than five days. Its major components included a dream guessing game, a gambling game which involved two clans playing against each other, taking turns tossing beans or seeds, and children going door to door begging for maple sugar candy.

The remaining Iroquoian ceremonies were calendrical ceremonies, which is typical of a primitive agricultural society. They all were fairly short, lasting perhaps several hours. The format was similar. First a sachem made a preliminary speech invoking whichever spirit was being honoured and explaining the purpose of the ritual. This is called a Thanksgiving Speech. We can visualize Ost-Toch as a child listening to her Mohawk step-father addressing the assembled community. Next comes a tobacco blessing, then a ritual dance associated with this particular ceremony, a feast, social dances for fun and a concluding Thanksgiving speech by the sachem.

The other major calendrical ceremonies were the Maple ceremony held when the sap ran, Sun Ceremony performed on the first warm day of spring, Thunder Ceremony performed at the first thunderstorm of spring, Seed planting, Bean harvest, New Corn, Green Corn and Corn Harvest.

False faces are frequently associated with the Iroquois. They were the most prominent of a number of curing societies and anyone who felt a need (frequently expressed in a dream) for a cure by the false faces would request the society to perform a ritual in his longhouse.

The rituals were very short. A team of false face members (wearing their masks and thus impersonating spirits) would enter the longhouse, sealing the doors. No one was allowed to enter during the ritual, else the ritual would be ruined and must be performed again. After a short dance, the false faces leave (with the patient believing he has been cured). The Iroquois also relied upon healers who used herbal remedies (some of which seem to have been beneficial...willow bark was used to treat fevers, and contains the same substance found in aspirin), set broken bones skillfully and even performed minor surgery. They were probably at least as good as the European doctors of the era. [90]

The Iroquois had an ill-deserved reputation for being warlike. This was due to two factors - fighting the French and a period from about 1645 to about 1680 when they were much more warlike than normal. They were not out to destroy other tribes and in fact were no more warlike though than their Iroquoian neighbours (like the Huron) and only somewhat more warlike than their Algonquoian neighbors. Prior to 1645, the Iroquois lived in close proximity to the Huron, the Wenro, the Neutral, the Conestoga, the Petun, the Erie, and the Susquahanna, and had lived close to them for generations. Within a generation or so, all these tribes were destroyed, scattered, or subjugated.

Prior to the coming of the whites, Indian warfare had been chronic but relatively low tempo. There was nothing to gain by destroying a neighbouring tribe. Doing so would entail such casualties to one's own tribe that it would expose you to attack.

---

[90] Bryan Brown

Warfare was a bloody "sport" which killed a few people every year, but never escalated to the tempo of mass destruction.

Then the white settlers arrived. They introduced diseases and some tribes were hit worse than others. These diseases destroyed a balance of power between tribes which had existed for generations. Whites introduced guns which were a more efficient way to kill. Whites also introduced a motive for wars of mass destruction.

The motive was beaver. More specifically, beaver fur which could be traded for European trade goods. The most important trade goods was guns. The tribes got in an arms race in which to survive and maintain power, they had to have more guns. This meant trading more beaver. Guns were used to seize territory from a neighbour, depriving him of his beaver and increasing one's own supply of beaver. This meant more guns and then more aggression.

So the opportunity for the Beaver Wars (disease and guns) plus the motive (control of the beaver trade) were both provided by white contact. So a situation where endemic low tempo warfare was a fact of life rapidly escalated it into a frenzy of killing.

The Iroquois' other ill-deserved reputation was for torturing prisoners. The Iroquois shared this practice with most other Eastern Woodlands tribes. During the Beaver Wars era, wholesale adoptions of all prisoners occurred to make up for massive battle losses, but the evidence is that prior to the Beaver Wars, most adult captives of both sexes (and teenage boys) were routinely executed, while children and teenage girls were incorporated into the tribe. It would seem that even during the relatively peaceful period before the Beaver Wars, torture was a practice that would have been very common in a Mohawk village, probably happening as often as several times a year, and sometimes involving multiple prisoners.

Torture involved an elaborate human sacrifice ritual to the sun and the god of war. The tribes believed that one who died bravely would be honoured with special status and happiness in the afterlife. The prisoner sometimes went through a pseudo-adoption into the tribe before execution (so that, symbolically, they were executing one of their own) and was the guest of honor at the war party's victory celebrations prior to execution. [91]

As early as the 1630s, smallpox had reduced the Mohawk's population and the trade wars of the 1640s and afterwards took a heavy toll on the male members of Iroquois society. During the 1660s the tribe had as many as 500 warriors but by 1698 the figure had been lowered to 110. By 1671 two of the Mohawk castles had been abandoned, and in that year Caughnawaga Castle inhabitants left and settled near Montreal. Only their lower castle at the mouth of the Schoharie Creek and the upper castle at Canajoharie remained. Ots-Toch therefore watched her tribe diminish in her lifetime.

[91] Bryan Brown

Reid states that Cornelis Antonisse Van Slyke, alias Broer Cornelis, married a Mohawk woman and later refers to two of their children (Jacques and Hilletie) as half-breeds. He does not mention Ots-Toch by name but to some readers the term "half-breed" would indicate that the mother was full-blooded. [92] After much research into Ots-Toch and the times she lived in, I have concluded that the use of the term half-breed was simply one of convenience and may have referred to any individual with any amount of native blood.

Sanders tells us that Jacques and Martin Van Slyke's mother was a Mohawk chieftain's daughter from Canajoharie Castle.

Pearson also has references to Jacques Cornelise Van Slyke as half-breed, an "indyan" or as having received land from the Mohawks because "he was of their people." Pearson also notes that Van Slyke was also sometimes called Jacques Cornelise Gautsh and then includes this intriguing footnote:

> "Gautsh, pronounced Hotch (nearly); can it be an abbreviation of Ots-Toch, his mother's name? A squaw was queen of the island which lies back of Washington street. She is buried on the island, under an old willow tree at the point towards the bridge. She had two children by a Frenchman - Mr. Harttell. Otstoch was like her mother, savage and wild. She married Cornelius Van Slyke. Kenutje, the second child, was small and handsome, like her father Mr. Harttell; she was very white. She married a Bratt." [93]

From this reference comes the story that Ots-Toch's mother was buried on Van Slyke Island, near present-day Schenectady.

Yet another controversy is created - that of a Mohawk woman named Kenutje being married to a Bradt, which is hotly contested by the Bradt family, of which the author is also a descendant. I have found no other evidence or mention of Kenutje other than this statement. Ots-Toch, however, is indeed fact - it is her heritage which is disputed, not her existence. After much research, the author is convinced that Ots-Toch was the daughter of Jacques Hertel, a Frenchman from New France (present-day Quebec) and a Mohawk woman.

Could the naming of Jacques Cornelise Van Slyke also hold a clue? It is speculation but why else does the French name of Jacques suddenly show up as the son of a Dutchman and Mohawk? Under Dutch naming conventions of the time, Cornelis and Ots-Toch's first two sons would be named after his father and her father. Following

[92] MV

[93] Statement of tradition in his family by Laurence R. Vrooman of Cortland County in HSP

Mohawk tradition, Ots-Toch's sons would be named after her father and maternal grandfather. Neither of their two sons was named after Cornelis' father Antonis, leading me to speculate that Marten and Jacques may have been named following Mohawk naming traditions. Further details are given in the chapter on Jacques Hertel and the reader is invited to form his or her own opinion after reading the facts presented.

One source makes the claim that Ots-Toch's father was Jacques Hartell [sic], a French trader or trapper from Montreal and her mother a Native woman from the French settlements to the north.

> "About 1620, a French trader named Hartell entered the Mohawk country and became enamoured of an Indian girl who owned the island in the river at Schenectady now called Hog Island. The Iroquois woman was possessed of land under the laws of the Five Nations. Hartell had two children by this woman - Ots-Toch who married Cornelis Antonissen Van Slyck, and Kenutje who married a Bradt.
> Ots-Toch was wild and savage like her mother while Kenutje was small and handsome and very white like her father, Hartell. The mother of these two French-Mohawk girls, at her death, was buried at the point of Hog Island toward the old highway bridge" [94]

Research proves this statement to be only partially correct. A permanent settlement was not established at Montreal until 1642, [95] so that city could not be the base for anyone in the 1615 to 1625 period. The site of Montreal was used as a sort of stopping-off point for the traders but it is unlikely anyone from the time period of interest would be referred to as "from Montreal". [96] In later years, it eventually became the centre of the fur trade business and for exploration. It is possible that later writers who were unfamiliar with the history of New France may have assumed that Montreal was the centre of New France all along. It would have been natural to assume that all traders came from Montreal. The statement that Ots-Toch's mother was from the native settlements to the north, nearer Quebec, is not in agreement with the words of the Mohawks themselves regarding the Van Slyke family and Ots-Toch, who they claim as one of their own. There would have been no benefit for the Mohawks to claim Ots-Toch unless she were Mohawk, because under the Mohawk matriarchal system of inheritance, Ots-Toch's children would be eligible for land, a valuable commodity the Mohawks would not grant except to their own people.

[94] History of the Mohawk Valley_ Nelson Greene V. II publ 1925 [p.334]
[95] CFN tells us that Montreal was established as a religious enterpise in 1642 but soon found itself in the midst of intensifying Iroquois raids.
[96] The original name for Montreal was Hotchelaga and it would be more conceivable that if Jacques were from that location, this would be the name passed down by writers, not that of Montreal.

Lineal descent in the Iroquois Nation ran in the female line with women being considered progenitors of the Nation. It was females who owned the land, and children, whether male or female, followed the status of their mother. If Ots-Toch was the daughter or granddaughter of a Sachem of the Mohawks, she, as an heir to the Lordship title, would be called Royaneh or Noble for life. Their were forty-eight original Royaneh families who were considered heirs of the Authorized Names for life and children born to the Royaneh families would be given an Authorized Name at either the Midwinter or Ripe Corn Festival.

The last mention of Ots-Toch is in Jasper Dankaert's journal when her daughter Hilletie refers to being driven out of the Mohawk village by her mother and siblings. No mention has been found of Ots-Toch after that time and it is not known when she died.

If she were Royaneh, Ots-Toch would, at her death, be honoured with the traditional funeral address for a chief woman:

"Now we become reconciled as you start away. You were once a chief woman in the Five Nations' Confederacy. You were once a mother of the nations. Now we release you for it is true that it is no longer possible for us to walk about together on the earth. Now, therefore, we lay it (the body) here. Here we lay it away. Now then we say to you 'Persevere onward to the place where the Creator dwells in peace. Let not the things of the earth hinder you. Let nothing that transpired while you lived hinder you. Looking after your family was a sacred duty and you were faithful. You were one of the many joint heirs of the Lordship titles. Feastings were yours and you had pleasant occasions. Your mind was amused but now do not allow thoughts of these things to give you trouble. Let not your relatives hinder you and also let not your friends and associates trouble your mind. Regard none of these things.

Now then, in turn, you here present who were related to this woman and you who were her friends and associated behold the path that is yours also. Soon we ourselves will be left in that place. For this reason hold yourselves in restraint as you go in that place. In your actions and in your conversation do no idle thing. Speak not idle talk neither gossip. Be careful of this and speak not and do not give way to evil behaviour. One year is the time that you must abstain from unseemly levity but if you cannot do this for ceremony, ten days is the time to regard these things for respect"

Perhaps these words were spoken for Ots-Toch at her death. A traditional Iroquois burial was a two-step affair. The body was initially privately buried first. About every 15 years, the population of Canajoharie would exhume the skeletons of all who had died over the preceding period and would hold a "feast of the dead". At the climax of this feast, the rarest of Iroquoian rituals, the skeletal remains were placed in a large pit and stirred together, intermixing the bones. This style of burial was another manifestation of the Iroquoian devotion to the group and to their communal style of living. In essence, the dead were symbolically united as one forever by this rite.

30

# CHAPTER 4

## JACQUES HERTEL, INTERPRETER TO SAMUEL DE CHAMPLAIN AND FIRST SETTLER AT TROIS-RIVIERES, NEW FRANCE

Jacques Hertel was born circa 1603 in Fecamp, a town on the coast of France on the English Channel, just north-east of Le Havre, in Normandy. It is about half-way between Le Havre and Dieppe, being slightly closer to Le Havre. His mother was Jeanne Miriot, his father Nicolas Hertel. [97]

Jacques came to Canada in 1613 or 1615 [98] and was employed by Champlain as an interpreter, which was not uncommon even at his young age. Champlain speaks of the arrival of three interpreters in 1613: Nicolas du Vigeau, Jacques Hertel and Thomas Godefroy. Hertel and others were identified as being from Normandy. [99] Jacques Hertel also appears on the Census of 1624, 1629 and 1635. In the last two, his date of arrival is given as 1615. Campeau says that Jacques came to New France in 1626 [100], but this is 12 to 13 years too late according to other records, including Champlain's own census.

For the purpose of my intent to support that Jacques Hertel was the father of Ots-Toch, born from a liaison with a Mohawk woman in New York, evidence that Jacques had opportunity to interact with the Iroquois tribes in the critical time period of 1616-1627 is important. It is during this time that Ots-Toch was born, and although the majority of reports put her birth at 1620, we can not be sure this is correct. No birth records have been found, nor are they likely to be, since Ots-Toch was not a Christian and therefore not baptised in a Christian ceremony. The birth of her son Jacques in 1640, [101] does give us a vague time frame for Ots-Toch's birth, although we do not know if Jacques was her first or second child. Ots-Toch may have been as young as 13 when her first child was born, so given a two year gap between births, we can put her age at the birth of Jacques as at least 15 years of age, possibly older. That gives us the latest date of

---

[97] DCB
[98] JR V.IX. Champlain's account says 1613
[99] JR
[100] MNF
[101] Jacques' date of birth is indicated by his death in 1690 at the age of 50.

birth for Ots-Toch of 1625. If Jacques were the first-born child, this estimate can be revised to 1627. Using Jacques Hertel's date of birth of 1603 we can also estimate a year for Ots-Toch's earliest date of birth. Assuming her father Jacques to be at least 13 years old (not an impossibility) when she was born, we have 1616 as the earliest possible date. These dates are given only to show the most extreme time range possible for Ots-Toch's birth, and therefore the beginning of the liaison of Jacques and his Mohawk companion.

It is also necessary to understand the relationships of the Native tribes when Champlain made his first expedition against the Iroquois in 1609. In 1535 Jacques Cartier visited the St. Lawrence and found the northern shore occupied by the Montagnais, almost up to the narrows of Quebec. From there to the Ottawa the Algonquins, conquerors of the Montagnais, lived. Beyond the Ottawa and still bordering the St. Lawrence, were the Hurons, who were allies of the Algonquins in their war with the Iroquois. The Iroquois Confederacy were hereditary enemies of the Hurons, the great trading nation in Huronia, in what is now Simcoe County, Ontario, Canada. The French under Champlain, having allied themselves with the Hurons in 1610, found themselves under attack by the Iroquois. The Dutch in the Mohawk Valley, eager to stop French expansion and wanting to secure the lucrative fur trade, allied themselves with the Iroquois and supported them in their expeditions against the French and Hurons. [102]

The Iroquois nation occupied the territory south of the St. Lawrence and south-east of Lake Ontario. The St. Lawrence, as the dividing line, was frequently the scene of battle between marauding parties of Native tribes. As Iroquois power grew in the 16th century, the Hurons retreated to the peninsula between Georgian Bay and Lake Huron, while the Algonquins retired to the upper Ottawa through the chain of lakes connecting the Ottawa River with Georgian Bay. Until the mid 17th century, this was the only route used for going to and from Huron country to Quebec. [103]

Jacques was one of several interpreters working for Samuel de Champlain in the newly formed New France. Champlain's method of training his interpreters was to choose young boys who he would send to live with the Native tribes for a year or two, often accepting in exchange a Native boy who was to learn French language and customs. Most of the interpreters had their whereabouts recorded; so far, a source has not been found to indicate what tribe Hertel lived with.

"The object of Champlain in enlisting Brule, Nicolet, Marsolet, Hertel, Marguerie and other grown-up boys for service in Canada from 1608 to 1620 was to educate

[102] Highlights of Huronia in *History of Huronia*: photocopies provided by Ste. Marie Among The Hurons Resource Library 1995
[103] TCNF:pp70,71

them as interpreters. They could all read and write; some of them were perfect scholars" [104]

There is mention of several of the interpreters and the tribes they were sent to live with. Etienne Brule was a Huron interpreter; Jean Nicolet, Jean Manet and Jean Richer were Nipissing interpreters; Nicolas de Vignau and Thomas Godefroy [105] were Algonquin interpreters; while Nicolas Marsolet [106] and Olivier Letardif were interpreters for the Montagnais. [107] A footnote in Samuel Champlain's book [108] adds to the list of interpreters the names of Jacques Hertel, LeBailif, Du Vernet, Jean-Paul Godefroy [109] and LaMontagne. The footnote goes on to add that these named individuals were not qualified interpreters in the time period of interest and that merely living with the Native tribes was not enough to be given the title interpreter. It is interesting to speculate on what is meant by this. Did Jacques simply choose to live with the native tribes, in the sense of being more of a freelance agent? Is this why he is sometimes referred to as an interpreter, and other times as a soldier?

Many of the boys sent to live with the tribes were adopted by the tribes and were captivated by a life unlike any other. This was the beginning of the group of men later known as the *coureurs des bois* (runners of the woods). [110]

Etienne Brule was sent to live with the Hurons in 1610, and Nicolas de Vignau went to live with the Algonquins in 1611. Champlain may have sent these young boys to live with many different tribes and Jacques may have been with a tribe that interacted with the Mohawks. It is almost an impossibility that he was sent to live with any Iroquois tribes due to their hatred of the French and Hurons. Ots-Toch and her mother were very

[104] *Jacques Hertel (de La Fresnaye)* by Madeline H. Carey, Scot Vandelinder, Arlene Coppernoll Cuba ; *Annals of the Ottawa* in Ottawa Evening Journal 12 Jan. 1889, copied from *The History of Brule's Discoveries and Explorations*
[105] Thomas Godefroy de Normanville was born circa 1610 at Lintot in Normandy. He died 1652 in Iroquois country. He lived with the Indian tribes during the Kirke brothers occupation of Quebec 1629 to 1632, then settled at Trois-Rivieres, where he continued to act as interpeter. Captured by Iroquois three times; Februrary 1641, the spring of 1648 and August 1652, he escaped the first two times. In 1652 however he was carried off to Iroquois country and killed.
[106] Marsolet was one of the eight left alive from the original twenty-four Frenchmen who wintered at Quebec in the winter of 1608. Etienne Brule and Marsolet are referred to as two of Champlain's boys. "The lads had well employed the long winter months by learning the Montagnais language and became valuable interpreters" SCFNF:108
[107] HNF:V.II Le comptoir 1604-1627
[108] SC:V.II
[109] Jean-Paul is often confused with Jean Godefroy de Lintot, brother of Thomas Godefroy de Normanville. Jean-Paul became a leading member of the Communaute des habitants and died in 1668 in France DCB:V 1: pp 339-340
[110] WFNF: 48 The men who later became known as the coureurs de bois were young, hardy and had a taste for adventure. They travelled by canoe all over Canada. Their food would consist of a little biscuit, peas, corn, and a few casks of brandy, and they would carry as little as possible in order to leave room for merchandise. If fish and game were scarce they ate moss, making a broth from it. CYC:108

anti-Christian, and as far as is known, were not among the group of Mohawks who eventually converted. It is far more likely that Jacques was with a tribe that had some interaction with the Mohawks.

In the autumn of 1609 Champlain returned to France leaving the factory (Quebec) with its fifteen interpreters and agents in charge of Captain Chauvin, Sieur de la Pierre. Trade had been thrown open in 1609 and in the summer of 1610 there were a large number of vessels in the St. Lawrence. Champlain returned to Quebec and prepared to meet the Algonquins and Hurons further up the river to accompany them against the Iroquois. At the mouth of the Richelieu River there was a fight between Iroquois and Champlain and the Algonquins. When the Hurons arrived the next day,

"Champlain persuaded the Hurons to take back with them a young French boy while he in his turn accepted a young Huron who later accompanied him to France." [111]

Only one expedition of 1609 had reached the interior and nothing had been done in the way of discovery. Agents had been sent to winter with the Hurons and Algonquins but any trader on the river could do the same. Bouvier, a stranger, had in fact sent one of his boys to winter with the Hurons that very year. [112] This supports the findings that Champlain routinely sent young boys to the Hurons and Algonquins to train as interpreters.

In mention of Champlain's trip to the Lachine rapids in 1611 to meet with the Algonquins and Hurons:

"..when on the thirteenth of June the first batch of two hundred Hurons appeared, with the French boy lent them by Champlain... Hurons and Algonquins having each accepted one of his boys, they all separated the best of friends with promises to meet again the following summer" [113]

Champlain's trip up the Ottawa in 1613 with Vignau and four other men to the Algonquin village on Lake des Allumettes in search of the northern sea, includes this statement:

"In fact, except for the two French boys and an odd interpreter or so, no Frenchman had until then advanced beyond the rapids of Lachine" [114]

[111] HNF:p 17
[112] ibid:p 83
[113] pp 80, 82
[114] TCNF:p 90

We also know that the French were exploring in Mohawk territory. As early as 1615, Etienne Brule, another of Champlain's interpreters, accompanied a contingent of Hurons into the Susquehannah to the south of the Iroquois tribes, in what is now southwestern New York state. Brule explored the regions, although his exact explorations are unknown. Like many of the early explorers and interpreters, he left no written record. [115]

Champlain, along with Father Joseph, a Recollet, and twelve Frenchman, spent the winter of 1615-16 among the Hurons on Georgian Bay and Lake Huron. The journey to the Huron nation was by way of the Ottawa River, Lake Nipissing and Georgian Bay, a long and difficult one. Champlain's enjoyment of exploring these regions made him oblivious to the difficulties.

"During the course of an expedition which the Hurons made against the Iroquois, he was able to visit Lake Simcoe, the Trent River, and the Bay of Quinte as well as that portion of New York State which borders on the eastern end of Lake Ontario." [116]

According to Biggar, the barter of furs at the rapids (Lachine) in the summer of 1617 was unusually large as all the tribes visited by Champlain in the winter of 1615 and 1616 now came down to the St. Lawrence for the first time. However the news that Dutch traders on the Hudson had succeeded in forming an alliance with the Iroquois confederation

"showed that little hope could henceforth be entertained of any trading connections in that direction" [117]

The hunting tribes were those furthest from the centres of trade at Montreal, Trois-Rivieres, Quebec and Tadoussac. They traded their furs to other Natives, not the French. The Native tribes in the middle, called middle traders, dealt with both French and other Natives. The Iroquois dealt with the Dutch settlers at Fort Orange, New York. A note from Marie de l'Incanation, the Ursuline Mother Superior at Quebec states:

"Their [the Iroquois] intention is to remain alone in all these regions so they may have all the beasts for food and the skins to give the Hollanders. It is not that they love the Hollanders but that they need someone by whose means they can obtain what they need from Europe; and as the Hollanders are closer to them, they trade with them more easily. " [118]

[115] PC
[116] ibid: p. 99
[117] ibid:p.106
[118] Word From New France: The Selected Letters of Marie de l'Incarnation translated and edited by Joyce Marshall, 1967

In New York, the Dutch had built Fort Nassau in 1614 but their fur-trading contact with the Iroquois was not really extensive until the founding of Fort Orange in 1624. In 1626, the Dutch almost lost their hold on the Hudson when the commander of Fort Orange sided with the Mahicans against their Mohawk enemies. The Mahicans were badly defeated and only some fancy negotiating by the new director of the colony, Peter Minuit, managed to salvage the situation and forge a friendship with the Mohawks. Even then, Minuit withdrew all of the settlers to the recently purchased Manhattan Island for their safety.

In the summer of 1624, there were more tribes at the barter in the Upper St. Lawrence than ever before. Champlain had not been beyond the rapids since 1615 but "owing to the annual winter visits of the interpreters" [119] and to the extension of French trade, new tribes continued to make their way to Lachine every summer.

"In early July 1624, six delegates from the Five Nations came to propose a treaty of peace and shortly thereafter, thirty-five Iroquois canoes came down the Richelieu River to barter furs with the Frenchmen for the first time" [120]

"In the summer of 1624 the concourse of savages at the barter in the upper St. Lawrence was greater than ever......owing to the gradual extension of the area in which the French merchandise circulated, fresh tribes continued to make their way nearby every summer to the place of barter. This summer was made especially noteworthy by the arrival of thirty-five canoes of Iroquois. Two years before this, two Iroquois warriors had come to the Montagnais of their own accord in order to try and conclude a treaty of peace. But as they were not official representatives Champlain induced four of the Montagnais, specially deputized to conclude a peace, to return with these Iroquois. On their arrival in the Iroquois country they were met with a good reception and a permanent treaty was drawn up. Thirty-five canoes of Iroquois had now arrived both to trade and to sign the peace. Although the nations and tribes were thus very various no difficulty arose, so perfect were the arrangements made by Champlain." [121]

Each nation had its own interpreter. After the ordinary business of the barter, there was the feast of friendship with presents given by both sides. Then followed the dances and other festivities. Finally the whole was brought to a close by the conclusion of the long-hoped-for peace between the Iroquois, the Hurons and the French. [122] Would it be surprising if Jacques Hertel were there? He would be 21 years old at that time, and a qualified interpreter. Ots-Toch's mother could as easily have been present.

[119] TCNF: p.123
[120] History of Canada by Lanctot
[121] ibid
[122] TCNF

From these references, we know that peace between the Iroquois and French in New France was achieved as early as 1622. This peace was broken in 1627 but for a five-year period, there was opportunity for Jacques Hertel to interact easily with the Mohawk tribes. When the Dutch moved upriver to set up Fort Orange (now Albany, New York) in 1623, they came much closer to the northern settlements, where the best furs were. The Iroquois, who had no allies with whom to trade furs, decided to try for the Dutch trade, which meant removing the Mahican tribes which lay between. It also meant the Iroquois had to divert some of their energies and resources from the raiding activities they carried out along the St. Lawrence River. To do this, they made peace with the Hurons and Algonquins in 1624, an action which brought them freedom from danger from the rear (northward) and the ability to safely attack the Mahicans whom they defeated in 1628. This opened the door for trade relations with the Dutch.

Throughout this time period, the French made sporadic attempts to establish trade relations with the Iroquois, but these were not successful in the long term and Champlain had abandoned those efforts by 1633. [123] We must remember that to establish trade relations with a native tribe, Champlain had to use interpreters, and this gives Jacques full opportunity to have interacted with the Mohawk tribes in the Mohawk Valley of New York.

"During the winter of 1625 Champlain remained in France....we are again without any record of what took place during the summer in the St. Lawrence valley. ... Champlain, on his return to Quebec in the summer of 1626, found everything in complete disorder..... During this time the annual barter [124] had been going on as usual further up the river. It was learned however from the Iroquois present that trouble had broken out between them and the Dutch and that five of the latter had even been massacred." [125]

"The savages who dwelt beside the Dutch had sent presents asking the Montagnais and Algonquins to help them against the Iroquois, who, when they had killed the five Dutchmen, had massacred twenty-four of that tribe." [126]

"It was agreed to wait (to make a decision re fighting the Iroquois) until the vessels had arrived, when the other nations should have come down for the barter. During the interval, however, some Algonquins went off on the war-path and a few light-

[123] CFN

[124] A journal entry from the Jesuit Relations for 1626 explains how the fur trade was carried on: "We see here (Tadoussac) not more than two ships once a year, about the beginning of the month of June. These two ships bring all the merchandise which these gentlemen use in trading with the Indians, that is to say, the cloaks, blankets, nightcaps, hat, shirts, sheets, hatchets, iron arrowheads, bodkins, swords, picks to break the ice in winter, knives, kettles, prunes, raisin, Indian corn, peas, crackers or sea biscuits, and tobacco. In exchange for thes they carry back the hides of the moose, lynx, fox, otter, but they deal principally in beavers."

[125] TCNF: pp127,128

[126] ibid: p 129

headed young Montagnais braves caught two Iroquois on Lake Champlain. Although Champlain was able to induce the savages assembled at the barter to send back these prisoners with presents and an expression of regret for what had occurred, yet his efforts were too late. On reaching the Iroquois country the embassy was at first well received, but when news was brought of the ravages committed else-where by the Algonquin warriors who had gone on the war-path, all the members of it were speedily massacred, without distinction of French or Indian" [127]

It is not known where Jacques Hertel was, and what he did, from the time of his arrival in New France in 1613 or 1615 until 1629 when the Kirke brothers from England seized control of New France. Mention is made in the Jesuit Relations that Jacques "took refuge with the savages"

Although we cannot at this point determine where Jacques spent the sixteen year period 1613 to 1629, we have mention of the interpreters and their way of life, in general. It is easy to speculate on Jacques' travels, and on his whereabouts. Knowing how the interpreters lived, and how much freedom of movement they had does give us an indication that Jacques could easily have journeyed to the Mohawk lands, or met Ots-Toch's mother in any number of places. From *Long Journey to The Country of The Hurons* by Father Gabriel Sagard we read:

"We know little of the mode of life of the armed men who went to Huronia. Usually the missionaries lived apart in their own cabins of bark, but these men, and also traders who went to Huronia, seem to have lived with the natives in their lodges. Here were dirt and squalor, lounging men, lascivious scenes, and no restraint from civilized traditions. It was easy to adopt native manners. The visitors hunted for their food as did the natives, or bought it from them. Intercourse with native women brought a race of half-breeds. Champlain said that such men cared only to hunt, fish, get drunk and sleep" [128]

"Robberies, murders, assassinations, lust and blasphemy were only too common among the factors and interpreters" [129]

In 1623 there is mention of a Recollet mission to Huronia and the fact that there were three Recollet priests and

"a rather motley force of thirteen so-called interpreters, hardy men, used to the life of the forest, and ready for any service" [130]

[127] ibid
[128] CH: pp xxx,xxxi
[129] ibid:p xiii; TCNF: p 177
[130] CH: p xxxiii

If we read Costain's description of Etienne Brule, possibly the most famous of Champlain's interpreters, we are perhaps given a glimpse of the life many of the interpreters lived.

"In his last appearances among white men he was dressed like an Indian, his powerful torso bared to the waist and tanned as brown as walnut. his hair, it may be guessed, was shocky and coarse. His eyes, when he became angry, which was often, had a reddish glint in them. He had gone native, living as the Indians did, taking brown-skinned wives wherever he went and putting them away as his fancy dictated" [131]

Sagard speaks of the country of the Neutral Tribe, which he states lay

"to the south 4 or 5 days journey from the Hurons, beyond the nation of the Quieunontateronons." [132]

and he goes on to add that the land extended over 100 leagues. [133] This Neutral nation was at peace and remained neutral with both Huron and Iroquois, with the result that

"members of either of the two nations were welcome among them and these did not dare to utter or do anything displeasing to one another when there, and often would eat together as if they had been friends. But if they met outside the [Neutral's] territory, there was no friendship any more and they would wage cruel war upon one another, and keep it up to the uttermost" [134]

As an interpreter, Jacques would have known of this tribe and it is possible that he and Ots-Toch's mother met in Neutral territory. It is even possible that this was the tribe Jacques lived with as a youth. Further mention is made by Sagard:

"One of our Frenchman had fallen ill among the Tobacco tribe, and his companions, who were going off to the Neutral tribe, left him there in the care of a savage..." [135]

In 1629 the Kirke brothers seized Quebec, and the French were no longer in control. Mention is made in several sources of the interpreters returning to live with the Natives and Jacques is specifically mentioned by Benjamin Sulte:

[131] W&G: p 78
[132] The tribe called the Quieunontatetonons by the Hurons, was the Weskarini, an Algonquin tribe living on the North side of the Ottawa River below Allumette Island
[133] A footnote states that the Neutral Nation was a confederation of Iroquois tribes living north of Lake Erie and along the Niagara River.
[134] CH:pp 151,158
[135] CH: p 194

"At the return of Champlain, he [Jacques] returned to Quebec with a thorough knowledge of the languages and customs of the Savages, having contracted some extremely useful friendships among the far distant tribes still unknown to the French. Meanwhile, information is sufficiently vague that we have reached the point of allowing ourselves to suppose that Jacque [sic] Hertel settled in Trois-Rivieres before the year 1636; we know that he must have frequently gone on the trading trips which were made each summer." [136]

It is not clear just who these "far-distant tribes" were, and this allows more speculation that they may have been the Mohawk. We will quite likely never know. The fact that he is said to have gone on the summer trading trips gives him plenty of opportunity for interaction with the Mohawk Tribe.

Sulte states that Jacques lived with native tribes during the years Quebec was occupied by the Kirke brothers from England.(1629-1633) According to Sulte, Hertel had acquired a taste for "la vïe des bois" [137] during his fourteen years of service. [138] Hertel returned to Champlain's service in 1633. [139]

The Jesuits state that Jacques Hertel "was long employed by Champlain as an interpreter and, upon the capture of Quebec, took refuge with the savages..." [140]

Did Jacques return to the tribe where he had spent his early years? Did he seek out Ots-Toch's mother and spend these years with the Mohawks? There is no record of his whereabouts, only the few vague references previously noted. We may speculate but that is all.

On Dec. 3 1633, the Hundred Associates Company granted Jacques Hertel two hundred acres of land in Trois-Rivieres, making him the first land-owner there. [141] Later volumes of the Jesuit Relations give us a description of his land. [142] At this time Hertel was granted the seigneury de La Fresnaye. [143] There is more of Jacques in 1633:

"as early as 1633 Jacques Hertel, a soldier who had spent the years of English occupation among the Indians, and Jean Godefroy, an interpreter, had been established at Trois-Rivieres, and in 1635 Champlain built a habitation there to help defend the little settlement. The Jesuits also established a permanent mission."

[136] HTR
[137] life in the forest
[138] this statement would imply that Jacques had been in New France since 1615
[139] DCB; HTR
[140] JR: V. IX, p. 305
[141] JR: Notes to Vol. IV, p. 261
[142] JR: 1759-91, p. 85:Half a league in front by two leagues in depth, conceded to the late Jacques Hertel, Sieur de la Frenaye
[143] DCB; HTR

Is it significant that Jacques is referred to as a soldier while Godefroy is listed as an interpreter? Or had Jacques taken up a new profession? [144] Jacques is elsewhere referred to as an "interpreter living in 1629 in Quebec (ville)" [145]

In a biography [146] of Francois-Joseph Hertel, the only known son of Jacques, we find the following:

"M. Jacques Hertel, Sieur de la Freniere, head of this family in Canada, was still a child of the beautiful country which gave us the de Longeuils, the de Repentigny's, the Godfroys, etc. and, one can say, the major part of the first inhabitants. He left Fecamp, his native village, to go to Canada, towards the beginning of the 16th century . . . . Taking pains, in 1626, to study the wild [Indian] languages, he became one of the most capable and useful of interpreters." [147]

It was not long before the French were beginning to expand their contacts with the Mohawk Valley tribes. It seems that they concentrated their efforts in the area around Oneida Lake. Their trading began to worry the Dutch. Finally, in 1634, the Dutch sent an expedition into Iroquois country to investigate the decline of the fur trade, possibly caused by French incursions, and to negotiate a new price structure for the furs. Harmen Meyndertz van den Bogaert was the leader of this 1634 expedition.

In 1633 the French were trading with the Mohawks. Harmen van den Bogaert states in his journal that at one of the villages he visited, the chief explained how the French had traded with them in August 1633 for French shirts, coats and razors. This same chief also told van den Bogaert that the French gave them six hands of sewant for one beaver as well as other gifts.

At that time, interpreters were well-rounded men. They were entrusted by government and by companies, negotiating affairs and maintaining relations with the Native tribes. Adopted by the nation, they were regarded as brothers and had great authority in the Councils. So it was for Jacques Hertel. At the same time that he was an interpreter, he was also a Lieutenant in the troops, which gave him entry into the better families. He benefited from their regard and was able to establish himself advantageously.

Jacques was granted two other parcels of land by Montmagny in 1636. In the records for Trois Rivieres, Jacques Hertel attended the baptisms of many children,

---

[144] *Word From New France: The Selected Letters of Marie de l'Incarnation* translated and edited by Joyce Marshall
[145] *The French Canadians 1600-1900* V.2 ed. by Noel Montgomery Elliot; *La Ville de Quebec Sous le Regime Francais* par Pierre Georges ROY, Vol. Premier, p.109.
[146] *Histoire des grandes familles francaises du Canada ou Apercu sur le Chevelier Benoist et quelques familles contemporaines* (Montreal: Eusebe Senecal, 1867)
[147] translated from the French by Dale T. Alexander 1995

including numerous Natives (children and adults) as early as 1636. [148] It is not known if Jacques was present at earlier baptisms since the Trois-Rivieres baptismal records do not begin until 1635.

In the spring or early summer of 1637, Jacques made a trip on the River des Prairies with Nicolet and St. Jean. The story of their adventure is told in the Jesuit Relations:

"They perceived a canoe prowling around the Islands on the lookout for some Hiroquois [sic]; they immediately fired several shots from the arquesbuses to summon it to them. The Savage who was in it, seeing the bark, brought his canoe alongside. After he had been questioned about various things, he was asked if he would not like to go to the three Rivers, as Monsieur de St. Jean and sieur Hertel desired to go there. He replied that he greatly wished to go there, but that the Hiroquois [sic] would be sure to kill him on the way. Sieur Nicolet rejoined that he ought to fear nothing when these two young men, both of them courageous, and children of brave Captains, were with him; that they were armed with good arquesbuses, and that no misfortune could befall him in their company." [149]

Jacques Hertel, already a Lieutenant in the troops, was elected syndic of Trois-Rivieres. [150] In 1641 Jacques, aged 38, married Marie Marguerie, age 15, the sister of his friend and fellow interpreter, Francois Marguerie. [151] Such seemingly young marriages among girls were not uncommon for that time period and location. Women in New France were in demand, and girls as young as thirteen married and raised families. New France had very few women and many settlers formed liaisons with native women. King Louis XIV of France wanted New France populated by French, not mixed-blood individuals, and he began the scheme known as the Filles du Roi (daughters of the King), wherein young impoverished girls were given a dowry if they would agree to sail to New France, and marry a settler. While Marie was not a Filles du Roi, she did come to New France at the urging of her brother Francois to help colonize the settlements.

[148] The baptism records for Trois-Rivieres begin in 1635
[149] JR
[150] DCB; HTR
[151] Francois Marguerie de la Haye, baptised 12 Oct. 1612 Rouen, Normandy France, spent his early youth with the Algonkins on Allumette Island. As an interpeter to Champlain he travelled a great deal, including to Huron country in 1636. He acted as guide and interpeter to the Jesuits on their trips and missionary endeavours until 1637. At that time he returned to Trois-Rivieres as chief interpeter of the village. In 1641 he and Thomas Godefroy were captured by Iroquois and kept prisoner for several weeks. He and Godefroy were used as guides in an Iroquois plan to attack Trois-Rivieres. Marguerie was released to negotiate with the authorities of Trois-Rivieres with Godefroy kept as hostage to ensure Marguerie's co-operation. Francois warned the governor not to accept the Iroquois proposals since it was a trap, and then he returned to the Indians so that his friend and fellow interpeter Godefroy would not be harmed. Eventually Jean Nicollet and Father Ragueneau negotiated on their behalf and the hostages were freed. Marguerie married Louise Cloutier in 1645. He drowned when his canoe capsized in the St. Lawrence River off Trois-Rivieres on 23 May 1648. He is buried at Quebec. DCB: V.1: pp 489, 490

Following is the marriage contract for Jacques Hertel, from the notarial records (Vol. 6, 1980), signed on 23 Aug. 1641.

Jacques Hertel, res: Trois-Rivieres. Origin: France, Normandy, Rural
Marie Marguerie, res: Trois-Rivieres. Origin: France, Normandy, Urban
Nicolas Hertel, res: France, Normandy, Rural. Father of groom, married, deceased.
Jeanne Miriot, res: France, Normandy, Rural. Mother of groom, married, deceased.
/ Marguerie, res: France, Normandy, Urban. Father of bride, married
Marthe Romain, res: France, Normandy, Urban. Mother of bride, married
Martial Piraube, notary

Following the marriage of Jacques Hertel to Marie Marguerie on 23 Aug. 1641, both of their names begin to appear together in numerous Trois-Rivieres baptism records. Most of these were Native baptisms. Their three children were baptised at Trois-Rivieres, as follows:

- Francois-Joseph Hertel baptised 3 July 1642. His uncle, Francois Marguerie was the godfather. Father Jean de Brebeuf [152] himself officiated.

- Marie-Madeleine Hertel, born 2 Sept. 1645, baptised 2 Sept. 1645.

- Marguerite Hertel, born 26 Aug. 1649, baptised 26 Aug. 1649

Jacques Hertel was elected official receiver for Trois-Rivieres for the Compagnie des Habitants in 1645. [153] He built a small house on his property at l'Arbe-a-la-Croix in 1644, which he abandoned in 1647 because of the fear of Iroquois attack.

In the spring of 1647 Jacques is mentioned in the Jesuit Relations as having carried, with three other residents of Trois-Rivieres, the Canopy at the procession of the Blessed Sacrament. On Easter Day of 1648, Jacques was named godfather of a young Huron boy named Sa:ondionrhens, from the village of la Conception. Jacques gave him the name of Charles. [154]

Jacques lived at Trois-Rivieres until his sudden and accidental death at the home of Antoine Derosiers [155] on 10 Aug. 1651. His wife Marie was only 25 years of age [156]

In the Jesuit Relations we read:

---

[152] Jean de Brébeuf, 1593-1649, was a Jesuit priest who was tortured and killed at St. Ignace, Simcoe County, Ontario by Iroquois who had overrun the Jesuit village St. Marie Among the Hurons. Father Brébeuf was made a martyr.
[153] HTR
[154] JR: 1647-48 p.81
[155] Antoine Desrosiers was married to Anne Du Herrison, who was the daughter of Michel Leneuf du Herisson, an imprtant official in Trois-Rivieres. DCB: V1:467
[156] Dictionnaire General du Canada_ by R.P.L LeJeune; _Can-Francais_ Vol. I & II; _JR: V. 36 p. 137

"On the 14th [of Aug. 1651], a shallop arrives [in Quebec] from Three Rivers, which brings news of the death of Monsieur Hertel, who died on St. Lawrence's day. Otsie'Ka moritur [Otsie'Ka died]." [157]

This is the first mention of Jacques as Otsie'Ka. It is not known whether this was a name given him by his native tribe, or by the Jesuits.

An inventory taken of Jacques Hertel's effects after his death, reads as follows in French:

"Dans l'inventaire des meubles de Jacques Hertel, en 1651, il est fait mention de cinq barriques de bouillon. Ce breuvage, qui n'est plus connu en Canada, etait, au dix-septieme siecle, tres repandu parmi les pauvres gens en Picardie. Le dictionnaire de Trevoux note qu'il avait beaucoup de rapport avec le chousset des Turcs, lequel est fait de pate crue mais levee, qu'on cuit dansun chaudron plein d'eau, et quand elle est rassise puis séchée , l'on en prend la grosseur d'un oeuf qu'on jette dans l'eau pourboire."

Translation: In the inventory of Jacques' effects in 1651, five casks of bouillon are mentioned. This beverage, which is no longer known in Canada, was, in the 16th Century, very widely known among the poor people of Picardy. The Trevoux dictionary notes that it had much in common with the chousset of the Turks, which is made from fermented corn pulp, cooked in a cauldron of boiled water until sticky, then boiled until dry, at which point a whole egg is thrown into the water. [158]

Sulte gives an additional comment on the death of Jacques Hertel's death at the home of Antoine Desrosiers.

". . . we do not have anything interesting to record in regard to it." ( . . . nous n'avons aucun fait interessant a constater a son egard. . . .) [159]

One would think that the sudden and accidental death of man aged 48 would warrant an explanation or a comment, but we are left to wonder how and why Jacques died. Jacques was buried in a side chapel of the parish church in Trois-Rivieres.

[157] JR
[158] translated by Rosemary Houston and Dale T. Alexander. The use of the egg would most likely have been to clarify the mixture, and Jacques would have used seagull or chicken eggs.
[159] HTR

44

# CHAPTER 5

## JACQUES CORNELISE VAN SLYKE ALSO KNOWN AS ACKES GAUTSCH OR BY HIS MOHAWK NAME IT-SY-CHO-SA-QUACH-KA

Jacques Cornelise Van Slyke was known as Jacques Cornelis Gautsch according to Prof. Jonathan Pearson who states:

"Gautsh, pronounced Hotch, could be an abbreviation of Ots-Toch, his mother's name".

Jacques' Mohawk name was It-sy-cho-sa-quach-ka, which may mean

"he who gathers flowers (or herbs) from the meadows" [160]

"Uhskoha" is the Mohawk word for "I will get it" and is pronounced as "osqucha" while "kahuta:ke" means "on the meadow" and is pronounced as "kayontochke". Perhaps Jacques' Mohawk name was "Uh-skoh-ha-kahuta:ke" or some combination of the two words that gave rise to the phonetic interpretation of It-sy-cho-sa-quach-ka.

Apparently Jacques was born and raised in his mother's longhouse among the Mohawks at Canajoharie New York, as were all his brothers and sisters. His son Harmen received a grant of three hundred morgens of land at Canajoharie from the Mohawks because

"his grandmother was a right Mohawk woman and his father born with us at Canajoharie" [161]

Jacques is referred to as part French, part Mohawk in Vrooman's *The Massacre* and a statement is made of a Native woman whose father was French and whose mother was Mohawk,
"Ah yes, a Frenchman's child reared by its Indian mother, and dismissed the father from his mind" [162]

---

[160] 1995 translation by Dorothy Leseur, a Mohawk woman living in Ontario
[161] HSCNY:234

Jacques is also said to be "formerly an Indian"

We first hear of Jacques on July 18 1661 when he, his father Cornelis Antonissen and thirteen other settlers petitioned Director-General Peter Stuyvesant for permission to purchase the native lands at Schenectady. [163] On the 21st day of the same month, Stuyvesant gave his permission on condition that the lands be transferred to the Director-General and his Council.

On the 27 July 1661 the Mohawks granted a deed to the lands known by the Dutch as the Groote Vlacte (Great Flats) and by the Mohawk as Schonowa. The signers of this deed were the three Mohawk chiefs - Contugo of the Bear Clan, Sonareetsie of the Wolf and Aiadans of the Turtle, and the witnesses were William Montagne and the brother of Jacques, Martin Maritsz Van Slyke who signed his name as Martin Mourisse.

Jacques was the fifteenth and last proprietor of Schenectady. These original fifteen settlers of Schenectady had left Rensellaerswyck in hopes of escaping the restrictions and conflicts there. Although too young to have been involved in active fur trading in the 1650s with eight of the original Schenectady proprietors [164], Jacques did trade with the natives at a later date. Seven of the fourteen proprietors had ties to Rensselaerswyck and many were closely associated with the Beverwyck community. Burke suggest that the Bradts from Norway, [165] who were Lutheran, and the Van Slykes "who were of mixed European-Indian descent" may have resettled at Schenectady in order to distance themselves from the established Dutch communities along the Hudson River.

On the 1 Aug. 1661 Jacques Cornelis bought a house, lot and barn in the colony of Rensellaerswyck. The contract of sale is as follows:

"Contract of sale between Hendrick Jochemsen and Frans Jansen Pruyn and Jacques Cornelissen van Slyck for a house, lot and barn in the colony of Rensselaerswyck.

[162] TM: pp 140, 202, 203
[163] HSC: p 9
[164] These eight men were: Arent van Curler, Pieter Adriaensen van Woggelum, William Teller, Gerrit Bancker, Sander Leendertsen Glen, Symon Volkertsen Veeder, Teunis Cornelissne Swart and Philip Hendricksen Brouwer.
[165] The author is descended from Albert Albertsen de Noorman aka Bradt, born Fredrikstad Norway in 1607, one of two brothers who settled at Rensellaerswyck in the 1630s.

"On this day, the 1st. of August 1661, appeared before me, Dirck van Schelluyne, notary public, and before the hereinafter named witnesses, Hendrick Jochemsz of the first part and Frans Jansz Pruyn and Jaques[sic] Cornelisz [Jacques Cornelissen Van Slyke] of the second part, acknowledging, the said Hendrick Jochemsz that he had sold, and Frans Jansz and Jaques Cornelisz that they had bought of him, a certain, the seller's, house and lot together with a barn [166] built by Jan Schoon, as they lie and are built and enclosed within the fence, with all that is fast therein by nail and earth and furthermore with such dominant and servient estates and rights as the seller acquired from Cornelis Cornelisz van Starrevelt and have by him hitherto possessed; said house and lot are standing and lying in the colony of Rensselaerswyck, bounded on the north side by Cors Boutsz, on the east and south sides by the streets and on the west side by the patroon of the aforesaid colony; which aforesaid house, barn and lot are sold and are to be delivered to the purchasers free and unencumbered, without any charges thereon or issuing out of the same, save the patroon's rights for which house, barn and lot said purchasers promise to pay the sum of eight hundred and forty guilders in good strung trading seawan, a just half in the latter part of the current month of August and the other half in the month of June 1662, each time promptly without further delay; and the purchasers shall enter upon and take possession of said house, lot and barn immediately, the seller to be holden in the months of September and October next at his own expense to face the house on all sides (except the stable) with brick. For the faithful performance of what is herein before written the parties hereto mutually bind their respective persons and estates, nothing excepted, subject to all courts and judges, and said house and barn shall remain as special security for the full payment of the aforesaid purchase money. Thus done and executed in Beverwyck in New Netherland, in presence of Cornelis Cornelisz van Starrevelt aforenamed and Marchelis Jans as witnesses hereto called. Signed Hendrick Jochemsz. This mark X was made by Jaques Cornelisz aforesaid, Frans Jansen Proum. Signed Coernelise Coernelissen van Sterrenuelt, Maercelys Jansen and D. V. Schelluyne, Not. Pub. 1661" [167]

In 1662 Jacques married Margaret or Grietje Ryckman, the daughter of Harmen Janse Ryckman from the Netherlands who had settled at Beverwyck. Grietje was born circa 1646 and died circa 1695 at Albany, New York. The first flat at Schenectady, which Jacques owned, was on the south side of the Mohawk River, to the west of the village proper, consisting of 40 morgens or almost 100 acres. Jacques was the original owner of this flat. This farm was still in the possession of the Van Slyke family as late as 1883. [168]

In 1663 a bond was issued from Frans Jansen and Jacques Cornelissen to Jan Cornelissen van der Heyden.

---

[166] something called a Schuyrbech: a combination of barn and hay rick with the rick on top of the barn for space reasons
[167] ERAR V.3:86
[168] History of the Mohawk Valley

"On this day, the 22nd of February 1663, Frans Jansz and Jaques [sic] Cornelisz [Jacques Van Slyke] acknowledge that they are well and truly indebted to Jan Cornelissz van der Heyden in the sum of six hundred and forty-four guilders and thirteen stivers, growing out of the matter of merchandise by them jointly received; of which said sum each promises to pay the just half in good, merchantable beaver skins, reckoned at eight guilders apiece, on the first of July next, punctually and without longer delay; therefore binding their respective persons and estates, nothing excepted, subject to the jurisdiction of all courts and judges. Done in Beverwyck, dated as above. Signed Frans Jansen. This mark A made by Jaques Cornelissz, aforenamed [a footnote states that Jacques Cornelissen Van Slyke, one of the sons of Cornelis Anthonissen van Schlick (Slyck) who was also referred to as Aques, Ackes or Akes Cornelissen] [169]

The early settlers laboured almost continuously. Only the weather, the Sabbath, and periods of prayer and fasting helped break the monotony of daily routine of work. Schenectady's settlers had a period of several years of good weather at its beginnings. the winter of 1658 and 1659 was severe however, and spring rains damaged the winter wheat and delayed planting. In 1659 the winter was also severe with heavy snowfalls. 1661 saw heavy flooding in June. Finally came a pleasant summer and winter in 1662 and 63. The only eventful weather happening was a small earthquake. In the spring of 1663 there were heavy rains, but a good harvest was still reported. In 1664, on May 13, Jacques Cornelissen Van Slyck [sic] was reported to be continuing his daily sowing. Many settlers made arrangements for indentured servants to work the land for agreed-on-periods of time. In July of 1663, Jacques Cornelise and Maritie Meynderts made a one-year arrangement with Gerrit Claessen van Nieukerck for cultivating, plowing, sowing, mowing, threshing, winnowing, cutting wood and whatever else was required in the running of their farms. Having hired Gerrit for one year starting with the harvest of 1663, Jacques was still recorded as "daily sowing" in the following spring. Apparently even hired help did not relieve a proprietor from all his duties of labour.

"Contract of Gerrit Claessen van Nieukerck to serve on the farm of Maritie Mynders and Jacques Cornelissen Van Slyke: On this day, the 7th. of July 1663, Maritie Mynders, widow of Jan Barentsz Wemp, and Jacques Cornelisz [Jacques Van Slyke] acknowledge that they have jointly hired Gerrit Claesz van Nieukerck farm servant, that he has bound himself faithfully to serve them on the farm at Schatechtede [sic] in tilling the land and what appertains thereto for the term of one year beginning next harvest time, and that she, Maritie Mynders, who has hired him for herself till that time, can spare him. For which service they, the hirers, at the end of the year promise to pay him, Gerrit Claesz, besides reasonable board during the year, the quantity of thirty-four beaver skins reckoned at eight guilders apiece, to wit, the half thereof in grain at beaver's price, and he other half, being seventeen beavers, in goods and

---

[169]ERAR V.3:212. Footnote adds to refer to ERAR 1:444, 453-454; History of the Schenectady patent pp 188-90; Van Rensselaer Bowier Mss p 2455-56, 800l Documentary History of New York, Oct. ed. 2:206

merchandise also at beaver's value. For the performance and satisfaction of these presents, the parties hereto mutually bind their respective persons and estates, nothing excepted, subject to the authority of all courts and judges. Done in the colony of Rensselaerswyck, dated as above. This mark was made + by Maritie Mynders, aforenamed. ACKES. This mark X was set by Gerrit Claessz, aforenamed. As witnesses: Jan Cornelisz van der Heyden, Cornelis Cornelisz Viele. D. V. Schelluyne Not. Pub. 1663" [170]

It is interesting to note that Jacques has now gone from a man who made his mark with an X in a contract dated August 1661, to a mark of A in Feb. 1663 and now in July 1663 his full name by which he was known, Ackes.

Marten Van Slyke, Jacques' brother, had half-ownership in a large island in the Mohawk River north of Schenectady. As Schenectady grew, it expanded to include this island, called Van Slyck's Island, and tradition says that Jacques' grandmother, Ots-Toch's mother, is buried at the eastern point of the island under a willow tree. This island was supposedly given to Ots-Toch and Cornelis Van Slyke as a wedding gift by the Mohawks, then half was awarded to Marten and when he died, his half went to his brother, Jacques. [171] The exact nature of the Island's ownership is contradictory. There is evidence of Jacques acquiring this land in 1664 when he leased half the Island from Maritie Meynderts (widow of Jan Barentse Wemp, [172]who had owned an island farm at Schenectady with Jacques' brother Marten Maurits [173]). [174] The document does state that Jacques and Maritie owned the land jointly. Jacques also received grants from the Mohawks as his birth right from his mother Ots-Toch.

In May 1664, Jacques leased one-half of Van Slyck's Island at Schenectady from Maritie Meynders. The contract follows:

"Lease of one-half of Van Slyck's Island at Schenectady from Maritie Meynderts to Aeckes Cornelissen Van Slyke: This day, the 13th of May 1664, Marrite Meyndertse widow of the late Jan Barentsz Wemp, acknowledges that she has let and Aeckes Cornelisz [otherwise called Jacques Cornelissen Van Slyke] that he has hired of her the just half of the farm [175] (the whole of which farm belongs to them jointly) lying

---

[170] ERAR V.3:222-223
[171] Ruby Hall p. 73 in Nelson Greene
[172] Maritie Meynderts married Sweer Teunise Van Velsen after Jan's death in 1663. She and her second husband were both killed at the Schenectady Massacre Feb. 1690
[173] Pearson states that Jan Barentse Wemp alias Poest, received a patent for the Great island immediately west of Schenectady and a house lot in the village on the west side of Washington Street, just north of State Street in 1662. Pearson states that this patent was also given to Jacques Cornelissen van Slyke, but Burke states it was to Jacques' brother, Marten Cornelissen. GFSS:289
[174]GFSSS: Pearson states that Marten was called Marten MAURITS and that he died in the fall of 1662, leaving his half of the island known as Van Slyke's Island to his brother Jacques Cornelissen van Slyke.
[175] This farm comprised the large island in the Mohawk river west of Schenectady now called Van Slyck's island. Pearson in ERAR tells us to see History of the Schenectady Patent

at Schenechtede [sic] upon which he, Aques [sic], dwells and which is known to him, for the term of four consecutive years, beginning on the date hereof or from the present sowing time, for the sum of one hundred and eighty beavers, or grain at beaver's price (the beaver reckoned at eight guilders apiece) a year, each time promptly without delay to be delivered at Schenechtede aforesaid. It is further stipulated that during the term of the lease the lessee shall have the use of a stallion and a gelding, the one called Beyert, the other Snoeck, the risk thereof to be borne by the lessor during the lease, but if the horses should perish through manifest neglect of the lessee, the charge shall be borne by the lessee. Furthermore, there shall be delivered to the lessee next spring two milch cows with their calves, if they then be with calf, which cows and expected calves the lessees shall keep for half the increase during the term of the lease, according to the custom of this country. Finally the lessee promises at the end of the lease to put again into the ground as much and similar seed grain as he now in company with the lessor has put into the ground and is still daily sowing, each party the first as well as the last year to receive the just half of the produce thereof and to bear and pay one-half of the expense, the fruits of the land for the other years remaining for the behoof of the lessee. For the performance and execution hereof the parties mutually bind their persons and estates, nothing excepted, subject to all courts and judges. All in good faith, done in the colony of Rensselaerswyck, dated as above. Signed: This mark + was made by Maritie Myndertsz, aforenamed. Ackes. Witnesses: Arnout Cornelis Vielen, Jan Cornelisz vander Heyden" [176]

In 1664 Jacques' name crops up again:

List of Debts which Mr. Arent van Curlar is to collect and receive for Gerrit Hendricxsz van Reis according to the above written power of attorney:

- Of Lambert van Valckenburch, [177]for shoes delivered, in beavers...20 gl
- Of Cornelis Dircxsz Vos, 1/2 beaver.....4 gl
- Jan Verbeeck, in seawan 3 gl
- Pieter Quackebos, 1 1/2 beavers....12 gl
- Cornelis Hoogeboom, 1 beaver......12 gl
- Marten Bierkaker's [178]wife, in seawan...27 gl
- Madam Dyckman, according to obligation dated 1/11 Oct, 1664, 16 beavers....128 gl
- Catalyna, the widow of Arent de Noorman [179] in beavers...36 gl, in seawan, 5 gl
- Akes Cornelisz, [180] in beavers ....16 gl, in seawan.....5 gl

[176] ERAR V.3:281-281
[177] This is yet another of the author's ancestors - her 9th great-grandfather Lambert Jochemse Van Valkenburg born circa 1614 in the Netherlands, who came to New Amsterdam in 1637 with his wife Annetie Jacobs. The author descends from two of his grandchildren through his son Jochem Lambertse: Isaac Jochemse and Jannetje Jochemse Van Valkenburg.
[178] Martin Hendricksen from Hamelwaerde, or Hamelworden near Freiburg on the Elbe, Hanover
[179] Arent Andriessen Bradt and wife Catalynte De Vos

- Cobus de looper, [181] in seawan, 14 gl
- Young Poentie [182], by settlement of accounts, in beavers....12 gl
- Jochem Ketlehem, 1/2 beaver......4 gl
- Pieter Adriaensz Gemackelick, in beavers....4 gl, and in seawan 2 -10 gl. [183]
- Barent Albertsz, [184]1 1/2 beavers....12 gl
- Harmen van Gansevoort, in seawan 14 gl, also per obligation 11 beavers or 88 gl
- Poulus, [185] the servant of Jan Eps in seawan 15 gl
- Pieter de steenbacker, [186]3 beavers.....24 gl
- Theunis de bierdrager, in seawan 6 gl
- Geertie Bouts, 1/2 beaver....4 gl
- Steven Jansz, in seawan 28 gl
- Jan Machielsz, 1/2 beaver....4 gl
- Anthony Jansz, per obligation in seawan 430 gl
- Marcelis Jansz per account, in seawan 300 gl
- Pieter Meusz, 3 1/2 beavers....28 gl
- Willem Brouwer, 2 1/2 beavers....20 gl

Signed Gerrit van Rys [187]

In 1664 Jacques mortgaged Van Slyck's Island for a debt to Sweer Teunis Van Velsen. It is difficult to imagine why he would need such a large amount of money.

"Appeared before me Johannes Le Montagne, in the service of, etc. in the presence of the honourable Jan Hendricksen Van Baelen and Jan Van Aken commissaries, etc., Jacus [sic] Cornelis dwelling at Schonhechteda [sic] who declared and

[180] Jacques Cornelissen Van Slyke, aka Akes
[181] Jacobus Teunissen de Looper
[182] Teunis Cornelissen van Vechten
[183] Pieter Adrianesen van Woggelum. There is an interesting account of his name Van Woggelum/ Woglom vs Mackelyck in Rosalie Fellows Bailey's _Dutch Systems in Family Naming New York - New Jersey_ Pieter Adriaensen aka Gemackelyck in 1652, Soogemacklick, then van Waggelen in 1678, and van Wuggelum in 1681. Soo gemackelyck means "so easy going" and this became Pieter's surname which shortened to Mackelyck then was abandoned in favour of Woggelum, a village in North Neth. which may be where the family originated.
[184] Barent Albertsen Bradt
[185] This might be Paulus Jansen, servant to Jan van Eps, killed in Schenectady massacre 1690. Paulus Jansen received in 1669 a patent for 1 1/2 morgens of land at Schenectady
[186] Pieter Jacobsen Borsboom,the brickmaker
[187] gl=guilders, a Dutch coin, now gulden, which in the 17th century, had the equivalent value of 6 guilders=one English pound sterling
seawan=sewant/zewant/wampum=a form of script in the colonies where coinage was rare. The value of a yard-long string of white seawan was 4 florins but this was an inflated price. 8 florin in seawan was only worth 3 florin in coin [Ref: Peter R. Christoph in _Bradt: A Norwegian FAmily in Colonial America_] Also: ERAR V.3: 304,305

acknowledged that he is well, truly and honestly indebted to Sweerus Teunise, in the sum of six hundred and ninety-three guilders in beavers, for goods and sundries to his content received; which aforesaid sum he, Jacus Cornelisse, promises to pay in the year of our Lord 1668, in the month of May; for the payment of said sum, pledging his person and estate, real and personal, more especially mortgaging the Island lying at Schonhechteda named Marten's Island, renouncing all exceptions which might militate against this obligation. Done in Fort Orange, the 3d July, A.D., 1664

The mark of ACKES, Jacus Cornelissen" [188]

A footnote explains that Jacus Cornelisse is

"Jaques Cornelise Van Slyck alias Gautsch alias Itsychosaquachka, one of the three children of Cornelis Antonissen Van Slyck alias Broer Cornelis and a Mohawk woman. Jaques had a brother Marten who gave name to the great Island lying west of Schenectady and a sister Hilletie who was a well known interpreter and married Pieter Danielse Van Olinda"

Frans Janse Pruyn, acting on Jacques' behalf in 1668, granted a house, lot, barn, garden and fruit trees in the colony of Rensselaerswyck to Jan Labatie who in turn granted the same properties to Barent Pieterse Coeymans five days later.

"Appeared before us, undersigned, commissaries of Albany, Frans Janse Pruyn, acting for Ackes Cornelise, who declares that in true rights, free ownership he grants, conveys and makes over by those presents, to and for the behoof of Jan Labatie, his heirs and successors or assigns, in the grantor's certain house, lot, barn, garden and fruit tress, standing and lying in colony Rensselaerswyck, according to the evidence of the vendue book of said colony bid off by said Labatie at public sale, of date the 16 of January 1664, extending and bounding on the westerly side the Herr patroon of the colony, northerly corst kouts [sic] easterly and southerly the public road, as the same lies in length, breadth and fence, free and unencumbered with no claim standing or issuing against the same, excepting the right of the patroon of the colony according to the descriptions and contents of the conditions and proposals of said vendue book, and by virtue of a conveyance of date the [illegible] of May, new style, 1665, in the Esopus; without the grantor's making the least claim thereto, also acknowledging that he is fully paid and satisfied therefore, the last penny with the first, therefore given *plenam actionem cessam*, and full power to the aforesaid Labatie, his heirs and successors or assigns, to do with and dispose thereof as he might do with his patrimonial estate and effects; promising to protect and free the aforesaid house, lot, barn, garden and fruit trees from all trouble, actions and liens of every persona as is right, and further, nevermore to do nor suffer anything to be done

[188] ERAR V.1: 354

against the same, with or without law, in any manner, on pledge according to law. Done in Albany, the 7th of January, 1668/9.

Frans Jansen Pruen [sic]

Witnesses Jan Verbeeck, Jan Thomase. In my presence: Ludovicus Cobes,

Secretary" [189]

By 1670 Jacques had built an inn at the corner of Washington Street and Cucumber Alley. He also had a house lot on the west corner of Washington Street and Cucumber Alley, with a front on the former street of 166 feet and extending back to the Binne Kill. The alley on the north side was the passage to the Binne Kill, which he could cross by means of a small boat, to his farm on Van Slyck's Island. By this date, Jacques and Grietje had at least four children, all born at Schenectady. No baptism records have been found for Jacques and Grietje's children, no doubt due to the burning of the town in February 1690. However Jacques' will lists his children as: Susanna, Grietje [190], Herman, Cornelis, Geertruyt, Marte, Helena, Fytie [191] and Lydia. If the order they are listed in his will is their birth order, and if we assign an arbitrary two years between births, we can deduce birth dates beginning with Susanna in 1663 to Lydia in 1679. These estimated dates fit well with marriages and births of their children, and these are the birth dates I have assigned in this book for convenience.

Tapping, or the selling of spirits, was a much sought-after privilege in the early settlements. In Schenectady, Jacques Cornelise Van Slyke and Cornelis Cornelissen Viele both wanted the right to serve liquor to the natives and this developed into a long-standing feud between the two men. In 1671 Viele petitioned the Albany courts for permission to tap liquor and to provide lodging and accommodation. Van Slyke was then the only village tapster, and this was a direct challenge to him. Their dispute over tapping rights and privileges created so much dissension that the case became the concern of the governor of New York. In 1672 Antonia Slaghboom the widow of Jonas Bronck and Arent Van Curlar, was given a licenses from Gov. Lovelace, in consideration of the loss of her husband and of her home by fire, to trade with the natives. It was thought that this would stop the quarrels of the other two tapsters, Cornelis Cornelise Viele and "Akes Cornelise Gautsch, the Indian" [192] Jacques was not successful in maintaining sole rights to tapping.

Prior to this,
"a petition of some patentees complaining about the tapping done by Cornelis Cornelissen Vielen" [193]

[189] ERAR V. 1: 453-454
[190] Grietje is the diminuitive for Margaret or Margrieta and that is likely the name she was baptised with.
[191] Fytie is the diminuitive for Sophia, and that may be the name she was baptised with.
[192] GFFSS:213
[193] ibid

In 1668 Jan Gerritsen van Marcken, the village schout, had also challenged Jacques' tapping rights, but he was not successful.

In 1678 fire destroyed the dwellings of Jacques Van Slyke and Sweer Teunissen van Velsen at Schenectady. On 29 January, 1678 they petitioned the courts at Albany for permission to tear down houses they owned outside Albany's walls and to be allowed to haul them away on their sleighs to Schenectady. On June 12, van Velsen had taken down his Albany house and carried it to Schenectady. [194] The house was hauled away on sleighs 30 Jan. 1678.

Schenectady had traditionally been a settlement of both farmers and traders, but after 1661 the villagers were limited to farming. Soon an illegal fur trade developed in Schenectady. In 1663 Stuyvesant tried to coerce the proprietors of Schenectady into signing a bond agreeing they would not continue trading at Schenectady with "any of the savages". They refused to sign and composed a letter of protest reminding Stuyvesant that a patent for land had been granted there to

"Jan Barents Wemp and Jacques N [Jacques Cornelissen Van Slyke] without such servitude or lien as is proposed in the aforesaid draft of the bond."

This referred to earlier privileges granted to Jan and Jacques as original settlers, in the form of permission to trade at the village. By 1669 there had been complaints that Schenectady residents openly traded with the natives, and so the court at Albany reiterated the prohibition against trade with the natives and fined any caught doing so. The villagers petitioned to have this restriction lifted, but were refused. In 1670 Schenectady's population was given permission to trade but only if they did so at Albany.

Albany continued to seek a monopoly on trade, and to prevent the illegal fur trade at Schenectady, Albany's courts ruled that all traffic of wagons and horses must obtain a license prior to departure from Schenectady. In resisting Albany authorities, traders at Schenectady resorted to bribery, threats, evasion and even violence. Albany magistrates complained of a lack of respect from Schenectady as a whole, including the Schenectady officials. In 1681 the Sheriff accused a Schenectady villager of "trading with an Indian" in the village. The resident interpreters, Jacques Cornelissen Van Slyke and Cornelis Cornelissen Viele, refused to act as interpreters in the matter, even though they were commanded to do so "in his Majesty's name." The Sheriff brought suit against Viele and Jacques for their refusal, but Viele stated that he did not refuse except conditionally, while Jacques claimed

"he was not commanded to do so in the King's name....or, at least, he did not hear it." [195]

[194] ARS II in MF
[195] ARS III 68-69 in MF:73

Jacques and his sister Hilletie were well known as interpreters and were much sought after. They were among the few of Schenectady's inhabitants who had contact with the colony's English hierarchy, and this was due to their position as interpreters at native conferences and as ambassadors to the Iroquois. Most of the residents of Schenectady were unknown beyond the village, but Jacques Van Slyke, referred to as a half-breed, was an exception, as were the rest of the Van Slyke, the Viele and the Glen families, who were in fact well known outside of the Mohawk valley community. Another sister to Jacques and Hilletie was Lea Van Slyke, who was called "the Indian wife of Claes Willemsen van Coppernol." Lea also lived at the village of Schenectady and although Burke refers to her with the comment that it is not certain whether she was a Mohawk woman or "another sister to the van Slycks", it appears she was indeed a sister. By 1707 both Jacques and Hilletie were dead; Lea, then married to an Englishman, Jonathan Stevens, survived them only a few years.

In 1679 and 1680 Jasper Danckaerts visited Schenectady from the Netherlands, keeping a journal of his trip. He mentions Jacques Cornelissen Van Slyke, who according to Danckaerts,

> "was also a half-breed, who had made profession of Christianity, and had been baptised, and who was not by far as good as she (Jacques' sister Hilletie), but on the contrary very wicked" [196]

Danckaerts goes on to add that he believes Jacques had been a good Christian until he was corrupted by the residents of Schenectady,

> "for this place is a godless one, being without a minister, and having only a homily read on Sundays."

Jacques' nephew Wouter, a full-blooded Mohawk according to Danckaerts, [197] lived at Schenectady with his uncle. Wouter spoke no Dutch and had abandoned all his native friends and family in favour of living as a Christian. He suffered from jeers and abuse from both the Mohawks and from the Christians. Dankaerts' notes that Wouter had

> "betaken himself entirely to the Christians and dresses like them. He has suffered much from the other Indians and his friends" [198]

According to Danckaert, Wouter's thoughts were occupied day and night by God and Jesus. Wouter was struggling to learn the Dutch language so he could be instructed in

---

[196] JD: 205

[197] The only way Wouter could be a full-blooded Mohawk and nephew to Hilletie and Jacques would be if he were the son of their deceased brother Marten Maurits. Marten is said by tradition to have taken an Indian wife before he died in 1662, and so a child of theirs could be considered, in Danckaert's eyes, to be full-blooded Mohawk.

[198] JJD

Christianity, and Jacques' sister Hilletie gave him what help she could. According to Danckaerts, Jacques Cornelissen not only failed to help Wouter, he actively hindered Wouter's desires.

"His uncle, with whom he lived, was covetous, and kept him only because he was profitable to him in hunting beaver. He therefore would hardly speak a word of Dutch to him, in order that he might not be able to leave him too soon and go among the Christians." [199]

Robert Sanders and Hilletie told Danckaerts that Jacques sent Wouter into the woods among the natives, to hunt for beaver so that he, Jacques, might profit. One story told to Danckaerts was of a time when Jacques and Wouter went out shooting for deer, and Jacques began to call Wouter a "stupid Indian" who could not shoot. Jacques claimed that he, a Christian, would have the better hunt than Wouter, and they separated. Wouter prayed to God to send him a deer and one appeared. He shot the animal but when he took the deer to his uncle, Jacques was angry that Wouter had shot something and he had not. When Wouter claimed that the deer was given to him in answer to a prayer to God, Jacques was ashamed. However, Danckaerts goes on to add that this did not change Jacques' actions for the better, although Hilletie was very much moved by the story, as was Danckaerts himself. Wouter related yet a second story of being sent an animal by God and how his heart was full with his love for God.

"in the presence of five or six persons who were well versed in the Mohawk language, and bore testimony that he (Wouter) said what she (Hilletie Van Slyke) interpreted, and that it was not enlarged" [200]

Next Wouter related a story of finding a bush in the shape of a man's hand, which he took as a sign from God. The bush, Wouter believed, represented a helping hand, one stronger and wiser than his. In Wouter's own words,

"It is true I have forsaken the Indians and have come among Christians, but this cannot help me unless a third power make me a true Christian and enable me to learn the language that I may inquire, read and enter into the grounds of Christianity" [201]

Wouter took the bush back with him to his uncle's house, and Danckaerts relates how he himself had seen it and held it. Wouter then presented the bush to Robert Sanders, who took it to Albany.

[199] JD:206

[200] ibid:208
[201] ibid:209

When Danckaerts asked Hilletie why she did not send Wouter to a place where he could learn the language and Christianity, Hilletie replied that her brother Jacques would never hear of sending Wouter away as he kept him

"as a kind of servant such as the English have, for the sake of vile gain, and although he (Wouter) was free and bound to nobody, would never speak a word of Dutch to him, so that he might not lose him."

The second difficulty according to Hilletie was Wouter's age, which she gave as either 24 or 26 years, and which would not make it easy to find a place for him to board. Danckaerts offered to take Wouter with him on his return to the Netherlands, where, he said, Wouter

"should never be our servant or slave....and if God should give him further the grace he would be our brother and as free as we were"

That same night, Wouter, Hilletie and her husband Peter Danielse van Olinda, Adam Vrooman and his wife Engeltie came to see Danckaerts about Wouter's possible future. It was decided that Wouter would go with Danckaerts, and the next morning, Friday April 26, 1680, Wouter was there early. As Danckaerts went around to say his goodbyes to Hilletie and others in the community, Jacques Van Slyke arrived. Jacques began to question Danckaerts as to Wouter's going to the Netherlands with them. He asked Danckaerts what trade they would teach Wouter, and who would be his security in the event he were captured by Turks. Jacques and Robert Sanders exchanged words and Sanders accused Jacques of only keeping Wouter for the profit Wouter brought to him. Danckaerts and his party eventually rode off, leaving Jacques still there. They arrived in Albany at Sander's house after a five hour ride. Danckaert's journal does not mention Wouter again, and nothing further is known of him. [202]

It was not unusual for natives and whites to live together in Schenectady for there and in Albany, they lived together, traded together, slept in the same rooms, and ate at the same table. The distinction between white and natives did not seem to be as sharp a line in the Mohawk Valley as elsewhere in the New World. Danckaerts mentions that the Dutch in these outlying communities had become wild and untamed, reckless, unrestrained, haughty and more addicted to cursing and swearing. Jacques' Mohawk nephew, Wouter, left Schenectady in 1680 to rendezvous with Jasper Danckaerts at Boston for a journey to the Netherlands. Nothing further is known of him. It is my belief that Wouter may have been a son of Jacques' brother Marten and this is discussed in the chapter on Marten.

Jacques' ownership of the First Flat above Schenectady was provided for by the Mohawks in their 1672 deed with the Schenectady magistrates. At the signing of this deed, the stipulation had been made that Jacques was to keep the first flat unless the

---

[202] ibid

inhabitants of Schenectady paid him "two rumlets of Brandy and one hundred beads of wampum" On the 13 July 1672 Jacques received two rumlets of brandy while the Mohawks received lead, powder, beer and a coat of duffels for their land. His sisters Hilletie and Lea also received several properties from the Mohawks. Gradually the Schenectady court awarded more land to other individuals but on 4 October 1683, representatives of the Mohawk tribe complained to Governor Thomas Dongan, stating that they had never meant to give up full control of their lands to anyone other than Arent van Curlar and the Van Slykes.

"That one Arent Van Corlaer bought all Schannectade, & payed them for it but now there be some who have bought only the Grasse, & pretend to the land Allso, they say Allso that they have bought the first flatt, but that is not so, for it belongs to Acques Cornelissen....for he is of their people, &.....that there are writeings made of a sale of land but It was never sold but only the Grasse tho it may be some drunken fellows may have made som Writeings without their knowledge. That they have only bought the grasse & are now going to live upon it, but they ought to pay for the land as well as the Grasse, & that they had given some to that woman (Hillah & another Lea who have the propirety of it) the other have only the grasse" [203]

The Mohawks referred to attempts made to dispossess Jacques (Akes) Cornelissen Van Slyke of his ownership of the first flat. Governor Dongan's reply revealed the dissatisfaction with the people of Schenectady with Jacques.

"The people of Schannectady say they sent Acques to purchase the Land in the name of their Town, and that Acques bought it in his own name, [204] & they sent allso one Kemel[205] to purchase it for the Towne; the Indians told them that Acques had bought & paid some part of the payment" [206]

Thus Viele and Jacques Van Slyke were once more opponents, this time over the acquisition of land from the Mohawks.

By 1683, there were many people who were dissatisfied with Jacques Cornelissen Van Slyke's handling of the land negotiation with the Mohawks, and they hired Cornelis Cornelissen Viele to act on their behalf. This may have been indicative of the divisions affecting Schenectady's first patentees and later arrivals who desired a more equitable share of village resources such as land. In November 1684 Governor Dongan issued a patent to Schenectady legalizing the earlier 1672 transfer of land negotiated by the Mohawks and the Schenectady magistrates. For a yearly stipend of 40 bushels of winter wheat, Dongan presented the community with a territory of 120 square miles. He then created an independent group of five trustees with authority to manage the unpatented

[203]MF:153-154
[204]The inhabitants of Schenectady later compensated Jacques van Slyke for the land.
[205]Most likely this is Cornelis Cornelissen Viele who was known as Keeman by the Mohawks
[206]MF:154

lands, even though this was protested by both the Mohawks and the villagers. The Mohawk tribes were becoming increasingly unhappy with the Dutch, and were being wooed by the French through the native leader Kryn.

By 1685 the English-French rivalry had become open conflict, as the French experienced a crisis in their fur trade, which was a lucrative business for them. By 1685 the French governor in New France was ordered to curb the aggression of the Iroquois and deal with threats to the French fur trade, no matter who these threats came from. By 1687 a French army was striking at both the English and the Iroquois.

Schenectady, throughout this time period, was of great assistance to the English and the services of the Dutch at Schenectady were in demand as interpreters. Cornelis Cornelissen Viele and Jacques Cornelissen Van Slyke had acted as interpreters since 1660. Jacques, who is described in official records as "formerly an Indyan", was trusted by the Mohawks due to his Mohawk blood. During a conference in 1688, representatives of the Mohawks proposed to Governor Andros that

"the propositions made yesterday to us, may be left in writeing [sic] with Akus the Interpreter, to whom wee may have recourse for information"

Burke states in *The Mohawk Frontier* that

"of all the seventeen interpreters, van Slyck may have been the best, and his services were in demand as far away as New York City, where in August 1687 he helped to examine a 'Christian Maquase brought a Prisonner from Cannada' " [207]

In 1687, when a French attack was anticipated, Governor Thomas Dongan wintered briefly at Schenectady. He received proposals from the Five Nations presented to him by Jacques Van Slyke and Daniel Jansen van Antwerpen. [208]

In 1689 the uprising initiated by the New York City militia and led by Jacob Leisler had far-reaching and divisive consequences for Schenectady. Leisler's Rebellion and the events surrounding it created dissension in the community over the issue of land ownership. The villagers divided into two groups - first settlers versus later arrivals, who both wanted access to land, the most valuable commodity known. Jacques Cornelissen, aged 49, aligned himself with the anti-Leislerian party in 1689, along with Willem Teller, Gerrit Bancker, and Pieter Danielsen van Olinda, all surviving village proprietors. Allied with them were the sons of original proprietors, such as Sanders and Johannes Sanderse Glen. Jacques' involvement was in having aided the Albany Convention with Indian Affairs. Others who opposed Leisler in 1689 were Adam Vrooman who later married Jacques' wife, Grietje Ryckman. Other names on this list are Sweer Teunissen van Velsen, Johannes Appel and Jan van Eps.

[207] MF:93-94
[208] MF

The pro-Leisler faction were a group somewhat younger in years who had arrived at Schenectady after its original settlement. These included Douwe Aukes, David Christoffelsen, Reynier Schaats and Reyer Schermerhorn. Symon Schermerhorn, Myndert Wemp, Johannes Pootman, Claes Fredericksen van Petten, Isaac Cornelissen Swits, and Arnout Viele. Many of the pro-Leisler individuals were of lesser means but this is not true of all, as the Schermerhorns, Myndert Wemp and Douwe Aukes all owned slaves. The Schermerhorns were the sons of Jacob Jansen who in 1660 was one of the principal traders at Beverwyck and who left a vast estate at his death in 1688.

Many families were divided by the Leisler Rebellion. Two of Jacques Cornelissen Van Slyke's daughters married two Bradt brothers, the sons of Arent Andreissen Bradt and Cathalynta de Vos. [209] These Bradt brothers were associated with the anti-Leislerian party but their sisters were the wives of Reyer Schermerhorn, Claes Fredericksen van Patten and Johannes Pootman, who were pro-Leislerians. Divisions at Schenectady continued even until the 1700s as evidenced by the signing of three addresses on 30 December 1701 to King William III signed by men who were in opposition to the Leislerian party. Three of Jacques Cornelissen Van Slyke's sons: Harmen, Cornelis and Martin, signed this document. They were three of nineteen Schenectady residents who did so. They were also opponents of Reyer Schermerhorn, and siding with the Van Slyke brothers were Samuel Bradt and Johannes Myndertse (both of who married sisters of the Van Slyke brothers), Adam Vrooman and his three sons: Jan, Hendrick, and Barent. Also against Schermerhorn were Pieter van Olinda who was married to Hilletie Van Slyke and their son Daniel. Another with ties to the Van Slyke family was Harmen Vedder who married Grietje Van Slyke, another daughter of Jacques Cornelissen [210].

At the beginning of 1690, war parties assembled at Quebec, Trois Rivieres and Montreal to attack New England and New York. The largest party consisting of 114 Canadians and 96 native warriors left Montreal in January headed for Schenectady. The invaders were led by Nicolas d'Ailleboust de Manthet, Jacques le Moyne de Sainte-Helene and Pierre Le Moyne d'Iberville, while the natives were led by Kryn. The attackers were under orders to inflict as much destruction against Schenectady and its inhabitants as they could. French prisoners taken later stated they had orders

[209]The author descends from the brother of Arent Andriessen Bradt, Albert Andreissen born ca 1607 in Frederikstad, Norway. The interlinking of families is very complex and tangled. Burke states in The Mohawk Frontier that "the most intricate relationships were among the van Slyck, van Olinda and Vrooman families." [MF:169] Jacques Cornelissen van Slyke's wife Grietje Ryckman, was sister to the first wife of Adam Vrooman. Adam was the brother of another of the author's ancestors, Eva Hendrickse Vrooman, who married Jochem Lambertse Van Valkenburg. Grietje Ryckman married her brother-in-law Adam Vrooman, after the death of his wife and her husband in 1690.

[210] Greitje, or Margaret van Slyke was the widow of Andries Arentsen Bradt, and she and Harmen Vedder were married on 10 December 1691.

"to murder and DeStroy all People they mett withall at Shinnechtady except Such as beg'd for quarters; as also to Burn ye Place and to take with them those that they could cary along"[211]

After seventeen days' march, the attackers reached Schenectady at eleven o'clock at night on February 9. Due to the extreme cold and knee-deep snow, they did not wait to attack but struck immediately. Schenectady had been built in the shape of a square palisade with only two gates. native women discovered in a shelter just outside the village, were forced to show the invaders the first gate, which was found to be open. The second gate was not found and the invaders encircled the village before attacking. The French method of attack was to divide into small groups of six or seven in front of each house, then enter the home, putting all who defended it, to death. Within two hours, the village had been taken by the French and many villagers lay dead.

According to the French, the only home not attacked was that of Sanders Glen [212] but when asked to surrender the following morning, Glen refused. The French promised Glen quarter for himself and his family if he surrendered, and this he did. At noon on Sunday, the French and natives left, taking 30 or 40 horses, and 27 captives as well as the severed head of the minister of Schenectady, Petrus Tesschenmaeker. Many of the sixty villagers who were killed had been burned in the fires that were lit when the houses were torched. The loss of life at Schenectady was greater than at any other town attacked by the French, due to the element of surprise and the ease with which the French and natives gained entrance to the village, making it impossible for soldiers and villagers to resist.

Reports stated that the devastation of Schenectady was almost total. All the houses, barns and cattle were destroyed except, as noted, the home of Sanders Glen. Of the 60 white villagers killed, 19 were men, 22 were young men, 7 were women, 1 was a young woman, and 11 were children. As well there were 9 soldiers from Connecticut, 16 slaves, 1 native, and 1 French female prisoner killed that night in the attack.

Accounts differ as to the number of survivors, with the French insisting they spared 50 or 60 people; two separate accounts of the attack stating that 25 survivors remained at Schenectady. However, records show that the heads of 50 Schenectady households were provided with aid at Albany in March. The discrepancy in numbers suggests that some of the inhabitants of the village may have been absent the night of the massacre. Jacques Cornelise Van Slyke was one of the twenty-five Dutch villagers who lived through the massacre. Shipping records [213] have revealed the name of Jacques as making a sailing voyage in 1690. The item reads Van Slyck, Akes Cornelissen, age 50,

[211] LIR in MF
[212] Robert Livingson stated that 6 or 7 houses had been spared. In June 1691 the Iroquois were known to be burning the deserted houses and barns near Schenectady and killing any livestock they found in the woods.
[213] Ship Passenger Lists, New York and New Jersey (1600-1825)" 1982 supplement by Boyer.

New York, 1690 but no ship is listed. [214]Apparently he died not too long after making the trip so he too may have been absent from Schenectady on the night of the massacre. His wife and children also survived the massacre.

There are many recorded tales of individuals and their plight. Symon Schermerhorn, although badly wounded, managed to escape to ride for five hours through the snow to reach Albany in order to spread the alarm. Riders were immediately sent to Esopus asking for assistance, and to Kinderhook and Claverack to warn farmers there. The cannon at Albany was fired to warn the nearby residents of Rensselaerswyck. On Monday February 10, a burial party was dispatched from Albany to Schenectady to attempt to bury the dead and to tend to survivors. A force of 140 Mohawks and Dutch pursued the French and natives and within a month, four prisoners were returned. Eventually 18 prisoners were released or escaped between 1690 and 1699. English captives often chose to remain among their native captors, but from the captives at Schenectady not one remained with the natives or French, not even, according to Burke, those most influenced by their stay with the Canadian natives such as Jan Baptist van Eps and Lourens Claesen Van der Volgen.

Most massacre survivors found refuge at Albany. On March 28, 1690, reference is made to supplies including clothes and material for clothing having reached Albany and being distributed to survivors of the Schenectady massacre. Albany became congested with the Schenectady survivors in February, then the arrival in May of troops from New England for an attack against Canada. Disease, consisting of smallpox and "the bloody flux" was prevalent during the spring of 1690. Jacques Cornelissen Van Slyke was at Albany on May 18, 1690

"lying....sick abed" [215]

Jacques may have been sick the previous fall, [216] but he testified against Robert Livingston on 1 April 1690 and was not noted as being in ill health at that time. He also traveled, apparently back to the Netherlands and home to Albany prior to May 1690. However he died soon after , having made his will on the 8th day of May 1690. In his will, Jacques expressed the intention that his wife and children should return to burnt-out Schenactady and reoccupy the family's property.

The will of Jacques Cornelissen Van Slyke follows:

"In the name of God, Amen. Know all men whom it may concern, that on this eighteenth of May anno sixteen hundred and ninety, at Albany, being in the second year of the reign of William and Mary, King and Queen of Great Britain, Jaques Comelisse van Slyck, residing at Schennechtady, lying here in the city aforesaid Sick

[214]Early New Yorkers and Their Ages by K. Scott, p.295.
[215] MF:199
[216]Yates states that he died of pulmonary disease, but does not give his source for this.

abed, but having to all outward appearances the perfect use and command of his understanding, faculties, memory and speech who, considering the frailty of human life and the uncertainty of the hour of death, has of his own motion, without inducement, persuasion or misleading of anyone, but moved thereto voluntarily after mature consideration thought it advisable not to leave this world without first having disposed of his temporal effects granted to him by the Almighty. Commending first and. foremost his immortal soul into the hands of God and his body to a Christian burial, he nominates, constitutes and appoints his wife Gerritje Ryckman his sole and universal heir of all his estate and effects, in manner following:

So soon as their son Herman enters the marriage state, she shall first of all let him have by way of gift fourteen morgens of land lying above Schanechtady, on the first flat, above Sassiasn, the testator's wife to have the use of all the other land, grounds, houses and buildings belonging to him, but the whole of the personal estate and effects she, shall be at liberty to use, spend, sell, alienate and dispose of. as she pleases, in like manner as the testator in his lifetime could do, without rendering an accounting or inventory, much less furnishing bond or security, to any relatives, to the guardians of his children or children's children, to the honorable orphan masters or constables, to the inferior and supreme courts of this government, or to any person whomsoever, all and singular of whom he excludes and shuts out, notwithstanding that some law or laws may direct otherwise, which he wills shall in this case be inoperative and of no effect, appointing her as executrix and administratrix during the time of her widowhood; but if she again enters into the marriage estate, she shall to the children begotten by them, to wit:  Susanna, Grietje, Herman, Cornelis, Geertruyt, Marte, Helena, Fytie, Lidia and those who may still be procreated by them, apportion and relinquish the just half of all the estate and effects to said children then living, wherein each child shall equally participate without any difference by reason of sex, without prejudice to the donation of fourteen morgens of land to Herman as herein-before written.

And although the daughters have likewise their interest in the lands, the testator wills that said lands shall remain in the possession of the sons subject to a proper appraisal, and the value of each daughter's portion be paid within the five following years, each year a just fifth part; which lands also may not be sold or alienated by the sons but must descend to each son's male child or children, and failing of these, to the nearest relatives in the male line, who may lawfully bear the name of Van Slyck and be of the testator's lawful seed; but the male lineage failing, the nearest female line shall inherit and succeed to the aforesaid estate even as the male line, because the testator expressly wills and desires that the aforesaid land shall not be alienated from his future blood and lineage but must always return thither again. But if his aforesaid wife marries again, she shall immediately, before the solemnization of such marriage, cause to devolve upon those who are of age their portion and (under, sufficient security) retain the minor's portion and enjoy the use and profits thereof until the time of the majority of each, with the understanding that whoever is of age may demand his portion without waiting until the majority of the younger; therefore she is holden to do by those underage in all ways as an honorable, faithful mother ought to do by her child or children, Without any reserve or exception.

And in order that all, the aforesaid conditions may in honest simplicity and justice be carried out, the testator appoints Mr. Pieter Schuyler, Mr. Dirk Wessells and Johannes Glenn as guardians over his minor children, who also shall be Joined with his aforesaid wife, to act as mediators in case any difference or misunderstanding arise between her and the children and to settle the same in love and friendship, so that the maternal and filial affection be not extinguished and that the testator's aforesaid will be not broken and Violated; which burden, by the testator's humble request, their honors will please take upon themselves, since Christian duty obligates us to assist the widows and orphans by word and deed.

All that is herein before written the testator declares to be his testamentary disposition and last will, which he desires to have effect from the weightiest to the least article thereof, whether as will, codicil, gift in anticipation of death or among the living, or any other bequest however it may be named, notwithstanding that all the formalities required by the laws of this government may not be observed herein, desiring that the utmost benefit of the law may be enjoyed herein for the maintenance of the same.

Thus done, signed and scaled on the 8th of May 1690, at Albany as aforesaid.

This is signed A C K E S by JAQUES CORNELISE
VAN SLYK with his own hand (L. S.)
Signed and sealed
in our presence,
A. Appell
Jacob Staets, chirurgeon
In my presence,
JAN BECKER" [217]

Jacques was 50 years old when he died, leaving a widow, Margaret, daughter of Harman Janse Ryckman of Albany. Margaret, or Grietje, as she was called, married her brother-in-law Adam Vrooman on the 21 Feb. 1692 in Albany New York. [218] Adam's wife, Margaret's sister, Engeltie, [219] had been killed at the massacre at Schenectady, along with their infant son. By Jan 13, 1697 Grietje Ryckman was dead, Adam Vrooman marrying for the third time in Albany to Grietje Takelse Heemstraat. [220]

[217] ERAR: V. 4 pp 119-121
[218] HSCNY:234
[219] There is confusion over the first wife of Adam Vrooman, with some sources claiming her as Engeltie Ryckman, sister of Margaret Ryckman, and others stating she is Engletie Blom. It is outside the scope of this genealogy to attempt to discuss this and interested readers should refer to the several books which mention her.
[220] GDS

64

Jacques was either very well respected and liked or actively disliked. He had one camp of followers who respected his dealings with the Mohawks and his abilities as an interpreter (which was more than just translating the words - it involved a great deal of diplomacy.) but another group in Schenectady appears to have resented him very much. This group petitioned to have him removed as interpreter, and argued that he rather nicely managed to line his own pockets in the transaction with the Mohawks to buy Schenectady. The land was put in his name but was supposed to be purchased on behalf of all 15 proprietors. The problem was that the Mohawks wouldn't sell the land unless it were in the name of one of their own. It appears that some Schenectady residents resented his land holdings and his favour with the Mohawks - understandable since he was half Mohawk!

Dankaerts thought him self-serving in regards to his nephew Wouter, as did his sister Hilletie, but I see a man who was raised as an Indian with different values and culture who was in his own way very concerned for Wouter - one of the objections he raised at Wouter's leaving with Dankaerts for the Netherlands was who would care for Wouter when they tired of him, or he became ill. This does not sound like the self-serving man Danckaerts portrays. Jasper was of course, very pious, a devout Labadist and had no use for the rough and ready settlers - he thought them a sinful lot, and was very disparaging in his remarks. So although his journal is a wonderful read, it is coloured by his own prejudices.

# CHAPTER 6

## HILLETIE CORNELISE VAN SLYKE

Hilletie Cornelise, sister of Jacques Cornelise Van Slyke, was, according to Jonathan Pearson,

"a half-breed, her mother being a Mohawk woman, her father Cornelis Antonissen Van Slyke"[221]

It is not clear what name Hilletie was given at birth, but we know that she was given the name Hilletie, sometimes written as Eltie, Illetie or Alleta, by the Christian woman with whom she went to live as a young adult. [222] This woman's name is not recorded but Danckaert tells us that she was a wise woman, sharp in trading with the natives and well as the local settlers. According to Danckaerts she was married for the second time to a papist who stayed at home while she traded throughout the country. It would be interesting to try to discover who this woman was.

Jasper Danckaerts, who visited Schenectady from the Netherlands in 1680, met Hilletie when she brought her four year old son to him to see if Danckaerts could do anything to cure the child's muteness. It is assumed from the birth dates that this was her first born child, Daniel Pieterse. Danckaerts wrote in his journal of Hilletie's compelling tale of her childhood and of her conversion to Christianity. Hilletie, with many tears, told Danckaert how moved she was to be allowed to see him, and to speak with him.
"....that I am so fortunate; that God should permit me to behold such Christians, whom I have so long desired to see, and to whom I may speak from the bottom of my heart without fear. "

Hilletie surprised and touched Danckaerts with her honesty and openness and her genuine love of God. As they talked, she told him of her early years, stating that she was born of a Christian father and an Indian mother of the Mohawk tribes. Her mother had

---

[221]GDS:229. Pearson further states that Jacques Cornelisse van Slyke was the half-breed son of Cornelise van Slyke and "his wife, a Mohawk chieftan's daughter." This is one of two versions of Ots-Toch's parentage, the other being that she was the daughter of a Frenchman from New France named Jacques Hartell [sic].
[222]JD

remained with the Mohawks, having a deep hatred of Christians. Hilletie and her brothers and sisters lived with their mother, but sometimes they went with her mother among the Christians to make purchases, and the Christians began to take a liking to Hilletie,

"discovering in her more resemblance to the Christians that the Indians, but understand, more like the Dutch, and that she was not so wild as the other children. They therefore wished to take the girl and bring her up, which the mother would not hear to, and as this request was made repeatedly, she said she would rather kill her." [223]

Hilletie at first had no wish to leave, and her mother Ots-Toch did nothing more than continually express her hatred of the Christians. Then Hilletie began to doubt what her mother was saying against the Christians

"the more so because she never went among them (Christians) without being well treated" [224]

Hilletie began to feel a longing towards the Christian religion and a love of God.

"Her mother observed it and began to hate her and not treat her as well as she had done before. Her brothers and sisters despised and cursed her, threw stones at her, and did her all the wrong they could" [225]

Finally Ots-Toch and her brothers and sisters could stand no more, nor could Hilletie continue to live with them. Her mother told Hilletie to leave, and she went to live with the Christians who had wanted her. They gave her the name of Eltie or Illetie, sometimes written Aletta, or Hilletie. Hilletie lived with a woman who taught her to read and write. She learned the Dutch language and was able to read the New Testament. Finally she was baptised in the Christian faith. [226] Hilletie was still subjected to scorn and abuse from those around her, telling Danckaerts that she

"grieved over [them], not daring to speak out my heart to any one, for when I would sometimes rebuke them a little for their evil lives, drunkenness and foul and godless language, they would immediately say 'Well, how is this, there is a sow converted'......... words which went through my heart, made me sorrowful, and closed my mouth"

Hilletie appears in the records as an interpreter, under the names of Hilletie Cornelissen and Hilletie Pieterse. It was not uncommon for Dutch women to take a

---

[223] JD:263
[224] JD:263
[225] JD:263
[226] There is no surviving record of baptisms at Schenectady before 1694.

patronymic based on their husband's rather than their father's first names. Thus the name Hilletie Pieterse is written, based on her husband Pieter Danielse Van O'Linda.

For many years Hilletie, along with Jan Baptist Van Eps and Lourens Claese van der Volgen, was employed as a provincial interpreter to the Native tribes, for which she was paid 20 pounds per year. The Mohawk sachems gave her the Great island in the Mohawk River at Niskayuna in 1667, which Van Olinda sold to Captain Johannes Clute in 1669. They also gave her land at the Willow Flat below Port Jackson and at the Boght in Watervliet. She married Pieter Danielse Van Olinda, a Dutch tailor turned farmer. Danckaerts had the following to say about Pieter.

"Her (Hilletie's) husband is not as good as she is, though he is not one of the worst; she sets a good example before him and knows how to direct him." [227]

In 1689 Jacob Leisler of Leisler's Rebellion sent an army to Albany to take the fort. When a force of Mohawk warriors arrived at the Fort in support of Albany's mayor Pieter Schuyler, Hilletie accompanied them as an interpreter. [228]

Hilletie died 10 February 1707. Pieter Danielse made his will August 1, 1715 and it was proved on Dec. 27, 1716. His will provides ten shillings to his eldest son Daniel born circa 1676. To his second son Jacob born circa 1678 he left the use of his land called the Willow Flat, above Schenectady. This land was patented to him and to Willem van Coppernol until his son Mattias born circa 1680 [229] died.

[227] JJD
[228] BNFA
[229] SC:26

# CHAPTER 7

## LEA CORNELISE VAN SLYKE

Not much is known of Lea or Leah as her name is sometimes written. In 1678 she appears in the records working on a farm with her first husband Claes Willemse van Coppernol in Catskill NY. In 1679 they were living on the Schenectady patent, apparently working the farm of Willem Teller. [1]

One interesting occurrence involving Lea came about in 1683. Albert van Eeckelen, the sixteen year old orphaned nephew of Dirck Albertsen Bradt, [2] was tomahawked and seriously injured at Dirck's house while sleeping. A Mohawk named Unochschonie was arrested and charged with the crime. Unochschonie claimed that he was sleeping in Dirck's house that night when another northern native named Wattkeense entered and attacked Albert. However Albert survived and claimed that he had locked all the doors to the house and that only he and Unochschonie were there at the time of the attack. The courts then informed the Mohawks of the crime and Unochschonie confessed. He stated he had gone to Dirck Bradt's house to borrow powder so he could hunt ducks for the wife of Claes Willemse (van Coppernol) at Schenectady. Unochschonie admitted that he had intended all along to steal the powder if Dirk would not lend it but added that the devil had encouraged him in this behaviour.

The court then issued a proclamation about the prohibition against allowing natives to lodge in white settler's homes. Unochschonie was put in jail to await the arrival of the Mohawk sachems. Two months later in June 1683 the sachems took Unochschonie into their custody guaranteeing he would not return. [3]

Claes and Lea settled on her land at the Willegen, near Port Jackson New York and had a son Willem Claessen van Coppernol born circa 1690. In 1692 Claes died leaving her a widow with a two year old son.

By 1693 Lea was married to Jonathan Stevens from New England. She and Jonathan had four children - Annatje, Nicolas, Dina and Arent. However there is a discrepancy in the dates of birth of these children and the estimated date of birth for Lea herself. Annatje was born in 1695 and Arent, her last, in 1702. Lea's date of birth is estimated as early as 1646 and probably no later than 1650, making it unlikely she would

---

[1] HSC
[2] Dirck was the brother of the author's ancestor Jan Albertsen Bradt
[3] BNFA

be bearing children at the age of 52. Jonathan's date of birth is given as 1675 but it seems unlikely he would marry a woman 20 or more years his senior. Descendants of Lea will want to investigate further.

# CHAPTER 8

## MARTEN MAURITS, SON OF CORNELIS VAN SLYKE

Not much is known of Marten Maurits Van Slyke. In keeping with Dutch naming patterns of the time, and patronymics, his name should have been recorded as Marten Cornelissen Van Slyke, but all the records I have found record him as Marten Maurits. There were variations in spelling, such as Martin Mourisz, Martin Mourisee, Marten Mouritsen and Marten Mouwerensz. However there is too much evidence pointing to his being a Van Slyke to not include him in this genealogy. A possibility which has occurred to the author is that Marten may have been a son of Ots-Toch by a Mohawk warrior, raised with the Van Slyke children and given his surname by Cornelis.

Tradition claims that Marten married a Mohawk woman, had at least one child, and lived with her until his death in 1662. It may be that Wouter, the "full-blooded Mohawk" nephew of Jacques Cornelise Van Slyke referred to by Danckaerts, was a son of Marten. It would make sense for a man like Jasper Danckaerts to refer to an individual of mixed parentage as full-blooded. Marten himself was at the least one quarter Mohawk (more if he was sired by a Mohawk man) and his children by a Mohawk woman would likely be thought of as full blooded Mohawks by white settlers.

There are few documents relating to Marten. He was a witness to the July 27 1661 deed between Arent van Curlar and the Mohawks, signing his name "Martin Mourisee" [1] . Marten and Jan Barentse Wemp acquired land at Schenectady and on Marten's death this property passed to his younger brother Jacques Cornelissen Van Slyke.

In August 1662 his name appears in the court records on a bond:

"Bond of Marten Mouritsen [2] to Jeronimus Ebbingh: On this day, the 10th. of August 1662, Marten Mouritsz, dwelling in the colony of Rensselaerswyck, acknowledges that he is well and truly indebted to Mr. Jeronimus Ebbingh, trader at Amsterdam in New Netherlands, in the sum of one hundred and sixty-three guilders, 11 stivers, 8 pence in beavers, together with twenty guilders in good strung seawan, growing out of the matter of merchandise delivered in the year 1661 and by him to his content received of Lodewyck de Rooy, late servant of Mr. Ebbingh; which said sum of fl

---

[1] Nelson Greene states that Marten was Cornelis' second son but does not give a source for this information.
[2] ERAR V.3:172: Marten Cornelissen van Slyck, alias Marten Maurits, a half breed who at an early date obtained Van Slyck's island, west of the city of schenectady. He died in 1662. See _History of the Schenectady Patent_p.77

163-11-8 (163 guilders, 11 stivers, 8 pence) in beavers and fl. 20 in seawan, he Marten Mourisz, promises to pay to said Mr. Ebbingh or his order, in the business season or at the latest in the month of July 1663, punctually and without further delay (and the seawan also in beavers, reckoned at 18 gl. a beaver); with yearly interest thereon at ten percent beginning on the 1st. of July last and running till the full payment thereof: therefor binding his person and estate, nothing excepted, subject to the authority of all courts and judges. All in good faith. Dates as above and signed in the presence of Lambert van Neck and Gerrit van Tricht, as witnesses thereto called. This mark MM was made by Marten Mourisz, aforenamed. Witnesses: Lambert Van Neck, Gerrit van Tricht. 1662" [3]

In Sept. 1662 Marten is mentioned again when he hired a farm labourer for his lands

"Indenture of service of Hendrick Arentsen as farm hand to Jan Barentsen Wemp and Marten Mauritsen: On this day, the 16th. of September 1662, Jan Barentsz Wemp and Marten Mouwerensz [sic] [4] have hired, and Hendrick Arentse de suyckerbacker (the confectioner) has bound himself to serve them in cultivating, plowing, sowing, mowing, threshing, winnowing, cutting wood, and whatever else pertains thereto; and likewise to perform all further service possible that may be asked of him on their farm lying at Schenectede [sic], to him, Hendrick, known for the time of one year beginning from the date hereof; for which service, they, Jan Barentsz Wemp and Marten Mouwerensz [sic] promise to pay the sum of three hundred guilders in beavers, at eight guilders each, or in grain or other wares at beaver's value, to be paid here in the Fuyck [Beverwyck] to said Hendrick Arentsz or his order; and he, Jan Barentsz, is bound for the full payment of said stipulated hire as his own debt. All in good faith, ate as above, in the colony of Rensselaerswyck. This mark I B W was made by Jan Barentsz Wemp. This mark M M was made by Marten Mouwerensz. Henderck Arenst [sic] [5]

Marten is said to have died in the fall of 1662 and we know he was alive in September of that year. After that there is no further record of him. Did he die in the smallpox epidemic that swept through Beverwyck and surrounding towns in 1662?

---

[3] ERAR V.3:172

[4] ERAR V.3:188: Marten Mauritsen van Slyck, who seems to have died soon after the date of this extract. He and Jan Barentsen Wemp owned the large island lying west of the city of Schenectady, which was at first called Marten's Island, and afterwards Van Slyck's Island. See HSP p77

[5] ERAR. V.3:187

# CHAPTER 9

## JACQUES HERTEL AND HIS WIFE MARIE MARGUERIE

While this family is not the main focus of this book, it was felt that their inclusion in a small way was both important to an understanding of Jacques Hertel, the man, as well as being historically necessary. The following chapter is a brief glimpse into this family starting with Jacques' wife, Marie Marguerie. Much more information is available to those interested in reading more about Jacques Hertel and Marie Marguerie's legitimate line.

We find mention of Marie in Raymond Douville and Jacques-Donat Casanova's book, in an article about women in New France.

Marie Marguerie, a native of Rouen, arrived in New France in 1639. She responded to an appeal from her brother Francois, explorer and companion of Champlain, who became an interpreter of the Native languages. Francois went to the town of Trois-Rivieres; Marie followed. There she met Jacques Hertel a native of Fecamp, from Normandy like herself and more, "one of the first and most notable inhabitants of the place."

They married in 1641. Three children were born, of which Francois became one of Canada's most illustrious heroes, the equal of [Father] Le Moyne in boldness and bravery. Francois Hertel was always under Le Moyne's superiority. He was educated in the heritage bequeathed to him by his mother. Jacques Hertel died suddenly on 10 Aug. 1651. He is buried in the side chapel of the parish church that he had constructed at his expense two years before, in deference to the fulfillment of a vow: the resistance of the Trois-Rivieres post against a Native attack.

Marie Marguerie had twenty-five years of hardship in New France but she was much sought after by the single men of the colony. Some senior officers in the entourage of the Governor and the Intendant courted her. She hesitated to decide even though she was now alone in the country with her three children. Her brother Francois had drowned in crossing the St. Lawrence River across from Trois-Rivieres five years earlier. She could have returned to France where some officials offered her marriage, but she preferred to wait, because her children had been born in New France.

Two years after the death of Jacques, she married Quentin Moral de Saint-Quentin, who was still only a humble colonist [1], after having been a soldier, but who became a King's lieutenant, then a civil and criminal judge. Four daughters were born of this union which lasted for thirty-five years. Marie Marguerie had never left her port of registry in New France. Quentin Moral died in 1686, in Trois-Rivieres. Marie Marguerie died on 24 Nov. 1700 and, the day of the funeral, the cure of the parish of Trois-Rivieres, le Recollet [Father] Luc Filiastre, bestowed the following eulogy:

"This day, 26 Nov. 1700, Marie Marguerie, the widow of Saint-Quentin has been buried She died after having received the last sacrament with all the marks of a singular devotion, having lived more than 50 years in the service of all of the inhabitants of this village, assisting them in their need with charity and an incomparable zeal; remarkably, she gave her full attentions to the service of the church, acting as sacristine and taking great care of the church furnishings. She was buried, according to her wishes, beside the body of M. Hertel, her first husband." [2]

Tanguay shows Quentin Moral de St. Quentin born 1622; buried 9 May 1686 at Three Rivers married in 1652 to Marie Marguerie born 1626; widow of Jacques Hertel; buried 26 Nov. 1700. There were children from her second marriage.

The *Dictionary National des Canadiens Francais, 1608-1760*, by Monseigneur Lussier (Montreal: Institut Genealogique Drouin, 1965), gives the following marriage: Quentin Moral de St-Quentin, Lieutenant of the King, married in 1652 [no exact date given] to Marie Marguerie, daughter of Francois Marguerie and Marthe Romain, of St.-Vincent de Rouen, Normandy.

[1] V. XLVII p. 315 Qeuntin Moral de St. Quentin, a Lt. of the king, md. 1652 at the age of 30, the widow of Jacques Hertel.
[2] NF

# CHAPTER 10

## FRANCOIS-JOSEPH HERTEL AND MARGUERITE DE THAVENET

The only known son of Jacques Hertel and Marie Marguerie was Francois-Joseph, born at Trois-Rivieres in 1642. His baptism record follows: [3]

Francois Hartel [sic], baptised 3 July 1642
Witnesses:
Jacques Hertel, father (married)
Marie Marguerie, mother (married)
Francois Marguerie, uncle (unmarried)
Marguerite Couillart (married)
Jean Nicolet (married)
Jean De Brebeuf, clergy

Joseph-Francois Hertel de La Fresniere was captured and adopted by the Iroquois in 1661, escaped and took part in retaliatory raids accompanying Frontenac to Lake Ontario in 1673. Fined and jailed briefly for illegal fur trading activities, his knowledge of Native languages and warfare was too valuable to waste. He became a soldier.

Under Frontenac's orders he led expeditions using the Native method of rapid movement and ambush, including the raid on Salmon Falls in New England where forty-three English were killed. Hertel became known as *The Hero* by the French and *The Terror of the English* by the English. He was the Commander of Ft. Frontenac from 1709-12 and by his marriage with Marguerite de Thavenet, inherited the Chambly seigneury. [4]

Francois-Joseph was captured at Trois-Rivieres and presumably taken into New York State by the Iroquois in 1661 at the age of 18. While in custody, he was tortured, a common fate of Iroquois captives. He wrote to his priest, Father Le Moine/Moyne who was at Onondaga.

"The first [letters] are from a youth of family, who was captured this summer at Trois-Rivieres. He is of comely appearance and delicate, and was the sole delight of

---

[3] RBMQ
[4] CE

his mother, to whom he also writes. His name is Francois Hertel. His words, then, are as follows:" [5]

(Note that this letter was written on birch bark.)

My Reverend Father,
On the very day when you departed from Trois-Rivieres, I was captured, toward three o'clock in the afternoon, by four of the lower Iroquois. The reason why, to my misfortune, I did not make them kill me was that I feared I was not well prepared to die. My Father, if you should come hither, and if I could thus have the happiness to confess, I believe that you would receive no injury; and I believe that I could go back with you if you could come. I pray you, take pity on my poor Mother in her great affliction. You know, my Father, the love she bears me. From a Frenchman captured at Trois-Rivieres on the first day of August, I have learned that she is well, and that she takes comfort in the thought that I shall be near you. There are three of us Frenchmen alive here. I commend myself to your good prayers, especially to the holy Sacrifice of the Mass, and pray you, my Father, to say a Mass for me. I beg you to pay my respects to my poor Mother and to comfort her, if you please.

My Father, I pray you, bless the hand that writes to you, which has had one finger burnt in a Calumet as reparation to the Majesty of God, whom I have offended. The other hand has a thumb cut off, - but do not tell my poor Mother.

My Father, I beg you to honor me with a brief word from your hand, and to tell me whether you will come before Winter.
          Your very humble and
          very obedient servant,
          Francois Hertel

Another letter, written on a piece of gunpowder wrapping-paper, was again to his priest, and another which follows below, to his mother:

My very dear and honoured Mother,
I well know my capture must have greatly afflicted you. I ask your forgiveness for having disobeyed you. My sins have brought me to my present condition. Your prayers and Monsieur de St. Quentin's and my sisters' have restored me to life. I hope to see you again before Winter. I beg you to ask the good Brethren of Notre Dame to pray to God and the blessed Virgin for me, my dear Mother, and do you also, and all my sisters. From
          Your poor Fanchon

[5] J.R. V.47 1661-63 p.33

Francois was adopted while held in captivity by the Mohawks, a not uncommon tradition of the natives. One account of his captivity says that he was adopted by an old Native woman. Francis Parkman, in his writings, says that they often adopted their captives. He adds that normally, their acts of cruelty were not done out of hatred for their enemy. Rather it was in some way, a measure of respect and honour for the courage of their foes. Parkman goes on to say that this respect for the enemy often ended with the victim being eaten.

In 1664, Francois-Joseph Hertel married Marguerite De Thavenet. She was born in 1646, the daughter of Raymond De Thavenet (a captain in the Brimon regiment) and Elisabeth De Mancelin. Marguerite came out to Canada to assist Madame de la Peltrie in her work in educating Native maidens. Marguerite's younger sister, Marie-Francoise De Thavenet was engaged to (but never married) Jacques De Chambly. He was the founder of Chambly and later governor of Acadia and of Martinique. Marie-Francoise became his heiress, and on her death, his Canadian properties were bequeathed to her older sister Marguerite. The seigneury of Chambly thereby came into the Hertel family, thus adding to their own fief of Hertel at Trois-Rivieres.

Francois was married 2 September 1664 in Montreal [6] and the record of this marriage follows:

> Joseph Hertel [sic], res: Trois-Rivieres; signed the roll
> Marguerite De Thavenet [sic], of this parish [Montreal]; signed the roll
> Jacques Hertel, father of groom, married, deceased
> Marie Marguery [sic], res: Trois-Rivieres, mother of groom
> Raymond De Thavenet, officer, father of bride, married
> Elisabeth De Manselin [sic], mother of bride
> Zacharie Dupuis, junior officer
> Charles Daillebout/Desmusseau, knight, noble or seigneur
> Charles LeMoyne, a professional of some kind

Francois and Marguerite had a large family [7] with several sons, all of whom became well-known soldiers and many of whom fought with their father. His three eldest fought with him at Salmon Falls as did his nephew Lewis Crevier. His known children were:
  • Zacharie Hertel de La Fresniere born circa 1665 married 1695 Charlotte Godefroy
[8]

[6] Vol 5, 1980; parish #391, Notre-dame-de-Montreal.
[7] Further information on descendants may be found in DGFQ
[8] Zacharie Hertel was wounded in the knee at Salmon Falls and this wound left him crippled the rest of his life. Despite his wound, Zaccharie took part the next year in a combat which left him a prisoner in the hands of the Iroquois, where he remained for three years. DCB: Vo. II p 283

• Jacques Hertel de Cournoyer born 19 March 1667 Trois-Rivieres married 1691 Marguerite-Thérèse Godefroy

• Jean-Baptiste Hertel-de-Rouville born 26 Oct. 1668 Trois-Rivieres, died June 1722 Ile Royale [9] married 1698 Jeanne Dubois

• Joseph born circa 1671 married 1698 Catherine Philippe

• Louis Hertel de Saint-Louis born 14 May 1673 Trois-Rivieres married 1730 Marie-Catherine d'Ailleboust

• Rene Hertel de Chambly born 26 March 1675 Trois-Rivieres

• Lambert Hertel de Cournoyer born 17 October 1677 Trois-Rivieres

• Marie-Francoise born 4 Novemeber 1679 Trois-Rivieres became an Ursuline nun

• Michel Hertel de Chambly born 11 October 1685 Trois-Rivieres

• Marguerite-Thérèse born 23 October 1690 married 1710 Jean-Baptiste Boucher

• Claude Hertel de Beaulac born 2 January 1692 Trois-Rivieres married 1729 Geneviève Mirambeau

• Pierre Hertel de Moncours born 19 March 1687 Trois-Rivieres died 28 Feb. 1739 [10] married 1721 Marie-Thérèse d'Ailleboust

Francois was the Commander of Ft. Frontenac from 1709 to 1712 [11] Under Frontenac's orders he led expeditions using the Native method of rapid movement and ambush. Twenty-nine years after his capture by Iroquois, Francois Hertel, led the attack of French and Natives on the Fort and Settlement of Salmon Falls. He took with him three of his sons, 27 Frenchmen, 20 Socoquis and 5 Algonquins. Fifty-four prisoners were taken by Hertel, forty-three English were killed, all the houses burned, the countryside ravaged, all dwellings burned, and more than 2000 head of stock killed. The only loss to the French-Indian side was one Frenchman killed and two wounded.

Francois Hertel was ennobled in 1716 after long delays owing to his humble birth, his letters of nobility not granted until then. Six years later he died and was buried at Boucherville, New France 22 May 1722. [12]

[9] Like his brothers, Jean-Baptiste soldiered at an early age. He took part in the campaign against the Senecas in 1687 and then in his father's raid onSalmon Falls in 1690. DCB: V.II pp 284, 285
[10] Pierre Hertel de Moncours was a soldier in the Colonial Military. He married Therese d'Ailleboust de Perigny at Montreal in 1721 and had two children. In 1731 he commanded the garrison of Fort Sain-Frederic at Lake Champlain, built by his brother Zacharie. He died 28 Feb. 1739. His son Pierre, an officer in the Colonial troops, was killed at Niagara in 1759. DCB: V. II p 284
[11] CE
[12] CE

# CHAPTER 11

## MARIE-MADELEINE HERTEL AND LOUIS PINARD

Madeleine Hertel was born 2 Sept. 1645 in Trois-Rivieres. On 29 Aug. 1658 at the age of thirteen she married Louis Pinard, a surgeon at the fort.

Louis Pinard, born July 12, 1634, was the son of Jean Pinard and Marguerite Gaignier of Notre-Dame de La Rochelle. He came to Canada circa 1648 as a surgeon and donné of the Jesuits. He returned to France in 1650 to complete his surgical studies and then came back to Trois-Rivieres in 1656 where he became the surgeon at the garrison. Pinard apparently took part in the expedition to Hudson Bay in 1685. In 1690 he became the surgeon-major of Trois-Rivieres.

After Marie-Madeleine's death, Louis married Marie-Ursule Pepin in 1680. Each of his wives bore him six children. He died and was buried at Batiscan on 12 January 1695. [1]

He and Marie had a son Claude who also became a surgeon. Louis and Marie's daughter Marie-Francoise married Martin Giguere dit Despins in 1682 and their lineage can be traced to the present day.

[1] DCB: V. 1: p.550

# CHAPTER 12

## MARGUERITE HERTEL AND JEAN CREVIER

Marguerite was born at Trois-Rivieres, New France on 26 Aug. 1649. She married Jean Crevier on 26 Nov. 1663 at the age of fourteen. Jean became the seigneur of Saint-Francois in 1663.

Jean Crevier de Saint-Francois, the son of Christophe Crevier dit La Meslée and Jeanne Enard, was born 3 April 1642 at Trois-Rivieres. Jean was a fur trader whose brother-in-law was Pierre Boucher, the man who founded Boucherville in New France. In 1678 Jean was one of 20 settlers summoned to Quebec by Frontenac to vote on whether or not "spirits" should be traded to the Natives. Jean voted in favour of it.

During a raid by the Iroquois in Aug. 1693 he was captured and carried off. As he was being prepared to be burnt alive, Major Peter Schuyler the commandant of the Albany garrison, ransomed him for 50 livres, but Jean died shortly afterwards of his wounds. His son Louis had previously been killed during Francois Hertel's expedition to Salmon Falls in 1690.

On 23 August 1700, his widow Marguerite Hertel, and their son Joseph, gave part of their seigneury to the Abenakis and the Sokokis, so that the Jesuits could open a mission. [2]

[2] DCB: V. 1: p. 550

# CHAPTER 13

## HARMEN VAN SLYKE, ELDEST SON OF JACQUES CORNELISSEN VAN SLYKE

Harmen Van Slyke was born ca 1680 according to Burke and 26 March 1704 according to Yates in HSCNY. However it seems clear that Harmen's marriage to his first wife occurred on 26 March 1704 so Yates has confused the marriage date with the baptismal date.

In the winter of 1695-96 the garrison at Schenectady consisted of a detachment under Lieutenant Bickford. On 10 January about midnight the whole guard except one, deserted, for a total of 16 deserters. Bickford, on discovering the desertion about 2 am, notified Col. Richard Ingoldsby of Albany and with 10 volunteers and 11 soldiers, Bickford started in pursuit. About 4 p.m. the next day, Jan. 11th., Bickford and his volunteers met up with the deserters and ordered them to lay down their arms. The deserters shot at the pursuers and a fight ensued. Five deserters were killed and two wounded, at which point the remaining men surrendered. Among the volunteers from Schenectady who accompanied Bickford were:

Harman Van Slyke, Ensign of the train bands of Schenectady
Gerrit Simons Veeder
Peter Simons Veeder
Albert Veeder
Gerrit Gysbert Van Brakel
Jan Danielse Van Antwerpen
Dirck Groot
Jonas LeRoy
John Wemp
Daniel Mutchcraft [Mascraft]
Thomas Smith

On 21 April 1696, the survivors of the deserting party were court-martialed and sentenced to be shot.

Harmen's military service was as a scout with the Mohawks in their war against the French and northern Indians, and as Captain of the 2nd Foot Company of Schenectady. He led 56 men recruited in the town. In 1715 his Lieutenants were Hendrick Vrooman and Jacob Glen. Among the privates was Fictoor Pootman aka Victor Putman.

Harmen was a Captain in a Schenectady Company in 1714 and an Indian trader in 1724. He received a grant of 300 morgens of land at Canajoharie NY from the Mohawks because

"his grandmother was a right Mohawk woman" and "his father born with us at Canajoharie". His father was Jacques Cornelise, son of Ots-Toch, the half French, half Mohawk woman who married his father Cornelis Antonissen.

The deed conveyed 12 Jan. 1713 and consisting of 2000 acres, stated:

"in consideration of ye love, good will and affection which
we do bear toward our loving cozen and friend Capt. Harmon
Van Slyke of Schenectady, aforesaid, whose grandmother was a
right Mohawk squaw and his father born with us in the above
said Kanajoree [Canajoharie].......it being his the said
Harmen Van Slyke's by right of inheritance from his father"

The deed was witnessed by Lea Stevens "interpreter to ye above deed" and the land included the Frey tract. Harmen deeded that portion back to Hendrick Frey of Zurich who had been given this by the Indians.

Harmen made his will 1 November 1731 and died in 1734 leaving twelve children. His sons Adam, James and Harmanus received half of his 2000 acres of land at Canajoharie known as Van Slyck's patent.

Harmen's actual date of birth is critical in determining the dates of birth for the remainder of Jacques Cornelise's children. Harmen, or Harmanus was the eldest son of Jacques Cornelis Van Slyke and Grietje Ryckman. If the date of birth of 1680 is correct, then it affects all the other children.

# CHAPTER 14

## WILLIAM NEEF, NEPHEW TO CORNELIS VAN SLYKE

William Pieterse Van Slyke was born in 1635 in Heyvelt, province of Utrecht, in the Netherlands. Willem arrived in New Netherland in 1660 on *De Trouw*, being listed as William Pieterse from Amersfoort. Amersfoort is only a few miles from Breukelen, the place of origin of Cornelis Van Slyke.

William was known by the name William Neef, meaning "nephew" in light of his being a nephew of Cornelis Antonissen. William married Baertie (1636-1699). He was in Beverwyck New York in 1666, when he sent to the Netherlands for an inheritance. Descendants of Willem might wish to pursue this lead further, as the inheritance may very well have been due to his father's death. A check of the Amersfoort records for that year may yield valuable information. He was the originator of the Van Slykes who settled on the west bank of the Hudson, now Greene county, New York. In 1768 he purchased and occupied a farm at Niskayuna, Schenectady county, New York.

Teunise Willemse, son of William Pieterse Van Slyke, was born in 1665 and died in 1748. Teunis married Jannetie Hendrickse Van Wie and in 1713, built a stone house on the west bank of the Hudson, one mile south of the present-day village of New Baltimore. In 1733 his was one of the four churches who received the deed for the land upon which to build the Dutch Reformed church at Coxsackie. The Boston Morning Journal of January 12, 1903, described the Bible once owned by Teunise Willemse Van Slyke as the oldest printed Bible on earth, made in Dordrecht, 1518-55, then owned by Benjamin Fredenberg Van Slyke, of Saginaw, Michigan, handed down from father to son, about four hundred years. [3]

[3] Hudson-Mohawk Genealogical and Family Memoirs, Cuyler Reynolds, Vol. 1. New York, Lewis Historical Publishing Company, 1911 : 1609

# BIBLIOGRAPHY

Following is the list of abbreviations to the references found in the footnoted chapters in this book.

BF: Bradt Family: A Norwegian Family in Colonial America. Peter R. Christoph, 1994

BRSRC: Baptism Record of Schenectady Reformed Church Schenectady New York 1694-1811 transcribed by Donald Keefer

CE: The Canadian Encyclopedia. 1993

CFA: Coppernol Family in America. Arlene Coppernol Cuba, 1970 Vol. I

CFN: Canada's First Nations. Olive Patricia Dickason. Toronto. McClelland & Stewart, Inc. 1992

CH: Sagard's Long Journey to the Country of the Hurons: The Long Journey to the Country of the Hurons. Father Gabriel Sagard. Ed. George M. Wrong. Trans. H.H. Langton, 1939.

CHA: Collections on the History of Albany. Joel Munsell, 4 vols. (1870) vol. III. p.58

CYC: Canada: Years of Challenge to 1814. Elspeth Deir, Paul Deir, Keith Hubbard. Holt, Rinehart and Winston of Canada, Limited, Toronto.

DCB: The Dictionary of Canadian Biography by University of Toronto Press:

DGFC: Dictionnaire Genealogique des Familles Canadiennes. Tanguay, 1887

DGFQ: Dictionnaire généalogique des familles du Québec des origines à 1730. René Jetté. 1983

DMV: Door to the Mohawk Valley. Millicent Veeder, 1947

EGNJ: The Early Germans of New Jersey. Theodore Frelinghuysen Chambers. Baltimore. Genealogical Publishing Co. Inc. 1982

EHS: Early History of Schenectady and its First Settlers by John Sanders

ERA&R: Early Records of the City and County of Albany and Colony of Rensselaerswyck, ed. A.J. F. Van Laer. Trans. Jonathan Pearson, 4 vols., 1869-1919

ESR: Settlers of Rensselaerswyck. A.J.F. Van Laer, 1980.

F&FMC: Forts and Firesides of the Mohawk Country New York: The stories and pictures of landmarks of the pre-Revolutionary War period throughout the Mohawk Valley and the surrounding countryside including some historic and genealogical mention during the post-War period. John J. Vrooman, 1943

GDS: Contributions for the Genealogies of the Descendants of the First Setters of the Patent and City of Schenectady from 1662 to 1800. Jonathan Pearson, 1873

GFSA: Contributions for the Genealogies of the First Settlers of the Ancient County of Albany, From 1630 to 1800. Prof. Jonathan Pearson, 1884

HCF: Histoire des Canadiens-Francais. 8 vols.

H&GDNF: History and General Description of New France. Rev. Pierre Francois Xavier de Charlevoix, S.J. Trans. by John Gilmary Shea, 6 vols.

HNF: Histoire de la Nouvelle France, 3 vols. Lescarbot, 1907-1914

HSCNY: The History of Schenectady County New York. Austin Yates. 1902

HSP: A History of the Schenectady Patent in the Dutch and English Times. Jonathan Pearson. Ed. J. W. MacMurray, 1883

HTR: Histoire de la ville des Trois-Rivieres et de ses environs. Benjamin Sulte Premeire Livraison Montreal: Eusebe Senecal 1870

JD: Journal of Jasper Danckaerts, 1679-1680. Jasper Danckaerts. Ed. Bartlett Burleigh James and J. Franklin Jameson, 1913

JR: The Jesuit Relations and Allied Documents: Travels and Explorations of the Jesuit Missionaries in New France, 1619-1791. Ed. Reuben G. Thwaites, 79 vols., 1896-1901

MM: Madame Montour et Son Temps. Simone Vincen, 1979

MF: Mohawk Frontier: The Dutch Community of Schenectady New York 1669 - 1710 by Thomas E. Burke Jr. 1991

MNF: Monumenta Novae Franciae, Vol. II: Etablisement a Quebec, 1616-1634. Lucien Campeau, S.I. 1979

MV: The Mohawk Valley: Its Legends and Its History. W. Max Reid 1901

NF: La Vie Quotidienne en Novelle-France; le Canada de Champlain a Montcalme. Raymond Douville and Jacques-Donat Casanova, 1964

NWI: New World Immigrants: A Consolidation of Ship Passenger Lists and Associated Data from Periodical Literature. edited by Michael Tepper. Volume 1. Genealogical Publishing Co. Inc. Baltimore 1988

NYHM: New York Historical Manuscripts Dutch. Trans. Arnold J. F. Van Laer, Ed. Kenneth Scott & Kenn Stryker-Rodda, 2 vols., 1974

OS: Old Schenectady. Roberts, c. 1905

PC: The Peoples of Canada, A Pre-Confederation History. J. M. Bumsted. Toronto. Oxford University Press, 1992

QAC: Queen Anne Chapel Records. Extracted from Register of Baptisms, Marriages, Communicants & Funerals begun by Henry Barclay at Fort Hunter January 26th. 1734, Montgomery County Dept. of History & Archives, Fonda, New York. by Maryly Penrose

RBMQ: Repertoire des Acts de Bapteme Mariage Sepulture et des Recensements du Quebec ancien, Vol 4. Montreal: University of Montreal Press, 1980, for parish #601: L'Immaculee-conception-des-Trois-Rivieres by Hubert Charbonneau and Jacques Legare

SA&M: Schenectady: Ancient and Modern. Monroe, 1914

SC: Samuel Champlain; Fondateur de Quebec et Pere de la Nouvelle-France, Histoire de sa Vie et de ses Voyages. N. E. Dionne, 1906

SCFNF: Samuel de Champlain: Father of New France. Samuel Eliot Morison. Toronto. Little, Brown & Company (Canada) Ltd. 1972

SCH: Schenectady County New York: Its History to the Close of the Nineteenth Century. Austin A. Yates, 1902

SPL: Ships Passenger Lists: New York and New Jersey (1600-1825) edited and indexed by Carl Boyer, 3rd. Newhall, California 1978

SWJP: Sir William Johnson Papers, 14 vols., 1972

TCNF: The Early Trading Companies of New France: A Contribution to the History of Commerce and Discovery in North America. H. P. Biggar, 1937. Augustus M. Kelly  Publishers, Clifton 1972

TM: The Massacre. Vrooman, 1954

UCR: Ulster County in the Revolution. Nathaniel Bartlett Sylvester

VVF: The Van Valkenburg Family In America: Genealogy of the known descendants of Lambert and Annatje Van Valckenburgh who migrated to New Amsterdam (New York) in 1642-44. Compiled by Paul I. Van Valkenburg. Vol. 1 Gateway Press Inc. Baltimore. 1981

W&G: The White and The Gold. Thomas B. Costain. Garden City NY. Doubleday & Company Inc., 1954

WFN: Word From New France: The Selected Letters of Marie De L'Incarnation. Translated and edited by Joyce Marshall. Toronto, Oxford University Press, 1967

# INDEX TO PART ONE

Clabbort: Thomas aka Chambers 15
Clacklayer: Pieter Jacobsz 16
Claes: Aeltje 8, 9
Claessen: Carsten 17
Cleyn: Uldrick 15
Clute: aka Knoet: Johannes 69
Cobes: Ludewyck - see Cobussen
Cobussen: Lowies aka Lodovicus/Ludewyck 11, 15, 53
Coeymans: Barent Pieterse aka Barent the miller 12, 51; Lucyas Pietersz aka Hout 16
Contugo: 46
Coorn: Nicolaes 10
Cornelis: Broer (see Van Slyke); Hilletie (see Van Slyke)
Couillart: Marguerite 77
Crevier: (aka dit La Meslee) Christophe 83; (aka de Saint-Francois) Jean 82; Joseph 83;
    Lewis 79; Louis 83
Croon: Adriaen Jansen 14
Cruyff: Eldert Gerbertsz 14
d'Ailleboust: see de Manthet; Marie-Catherine 80; Marie-Therese 80
d'Iberville: Pierre Le Moyne 60
Daillebout: Charles 79
Dankaerts: Jasper 30, 55, 68
de Beaulac: see Claude Hertel
de Boer: Thomas Jans 16
De Brebeuf: Jean 77
de Brouwer: Philip 15; Philip Hendrickse 17;
de Chambly: see Hertel; Jacques 79; Rene
de Champlain: Samuel 31, 32, 33, 34, 36, 40
de Cournoyer: see Jacques Hertel son of Francois-Joseph; see Lambert Hertel
de Goyer: Thys 16
de Hooges: Antony 8
De Hulter: Johanna 11
de la Fresnaye: see Jacques Hertel
de La Fresniere: see Joseph-Francois/Francois-Joseph Hertel; see Zacharie Hertel
de La Peltrie: Madame 79
De Looper: Jacobus Teunissen aka Cobus 51
de Manselin: Elisabeth 79
de Manthet: Nicolas d'Ailleboust 60
de Moncours: see Pierre Hertel
de Nooreman: Hans aka Carelsen 15
de Noorman: Arent aka Bradt aka Bratt 50; Catalyna 50
de Rooy: Lodewyck 73
de Rouville: see Jean-Baptiste Hertel
de Saint-Francois: see Jean Crevier
de Saint-Louis: see Louis Hertel
de Saint-Quentin: Quentin Moral 76, 78

de Sainte-Helene: Jacques le Moyne 60
de smit: Meyndert aka Van Iveren 15
de Thavenet: Marguerite 77, 79; Marie-Francoise 79; Raymond 79
De Vos: Catalynte 51, 60
de Wever: Jan aka Jan Martense aka Jan Van Alstyne 15
de Winter: Bastiaen 11
Dehennakarineh: aka Dekarihokenh 23
Derosiers: Antoine  43, 44
Desmusseau: Charles 79
Despins: dit name for Martin Giguere
Deyoenhegwenh: 23
Dircksen: Poulus 12
Dongan, Thomas 58, 59
du Vernet:33
du Vigeau: Nicolas 31, 33
Dubois: Jeanne 79
Dupuis: Zacharie 79
Dyckman: Madam 50
Ebbingh: Jeronimus 73, 74
Eldertsen: Isbrant 14, 17
Enard: Jeanne 83
Eps: Jan 51
Fanchon: see Francois Hertel
Filiastre: Luc  76
Flodder: Jacob Janse aka Gardenier 14
Fransman: Johan aka Jean Labatie 11, 15
Fredericksen: Carsten 12; Meyndert aka Van Iveren 15
Frey: Hendrick 86
Frontenac: 77, 80
Gaignier: Marguerite 81
Gardenier: Jacob Janse aka Flodder 14
Gautsh: Akes - see Jaques Cornelise Van Slyke
Gemackelyck: Pieter Adriaensen aka Soogemackelyck aka Van Woggelum 13
Gerbertsen: Eldert aka Cruyff 13
Giguere: Martin - aka dit Despins 81
Glen: Jacob 85; Johannes 64; Johannes Sanderse 59; Sanders 61; Sander Leendertsz  aka
         Alexander Lindsey 14, 18
Godefroy: Charlotte 79; Marguerite-Therese 79 Thomas 31, 33; Jean-Paul 33, 40
Graef: Cornelis Gerritsen 17
Groesbeek: Claes Jacobsen 14
Groot: Dirck 85
Heemstreet: Grietje Takelse 64
Helmsz: Jan 17
Hendericx: Jannetie 16
Hendrickse: Geurt 13 (see Van Schoonhoven)

Herbertsen: Anderien aka Andries Herbertsz 13, 17
Hertel: Claude 80; Francois-Joseph 41, 43, 75, 77-80, 83; Jacques 20, 28, 29, 31-34, 36-
    44, 75, 77, 79; Jean-Baptiste 79; Joseph 80; Lambert 80; Louis 80; Marguerite 43,
    83; Marguerite-Therese 80; Marie-Francoise 80; Marie-Madeleine 43, 81; Michel
    80; Nicolas 31, 43; Pierre 80; Rene 80; Zacharie 79
Hiathawa: aka Ayonhawathah 23
Hierman: Hendrick 15
Hoogeboom: Cornelis 50; Hoochboom: (Hoogeboom) Meuwes Pietersz 15
Hout: Lucyas Pietersz aka Coeymans 16
Hudson: Henry 1
Ingoldsby: Col. Richard 85
It-sy-ch-sa-quach-ka: see Jacques Cornelise Van Slyke
Jacobsen: Caspar 12; Claes aka Groesbeek aka Van Rotterdam 14 ; Frans 16; Rutger aka
    van Schoonderwoert 13, 15
Janssen: Marcellis 47; Paulus 51; Volckert 12
Jansz: Anthony 51; Marcelis 51; Steven 51
Jochimsen: Henderick 13, 15, 46; Tryn 12
Joques: Father Isaac 8
Keeman: see Kemel
Kemel: aka Keeman aka Cornelis Cornelissen Viele 58
Kenutje: 28, 29
Ketlehem: Jochem 51
Keyser: Dirck Dircksee 13
Kieft: William 9
Kip; Jacob H. 10
Kirke: brothers 38, 39
Knoet: see Clute
Kryn: 60
La Meslee: dit name for Christophe Crevier
la Montagne: 13, 33; Johannes 13
Labatie: Jean aka Johan Fransman 11, 15, 51
Le Baillif: 33
Le Montagne: Johannes 51
Le Moyne: see D'Iberville, De Sainte-Helene; Charles 79
Le Roy: Jonas aka Leonard Remi Le Roy aka Larroway 85
Leisler: Jacob 59, 69
Letardif: Olivier 33
Livingston: Robert 62
Loockermans: Jacob 12; Pieter 16
Lovelace: Governor 53
Machielsz: Jan 51
Manet: Jean 33
Marguerie: 32; Francois 42, 43, 75- 77; Marie 42, 43, 75-77, 79
Marsolet: 32; Nicolas 33
Mascraft: see Mutchcraft Daniel

Maurtis: See Van Slyke, Marten
Megaplonsis: Dominie 8
Meusz: Pieter 51
Meynderts: Johannes 60; Maritie 48-50
Minuit: Peter 36
Mirambeau: Genevieve 80
Miriot: Jeanne 31, 43
Montagne: William 46
Mourisse: Martin -see Martin Van Slyke
Mutchcraft: aka Mascraft Daniel 85
Neef - see Van Slyke, Willem
Nicolet: 32; Jean 33, 42, 77
Noldingh: Evert 15
Orenregowah: 23
Ots-Toch: aka Alstock 8, 10, 18-21, 25-30, 32, 34, 36, 38, 39, 45, 49, 68, 73, 86
Otsie'Ka: see Jacques Hertel
Pelen: Brant 9
Pels: Evert 15
Pepin: Marie-Ursule 81
Philippe: Catherine 80
Pieters: Hilletie aka Hilletie Van Slyke 68; Marritjen 8
Pinard: Claude 81; Jean 81; Louis 81; Marie-Francoise 81
Piraube: Martial 43
Pootman: (aka Putman) Johannes 60; Victor 85
Pouwell: Tomas 12, 15
Provoost: Johannes 11, 13
Pruyn: Frans Jansen 46, 47, 48, 51
Quentin: Moral - see Sainte-Quentin
Rams: Christiaen Pietersen 9, 10
Rastawenseronthah: 23
Reur: Henderick 14
Reyndertse: Barent aka de smit 12
Richer: Jean 33
Rierdrager: Teunis Jacobez 16
Roelofsz: Jan 15
Romain: Marthe 43, 76
Rooseboom: Hendrick 15
Ryckman: Engeltie 64; Harmen Janse 16, 47, 64; Margaret Harmense aka Grietje 47, 53,
    59, 63, 64, 86
Sa:ondionrhens: 43
Sanders: Robert 55, 56, 57
Sanders: see Glen
Schaets: Mother 13; Dominie 17; Reynier 59
Schelluyne: D. V. 17
Schepmoes: Jan Jansen 8

Schermerhorn: Jacob 13; Jacob Janse 60; Ryer 59, 60; Symon 59, 62
Schoester: Cornelis Teunisz aka Kees Schoester aka Cornelis Bos 15
Schoon: Jan 47
Schutt: Willem Janssen 12
Schuyler: Peter 63, 69, 83;Pieterse 13
Scounowee: 18
Segerse: Cornelis aka Van Egmont aka Van Voorhout 16
Shadekariwadeh: aka Sharenhowaneh aka Shoskoarowaneh 23
Sickels: Sacharias/Zacharias aka van Weenan 16
Slaghboom: Antonia 53
Smith: Thomas 85
Sonareetsie: 46
Soogemackelyck: Pieter Adriaensen aka Van Woggelum aka Gemackelyck 13, 51
St. Jean: 42
Staats: Abraham 8
Staets: Jacob 64
Stevens: Annatje 72; Arent 72; Dinah 72; Jonathan 10, 55, 72; Lea 86; Nicolas 72
Stuyvesant: Peter 17, 46, 54
Swart: Gerret 14
Swits: Isaac Cornelissen 60
Tappan: Jurian Teunisse: 11-13
Teller: John 18; Willem 59, 71
Tesschenmaeker: Petrus 61
Teunisse: Jurian aka Tappan 11-13
Teunissen: Cornelis (see Van Slyke)
Thomase: see Tomassen
Tomassen: Jan 12-14, 53
Tysen: Jaques 16
Unochschonie: 71
van Aecken: Jan 12, 51
van Aken: see van Aecken
Van Alstyne: Jan aka de Wever aka Martense 15
Van Antwerpen: Daniel Janse 59; Jan Danielse 85
Van Baelen: Jan Hendricksen 51
Van Brakel: Gerrit Gysbert 85
van Breuckelen - see Van Slyke
Van Buren: Hendrick 3
van Coppernol: Claes Willemse 10, 55, 69, 71; Willem Claessen 71
Van Curlar: Arent 10, 18, 19, 50, 53, 58, 73
van den Bogaert: Harman Meyndersen 9, 41
Van den Sliick: Splinter 4;
Van der Heyden: Jan Cornelissen 47-50
Van der Volgen: Laurens Claesen 62, 69
van Doesburch: Geertruy Andriesz 15
van Eeckelen: Albert 71; Jan 12

Van Egmont: Cornelis aka Segerse aka Van  16
Van Eps: Jan 59; Jan Baptist 62, 69
van Es: Cornelis aka Van Nes 15
Van Every: see Van Iveren
van Gansevoort: Harmen 51
van Hamel: Diederick 16
van Hoesen: Jan 16
Van Iveren: Meyndert Frederickse aka de Smit 15
van Marcken: Jan Gerritsen 53
Van Mijnden: Wouter 4
Van Neck: Lambert 74
Van Nes: Cornelis Hendrickse aka Van Es 15
van Nieukerck: Gerrit Claessen 48
van Nortstrant: Jacob Jansz 16
van Olinda: Daniel Pietersen 60, 68, 69; Jacob Pietersen 69; Matthias Pietersen 69; Pieter
        Danielsen  10, 51, 57, 59, 60, 69
Van Otterspoor: Jan Janse 11
Van Petten: Claes Frederickse 60
van Reis: Gerrit Hendricksz 50, 51
Van Rensellaer: Jeremias 14, 20; Kiliaen 3, 6, 7, 8, 20
Van Rotterdam: Claes Jacobse aka Groesbeek 14, 15
Van Ruele - see Van Ruwiel
Van Ruwiel: 4, Gijsrcht, Splinter 6
van Rys: see Van Reis
van Schelluyne: Dirck 14, 46, 47, 49
van Schoonderwoert: Rutger Jacobse 13, 15
Van Schoonhoven: Geurt Hendrickse 13
van Slechtenhorst: Gerret 15
Van Slijk, Van Slicht, Van Slyk, Van Slyck, Slijk, Van Slyken, Van Slijcken - see Van
        Slyke
Van Slyke: Adam Harmanse 86; Antonis 4, 28; Cornelis 53, 60, 63; Cornelis Antonissen
        1, 3, 6-15, 17-21, 27-29, 46, 48, 49, 51, 67, 86;  Elizabeth 3, Fytie 53, 63;
        Geertruyt 53, 63; Grietje 53, 60, 63 ; Harmanus Harmense 86; Harmen 45, 60, 85,
        86; Helena 53, 63; Herman 53, 63; Hilletie 10, 18, 19, 27, 30, 51, 54-57, 60, 64,
        67; Jacques Cornelise 10, 17-20, 27-29, 32, 45-54, 56-62, 64, 67, 73, 86; James
        Harmense 86; Lea 10, 12, 18, 55, 57, 71-73; Lydia 53, 63; Marte 53, 63; Marten
        10, 18, 28, 29, 46, 49, 51, 57, 73, 74; Martin 60; Pieterse 3; Susanna 53, 63;
        Teunis 4; Teunis Willemse 87; Wouter 55-57, 64, 73; Willem Pieterse 3, 87;
van Starrevelt: Cornelis Cornelisz 47
van Tienhoven: Cornelis  9, 19
Van Tricht: Gerrit 74
van Valckenburg: Lammert/ Lambert 16, 50
van Vechten: Teunis Dircksz. aka Poentie 14; Teunis Cornelise aka Young Poentie 51
Van Velsen: Sweer Teunis 51, 52, 54, 59
van Voorhout: Cornelise Cornelisz aka Segerse aka Van Egmont 14, 16

van Weenan: Sacharias/Zacharias aka Sickels 16
Van Wie: Jannetie Hendrickse 87
Van Woggelum: Pieter Adriaensen aka Soogemackelyck aka Gemackelyck 13
Vander Donck: Adriaen 9
vander Heyder: Jacob Tyssen 13
Vedder: Harmen 60
Veeder: Albert 85; Gerrit Simons 85; Peter Simons 85
Verbeeck: Jan 13, 50, 53
Viele: Arent Cornelise 18, 50; Arnout 60; Cornelis Cornelise aka Keeman aka Kemel 49,
    53, 54, 58
Vos: Cornelis Dircxsz 50
Vries: de maile 16
Vrooman: Adam Hendrickse 59, 60, 64; Barent 60; Hendrick 60, 85; Jan 60
Wattkeense: 71
Webber: Anneke Jans aka Bogardus 14
Wemp: Jan Barentse 13, 14, 48, 49, 54, 73, 74; Meyndert 60
Wendel: Evert 16
Wessels: Dirk 63

# PART TWO

# CHARTS

Pages 101 to 181

# PART TWO: CHARTS

## SECTION A

### DESCENDANTS OF ANTONIS (TEUNIS) VAN SLIJK

First Generation

⅄1 Antonis (Teunis) VAN SLIJK, born abt 1580 at Netherlands.

    BIRTH: estimate of date of birth based on birth of son Cornelis

  Antonis (Teunis) VAN SLIJK married (1) ? (___).

  Children:
+    2 M    i Cornelis Antonissen VAN SLYKE.
+    3 M   ii Pieter Teunis VAN SLYCK.

Second Generation

2 Cornelis Antonissen VAN SLYKE, born in 1604 at Breuckelen, Utrecht, Netherlands; died in 1676 at Canajoharie, NY, USA.

    BIRTH: Birth year based on age given at signing of contract in 1634

    MARRIAGE: The marriage date of 1635 to 1640 is based on the birth of children.

    AKA: Cornelis was known as Cornelis Antonissen; Cornelis Teunissen; Cornelis van Breuckelen; Broer (Brother) Cornelis; Brodeur; and Cornelis Antonissen Van Slyke/Slicht

    BURIAL: He is buried at the Second Dutch Reformed Church according to Munsell.

  Cornelis Antonissen VAN SLYKE married (1) Ots-Toch (___) abt 1635/1640 at Mohawk Castle, Canajoharie, NY. Ots-Toch, dau. of Jacques HERTEL and Mohawk Woman (___), born abt 1622 at Mohawk Castle, Canojaharie, NY USA.

  Children:
    4 M    i Marten Mouris VAN SLYCK, born abt 1635 at Canajoharie, NY; died abt 1662 at NY.
    5 M  ⅱ Jacques Cornelise VAN SLYKE, born abt 1640 at Canajoharie, Montgomery Co., NY, USA; died aft 11 May 1690 at Albany, NY, USA.

        OCCUPATION: Interpreter, trader and tapster in Schenectady NY

        BIRTH: Birth date of 1640 is based on death in 1690 at age 50.

        MARRIAGE: Ancestral File LDS Library. Also based on estimated births of children

        DEATH: Will dated May 11, 1690 made while ill at Albany New York.

        RESIDENCES: Canajoharie, New York and Schenectady New York

        AKA: Jacques was known as Akes Cornelise; Akes Gautsch; his Mohawk name was It-Sy-Cho-Sa-Quash-Ka

Jacques Cornelise VAN SLYKE married (1) Margarita (Grietje) RYCKMAN in 1662 at Schenectady, NY. Margarita, dau. of Harmen Janse RYCKMAN and unknown (___), born abt 1640; died in 1695 at Albany, NY, USA.

COMMENT: Grietje is the Dutch diminuitive for Margaret.

NOTE: Grietje married Adam Vrooman after the death of Jacques Van Slyke in 1690.

6 F   iii Hilletie Cornelise VAN SLYKE, born abt 1644 at Canojoharie, NY; died on 10 Feb 1707.

OCCUPATION: Indian Interpreter

Hilletie Cornelise VAN SLYKE married (1) Pieter Danielse VAN OLINDA. Pieter, died in 1716.

AKA: Pieter was also known as Van Der Linde

NOTE: Pieter sold land given to his wife Hilletie by the Mohawks, in 1669. This land was the Great Island at Niskayuna.

DEATH: In his will, Pieter mentions his children Daniel the eldest son, Jacob and Matthys (non compos.)

7 F   iv Lea VAN SLYKE, born abt 1646 at Canajoharie, NY; died in 1692 at Port Jackson, NY. She married (1) Claes Willemse VAN COPPERNOL. Claes, born abt 1646/1654; died in 1692 at Schenectady, NY.

NOTE: Claes hired the farm of William Teller at Schenectady, and later settled on his wife's land below Port Jackson.

Lea VAN SLYKE married (2) Jonathon STEVENS on 24 Jul 1693 at Schenectady, NY. Jonathon, born in 1675 at New England.

3 Pieter Teunis VAN SLYCK, born at Netherlands.
  He married (1) -- (___).

  Children:
8 M   i Willem Pieterse VAN SLYCK, born in 1635 at Beverwijck, Netherlands.

NOTES: Willem Pieterse from Amersfoort arrived at NY April 1660 on DE TROUW. De Trouw (The Faith) sailed Dec 23, 1660 with Captian Jan Jansz Bestevaer. Willem is shown on the passenger list as Willem Petersen from Amersfoort. Willem was known as Willen NEEf meaning "nephew" due to his status as the nephew of Cornelis Antonissen Van Slyke.

RESIDENCES: His descendants settled in Albany NY

Willem Pieterse VAN SLYCK married (1) Baertie (___) in 1658 at Kinderhook, NY. Baertie, born in 1636 at Kinderhook, NY; died in Dec 1699 at Albany NY.

9 F   ii ELizabeth VAN SLYKE, born abt 1640.

BIRTH: Birth date estimate based on date of birth of her husband in 1637.

ELizabeth VAN SLYKE married (1) Hendrick Cornelissen VAN BUREN. Hendrick, son of Cornelis Maessen VAN BUREN and Catalyntje aka Van Alstyne MARTENSE, born on 30 Jun 1637 at Atlantic Ocean.

BIRTH: Hendrick was born on board the ship "Rensellaerswyck" on 30 June 1637 as it crossed from the Netherlands to the New World.

RESEARCHER: Much of the data on the children of this family comes from Brenda S. Whelpy in Texas and Mike Wolfe in CA

SOURCE: LINEAL ANCESTORS OF RUFUS RENNINGTON YOUNG AND JANE VOSBURGH AND THEIR DESCENDANTS by Charles Henry Cory

# PART TWO: CHARTS


## SECTION B


## DESCENDANTS OF CORNELIS ANTONISSEN VAN SLYKE

--------------------------------------------------------------------------------

First Generation

1 Cornelis Antonissen VAN SLYKE, born in 1604 at Breuckelen, Utrecht, Netherlands; died in 1676 at Canajoharie, NY, USA.

   BIRTH: Birth year based on age given at signing of contract in 1634

   MARRIAGE: The marriage date of 1635 to 1640 is based on the birth of children.

   AKA: Cornelis was known as Cornelis Antonissen; Cornelis Teunissen; Cornelis van Breuckelen; Broer (Brother) Cornelis; Brodeur; and Cornelis Antonissen Van Slyke/Slicht

   BURIAL: He is buried at the Second Dutch Reformed Church according to Munsell.

Cornelis Antonissen VAN SLYKE married (1) Ots-Toch (____) abt 1635/1640 at Mohawk Castle, Canajoharie, NY. Ots-Toch, dau. of Jacques HERTEL and Mohawk Woman (____), born abt 1622 at Mohawk Castle, Canojaharie, NY USA.

Children:
      2 M      i Marten Mouris VAN SLYCK, born abt 1635 at Canajoharie, NY; died abt 1662 at NY.
    + 3 M     ii Jacques Cornelise VAN SLYKE.
    + 4 F    iii Hilletie Cornelise VAN SLYKE.
    + 5 F     iv Lea VAN SLYKE.


Second Generation


3 Jacques Cornelise VAN SLYKE, born abt 1640 at Canajoharie, Montgomery Co., NY, USA; died aft 11 May 1690 at Albany, NY, USA.

   OCCUPATION: Interpreter, trader and tapster in Schenectady NY

   BIRTH: Birth date of 1640 is based on death in 1690 at age 50.

   MARRIAGE: Ancestral File LDS Library. Also based on estimated births of children

   DEATH: Will dated May 11, 1690 made while ill at Albany New York.

   RESIDENCES: Canajoharie, New York and Schenectady New York

   AKA: Jacques was known as Akes Cornelise; Akes Gautsch; his Mohawk name was It-Sy-Cho-Sa-Quash-Ka

Jacques Cornelise VAN SLYKE married (1) Margarita (Grietje) RYCKMAN in 1662 at Schenectady, NY. Margarita, dau. of Harmen Janse RYCKMAN and unknown (____), born abt 1640; died in 1695 at Albany, NY, USA.

   COMMENT: Grietje is the Dutch diminuitive for Margaret.

--------------------------------------------------------------------------------
Second Generation

--------------------------------------------------------------------------------

NOTE: Grietje married Adam Vrooman after the death of Jacques Van Slyke in
1690.

Children:
+     6 F      i Susannah VAN SLYCK.
+     7 F     ii Margareta (Grietje) VAN SLYCK.
+     8 M    iii Harmen VAN SLYKE.
+     9 M     iv Cornelis VAN SLYKE.
+    10 F      v Geertruyt VAN SLYKE.
✗ +  11 M     vi Marten VAN SLYCK.
     12 F    vii Helena VAN SLYKE.
     13 F   viii Fytje VAN SLYCK, born in 1680 at Schenectady NY.

              NAME: She is listed as Fytie in her father's will of 1690. Probably nickname
              for Sophia.

              CHRISTENING: A note from W. Barker re Montgomery Co. NY states that there was
              a Fytie Van Slyke baptised in Albany 20 Jan. 1686.

              MARRIAGE: The same Fytie Van Slyke baptised 20 Jan. 1686 was married to Jacob
              Van Der Slyk [sic]. It is possible that this is Jacques and Grietje's daughter,
              in which case Lydia was born between 1687 and 1690.
              It is also possible that what appears to be a marriage record is a baptismal
              record with Jacob replacing the name Jacques.

+    14 F     ix Lydia VAN SLYCK.

4 Hilletie Cornelise VAN SLYKE, born abt 1644 at Canojoharie, NY; died on 10 Feb 1707.

     OCCUPATION: Indian Interpreter

Hilletie Cornelise VAN SLYKE married (1) Pieter Danielse VAN OLINDA. Pieter, died in 1716.

     AKA: Pieter was also known as Van Der Linde

     NOTE: Pieter sold land given to his wife Hilletie by the Mohawks, in 1669.
     This land was the Great Island at Niskayuna.

     DEATH: In his will, Pieter mentions his children Daniel the eldest son, Jacob
     and Matthys (non compos.)

Children:
+    15 M      i Daniel VAN O'LINDA.
+    16 M     ii Jacob VAN O'LINDA.
     17 M    iii Matthew VAN O'LINDA, born abt 1680.

              DEATH: He died unmarried according to Yates


5 Lea VAN SLYKE, born abt 1646 at Canajoharie, NY; died in 1692 at Port Jackson, NY.
     She married (1) Claes Willemse VAN COPPERNOL. Claes, born abt 1646/1654; died in 1692 at Schenectady,
     NY.

     NOTE: Claes hired the farm of William Teller at Schenectady, and later settled
     on his wife's land below Port Jackson.

Children:


--------------------------------------------------------------------------------
Second Generation

----------------------------------------------------------------------------------------------------

+    18 M     i William Claessen VAN COPPERNOL.

Lea VAN SLYKE married (2) Jonathon STEVENS on 24 Jul 1693 at Schenectady, NY. Jonathon, born in 1675 at New England.

Children:
+   19 F    ii Annatje aka Anna STEVENS.
+   20 M   iii Nicolas Hendricus STEVENS.
     21 F    iv Dina STEVENS, born on 5 May 1700 at Schenectady, NY.

             SP: Adam Vrooman; Grietje Van Slyck

             Dina STEVENS married (1) Samuel HAGEDORN.
+    22 M    v Arent STEVENS.


Third Generation


6 Susannah VAN SLYCK, born abt 1662 at Schenectady, NY; died in 1713.
  She married (1) Samuel Arentse BRADT bef 1684. Samuel, son of Arent Andriesse BRADT and Catalyntje DE VOS, born in 1659 at Schenectady, NY; died in 1713.

Children:
+   23 M    i Arent BRADT.
+   24 F    ii Margriet BRADT.
     25 F   iii Hanna BRADT, christened on 5 Jun 1692 at NY USA.
+   26 M   iv Jacobus BRADT.
     27 F    v Cornelia BRADT, christened on 30 Dec 1696 at NY USA.

             BAPTISM: RPDC extracts in New England Historical & Genealogical
             Register Vol. 18
             SP: Jannetje SCHERMERHORN, Adam VROMAN

     28 M   vi Johannis BRADT, christened on 1 Sep 1699 at Schenectady NY.

             BAPTSISM: Reformed Dutch Protestant Church extracts in New England Historical &
             Genealogical Register Vol. 18
             Listed at baptism as Joannes BRAT with no sponsors.

+   29 F  vii Cataleintje BRADT.
     30 M viii Ephraim BRADT, christened on 2 Jan 1704 at Schenectady NY U.
     31 F   ix Susanna BRADT, christened on 2 Jan 1704 at Schenectady, NY.

             BAPTISM: RPDC extracts in New England Historical & Genealogical
             Register Vol. 18
             SP: Jaacobus VAN DYCK & Jannetye VROMANS

             Susanna BRADT married (1) Bartholomew VROOMAN on 11 Mar 1726. Bartholomew, son of
             Johannes (Jan?) VROOMAN and Grietje Symonse VEEDER, born on 10 Jan 1703 at Schenectady
             NY; christened on 17 Jan 1703 at Schenectady, NY; died on 29 Mar 1771.

             BAPTISM: RPDC extracts in New England Historical & Genealogical
             Register Vol. 18


--------------------------------------------------------------------------------------------------

His father is listed as Johannes VROMAN instead of Jan VROOMAN, with his wife
Gesa SIMONS [VEEDER]. SP: Volkert SIMONSON [VEEDER] & Grietye HEEMSTRAET

    32 M    x Andreas BRADT, christened on 28 Oct 1706 at Schenectady, NY.
             He married (1) Anna DEGRAFF in 1743.
+   33 M   xi Samuel BRADT.
+   34 M  xii Ephraim BRADT.

7 Margareta (Grietje) VAN SLYCK, born abt 1665 at Schenectady, NY; died bef Dec 1733 at NY.
She married (1) Andries Arentse BRADT abt 1680 at Schenectady, NY. Andries, son of Arent Andriesse BRADT
and Catalyntje DE VOS, born in 1653 at Schenectady NY U; died on 9 Feb 1690 at Schenectady NY.

NOTES:
Andries and one of his children were killed in the Schenectady Massacre in
Feb. 1690. The child killed with him was a son, name unknown.

Children:
+   35 M    i Arent A. BRADT.
    36 F   ii Maria BRADT, born in 1684.

Did Maria marry her half-brother, Jacobus Vedder? Further investigation is
needed as it does appear that she did. Jacobus Vedder married a woman named
Maria and had no children.

+   37 F  iii Margarita BRADT.
    38 F   iv Bathsheba BRADT, born in 1688.

She m. Charles BURNS

Margareta (Grietje) VAN SLYCK married (2) Harmen Hermanus VEDDER on 10 Dec 1691.

COMMENT: I believe this is the Harman Veeder taken prisoner or missing after
the Buekendahl Massacre 18 July 1748 near Schenectady NY.

FATHER:
His father was also Harmen.

Children:
    39 F   v Margriet VEDDER, christened on 11 Apr 1694 at Schenectady NY.

CHRISTENING: Doop-boek of Reformed Protestant Dutch Church
Schenectady NY
SP: Harmen VAN SLYCK, Grietje RYCKMAN

    40 M  vi Jacobus VEDDER, christened on 15 Apr 1696 at Schenectady NY; died in 1762.

CHRISTENING: RPDC extracts in New England Historical & Genealogical Register
Vol. 18
Sp: Albert Vedder, Susannah Van Slyke

Jacobus VEDDER married (1) Maria (___).

There is some evidence pointing to Jacobus' wife Maria being his half-sister
Maria Bradt, with their mother being Margaret Van Slyke. Perhaps this is why
Jacobus and his wife had no children? Further investigation is needed on this.
Jacobus' wife Maria was alive as of July 1762 and was named as executor of his
will.

---

Third Generation

--------------------------------------------------------------------------------

41 F    vii Helena VEDDER, christened on 5 May 1700 at Schenectady NY.

        SIBLINGS: twin to Feytje.

42 F    viii Sophia (Fytie) VEEDER, christened on 5 May 1700 at Schenectady NY; died bef 1762.

        CHRISTENING:  RPDC extracts in New England Historical & Genealogical Register
        Vol. 18
        SP: Arent VEDDER, Sara GROOT, Cornelis VAN SLYCK, Hilletje CORNELIS

        SIBLINGS: Twin to Helena

        She is listed as the deceased sister, Suffia Pieters, of Jacobus Vedder in his
        will dated 1 July 1762. Her two children Harmanus Pieters and Margaret Pieters
        wife of James Sueter are provided for.

        Sophia (Fytie) VEEDER married (1) Mr. PIETERS.
43 F    ix Angnieta VEDDER, christened on 19 Apr 1702 at Schenectady NY.

        CHRISTENING:  RPDC extracts in New England Historical & Genealogical Register
        Vol. 18

        PARENTS:
        Parents listed at bptsm as Manus VEDDER & Margrieta VAN SLYK. SP: Jan Danielse
        VAN ANTWERPEN & Geertru VAN SLYK

        Angnieta VEDDER married (1) Johannes PEEK. Johannes, son of Jacobus PEEK and ELizabeth
        TEUNISE.
+  44 F    x Lydia VEDDER.
   45 M    xi Harmen Harmense VEDDER, died on 27 Jun 1763 at Albany NY.

        WILL: Harme Haramanes Vedder of Schonectady Albany Co. merchant, leaves
        everything to his daughter Susanna, widow of Nicolas A. van Petter and his
        brother Johannes Haramenes Vedder. Witnesses: Johans. Roseboom silversmiht,
        Symon Vroman and Mindert R. Wemple

46 M    xii Johannis Harmense VEDDER, died aft 1763.

8 Harmen VAN SLYKE, born abt 1675 at Schenectady, NY; died on 20 Dec 1734.

    CONFLICT:Harmen Van Slyke was born ca 1680 according to Burke and 26
    March 1704 according to Yates in HSCNY. However it seems clear that
    Harmen's marriage to his first wife occured on 26 March 1704 so Yates
    has confused the marriage date with the baptismal date.
    A second conflict occurs with Pearson giving Harmen a second wife, Antje Schell
    ca 1726. However, W. Barker quotes that the Schenectady baptism records show
    Marten Van Slyke as the husband of Antje Schell from 1727-1729. ACTION: The
    Schenectady records should be checked and this followed up.

    COMMENT:Harmen's actual date of birth is critical in determing the dates
    of birth for the remainder of Jacques Cornelise's children. Harmen, or Harmanus
    was the eldest son, according to John J. Vrooman in F&FMC. If the date of
    birth of 1680 is correct, then it affects all the other children.

    BIOGRAPHY: In the winter of 1695-96 the garrison at Schenectady consisted
    of a detachment under Lieutenant Bickford. On 10 January about midnight
    the whole guard except one, deserted, for a total of 16 deserters.

--------------------------------------------------------------------------------

--------------------------------------------------------------------------------

Bickford, on discovering the desertion about 2 am, notified Col Richard
Ingoldsby of Albany and with 10 volunteers and 11 soldiers, Bickford
started in pursuit. About 4 p.m the next day, Jan. 11th., Bickford and
his volunteers met up with the deserters and ordered them to lay down
their arms. The deserters shot at the pursuers and a fight ensued. Five
deserters were killed and two wounded, at which point the remaining men
surrendered. Among the volunteers from Schenectady who accompanied
Bickford were:
     / Harman Van Slyke, Ensign of the train bands of Schenectady
       Gerrit Simons Veeder
       Peter Simons Veeder
       Albert Veeder
       Gerrit Gysbert Van Brakel
       Jan Danielse Van Antwerpen
       Dirck Groot
       Jonas LeRoy
       John Wemp
       Daniel Mutchcraft [Mascraft]
       Thomas Smith
On 21 April 1696, the survivors of the deserting party were
courtmartialed and sentenced to be shot.

MILITARY:
Harmen's military service was as a scout with the Mohawks in their war
against the French and northern Indians, and as Captain of the 2nd Foot
Company of Schenectady. He led 56 men recruited in the town. In 1715 his
Lieutenants were Hendrick VROOMAN and Jacob GLEN. Among the privates was
Fictoor Pootman aka Victor PUTMAN.
       Harmen was a Captain in a Schenectady Company in 1714 and an
Indian trader in 1724.

RESIDENCES:
He received a grant of 300 morgens of land at Canajoharie NY from the Mohawks
because         "his grandmother was a right Mohawk woman" and "his father born
with us at Canajoharie". His father was Jacques Cornelise, son of
Ots-Toch, the half French, half Mohawk woman who married his father
Cornelise Antonissen.
The deed conveyed 12 Jan. 1713 and consisting of 2000 acres, stated:
                "in consideration of ye love, good will and affection which
                we do bear toward our loving cozen and friend Capt. Harmon
                Van Slyke of Schenectady, aforesaid, whose grandmother was a
                right Mohawk squaw and his father born with us in the above
                said Kanajoree [Canajoharie].......it being his the said
                Harmen Van Slyke's by right of inheritance from his father"
The deed was witnessed by Lea STEVENS "interpreter to ye above deed"
and the land included the FREY tract. Harmen deeded that portion back to
Hendrick FREY of Zurich who had been given this by the Indians.

DEATH: Harmen made his will 1 November 1731 and died in 1734 leaving
twelve children. His sons Adam, James (Jacob) and Harmanus received half of his
2000 acres of land at Canajoharie known as Van Slyck's patent.

Harmen VAN SLYKE married (1) Jannetie VROOMAN in 1704. Jannetie, dau. of Adam VROOMAN and Margrieta
(Grietje) Takelse HEEMSTRET, died bef 1727.

Children:
+    47 M      i Jacobus (James) VAN SLYKE.
     48 F     ii Engeltie VAN SLYKE, christened on 29 Jan 1706 at Schenectady NY.


--------------------------------------------------------------------------------

----------------------------------------------------------------------------------------

                         She married (1) Sander LANSING.
   +    49 F      iii Margarieta VAN SLYKE.
   +    50 F       iv Helena aka Lena VAN SLYCK.
        51 M        v Samuel VAN SLYKE, born abt 1710/1711 at Schenectady, NY; died in 1778.
        52 F       vi Catrina VAN SLYCK, christened on 13 Sep 1712 at Schenectady NY.

                         CHRISTENING: Sponsors: Hendrick Vroman, Cat. Lucassen. Source: W. Barker,
                         Montgomery Co. NY

        53 F      vii Jannetje VAN SLYKE, born abt 1715.
        54 M     viii Adam VAN SLYKE, christened on 10 Nov 1716 at Schenectady NY.

                         CHRISTENING: Sponsors: Wouter Vroman. Grietien Heemste (Heemstraet?)

        55 F       ix Geertruy VAN SLYKE, christened on 10 Jan 1719 at Schenectady.
   +    56 M        x Adam VAN SLYKE.
   +    57 M       xi Harmanus VAN SLYKE.

He married (2) Antje SCHELL in 1726 at Schenectady NY.

        Antje and Harmen had two children according to Burke in Mohawk Frontier.

   Children:
   +    58 M      xii Jacques (Akers) VAN SLYKE.
        59 M     xiii Gerrit VAN SLYKE, christened in Aug 1729 at Schenectady NY.

                         FATHER: It is not clear whether his father is Marten or Marten's brother
                         Harmen.

                         BAPTISM: Sponsors: Albert Van Sleek [sic], Maria Van Sleek


9 Cornelis VAN SLYKE, born abt 1676 at Schenectady, NY.

        BIRTH: I believe the dob is in error and is really the date of marriage, as is
        in error for his brother Harman. Both dob came from HofSC, NY by Yates.

        MARRIAGE:
        Cornelis md. Clara two days before the birth of their first child, Margriet.

   Cornelis VAN SLYKE married (1) Claartje Janse BRADT on 10 Feb 1696. Claartje, dau. of Jan Albertsen
   BRADT and Maria Moockers POST, born abt 1678 at NY USA.

   Children:
   +    60 F        i Margariet VAN SLYKE.
   +    61 F       ii Maria VAN SLYCK.
        62 M      iii Jacques VAN SLYKE, christened on 10 Oct 1697.
        63 M       iv Jacques (Akes) VAN SLYKE, christened on 19 Oct 1698 at Schenectady NY.

                         CHRISTENING: Reformed Protestant Dutch Chruch extracts in New England
                         Historical & Genealogical Register Vol. 18
                         SP: Harmen & Susanna VAN SLYK. Parents were listed as Cornelis VAN SLYK &
                         Clara JANSE

   +    64 M        v Johannes VAN SLYCK.
   +    65 M       vi Adriaen VAN SLYCK.
   +    66 M      vii Harmanus (Harme) VAN SLYCK.
   +    67 M     viii Hendrick VAN SLYCK.


-------------------------------------------------------------------------------------------------
                                      Third Generation

--------------------------------------------------------------------------------

```
    +     68 F     ix Helena (Lena) VAN SLYCK.
    +     69 M      x Antony VAN SLYCK.
    +     70 M     xi Albert VAN SLYKE.
          71 F    xii Geertruy VAN SLYCK, christened on 30 Oct 1709 at Albany, NY.
          72 F   xiii Catharina VAN SLYKE, born in 1711 at Schenectady, NY; christened on 6 Mar 1711.
    +     73 M    xiv Cornelius VAN SLYKE.
    +     74 M     xv Peter (Petrus) VAN SLYKE.
          75 F    xvi Susanna VAN SLYCK, christened on 24 Mar 1716 at Schenectady NY.
```

10 Geertruyt VAN SLYKE, born abt 1760. *1660*
    She married (1) Johannes Myndertse VAN IVEREN. Johannes, son of Myndert FREDERICKSE and Catharyn
    BURCHARTS, born in 1669 at Beverwyck, NY; died in 1757 at Schenectady, NY.

    NOTES:
    Johannes Myndertse Van Iveren, aka Van Every, was the son of Myndert Frederick
    se Van Iveren and Cathalyn Burger.

    Children:
```
          76 F      i Margarita VAN EVERY, christened on 8 Jun 1707 at Albany, NY.
          77 M     ii Jacobus VAN EVERY, christened on 22 Apr 1709 at Albany, NY.
```

11 Marten VAN SLYCK, born abt 1678 at Schenectady NY.

    CONFLICT: According to the Kelly transcript (1987) of the Schenectady church
    records, this Marten was the father of children by Antje Schell on the 1727-29
    baptisms, and not Harmen, his brother. Antje was called Antje Siel in the 1729
    baptismal records. The descendants of Antje need to check on this to ascertain
    which son of Jacques Cornelissen was the husband.

    Marten VAN SLYCK married (1) Grietje Gerritse VAN VRANKEN on 23 Mar 1701 at Schenectady NY. Grietje,
    dau. of Gerrit Claes VAN VRANKEN and Ariaentje ULDRICK.

    Children:
          78 M      i Jacob VAN SLYKE, christened on 8 Feb 1702 at Schenectady NY.

                    CHRISTENING: RPDC extracts in New England Historical & Genealogical Register
                    Vol. 18
                    Parents listed at bptsm as Marten Van SLYK and Grietje GERRIS. SP: Kornelius
                    Van SLYK & Geertru Van SLYKE.

          79 M     ii Gerrit VAN SLYKE, christened on 27 Feb 1704 at Schenectady, NY.

                    CHRISTENING: Sponsors; Klaas Gerrissen, Geertruy, Geertruy Gerrisen

    +     80 F    iii Margarita VAN SLYCK.
    +     81 M     iv Petrus VAN SLYCK.
          82 F      v Ariantie VAN SLYKE, christened on 21 Jun 1712 at Schenectady, NY.

                    CHRISTENING: Schenectady Reformed Church, Schenectady
                    Sp: Arent Brat; Marg. Brat. Parents: Mart Sleyck; Margarietie V. Franken

          83 F     vi Susanna VAN SLYKE, christened on 18 Dec 1714 at Schenectady, NY.

                    CHRISTENING: Sponosrs: Harmen Van Slyc, Lana Van Slyc


14 Lydia VAN SLYCK, born abt 1685 at Schenectady, NY, USA.
```

--------------------------------------------------------------------------------
Third Generation
```

-------------------------------------------------------------------------------------------

    MARRIAGE: According to Jack Middaugh, the church records show that Lydia and
Isaac married on 12 May 1705 and not 4 Oct. as my records show.

    Lydia VAN SLYCK married (1) Isaac VAN VALKENBURG on 4 Oct 1705 at Schenectady, NY, USA. Isaac, son of
Jochem Lambertse VAN VALKENBURG and Eva Hendrickse VROOMAN, born at NY USA; christened on 4 Jul 1686 at
Albany, NY, USA.

    1717:lived Albany, Rensslaerwyck & Verreberg, NY
!6 Sept. 1712: received a conveyance from Carl Hansen TOLL of a lot on the
south side of Union St., incl. the Court House lot 100 ft. x 210 ft. for 30 L.

  Children:
     84 M    i Isaak VAN VALKENBURG, christened on 10 Jan 1704 at Schenectady NY U.
     85 M   ii Jacobus VAN VALKENBURG, christened on 28 Oct 1705 at Schenectady NY U.
             He married (1) Margariet RETTELIEF on 30 Oct 1732 at Albany NY. Margariet, christened
             on 9 Jun 1706 at Albany NY.
+   86 F  iii Eva VAN VALKENBURG.
     87 M   iv Jochem Lambert VAN VALKENBURG, christened on 15 Jan 1710 at Albany NY USA.
             He married (1) Helena Susanna Magdalena WARNER in 1732. Helena, born on 7 Jun 1725;
             died on 1 May 1748 at Schoharie NY.
             He married (2) Maria BERRI in 1749 at Schoharie NY. Maria, born in 1727.
+   88 M    v Isaac VAN VALKENBURG.
+   89 F   vi Margarita VAN VALKENBURG.
     90 M  vii Harmen VAN VALKENBURG, christened on 2 Mar 1715 at Albany NY USA; died at Wysox, Pa
             USA.
+   91 F viii Jannetien VAN VALKENBURG.
     92 F   ix Geertruit VAN VALKENBURG, christened on 31 Jul 1720 at Schenectady NY U.
             She married (1) Cornelius AARDSCHE.
     93 F    x Lydia VAN VALKENBURG, born on 1 Sep 1725 at Schenectady NY U.

15 Daniel VAN O'LINDA, born abt 1676.
 He married (1) Lysbeth KRIGIER on 11 Jun 1696 at Schenectady, NY.

  Children:
+   94 M    i Peter VAN O'LINDA.
     95 M   ii Johannes VAN O'LINDA, born in 1699; christened on 3 Sep 1699 at Albany, NY.

            BAPTISM: Genealogies of First Settlers of Schenectday by Pearson

            NAME: aka John

+   96 M  iii Martin VAN O'LINDA.
     97 F   iv Maria VAN O'LINDA, born in 1704.

16 Jacob VAN O'LINDA, born abt 1678.
 He married (1) Eva DE GRAFF.

    d/o Claes de Graaf

  Children:
     98 M    i Peter VAN O'LINDA, born in 1712 at Albany, NY; christened on 17 Feb 1712 at Albany, NY.
     99 M   ii William VAN O'LINDA, born in 1716; christened on 13 Oct 1716.

            BAPTISM: Genealogies of First Settlers of Schenectday by Pearson

+  100 M  iii Martin VAN O'LINDA.
   101 M   iv Nicholas VAN O'LINDA, born in 1719; christened on 30 May 1719.
   102 F    v Helena VAN O'LINDA, born in 1721; christened on 12 Feb 1721.

-------------------------------------------------------------------------------------------
Third Generation

She married (1) Johannes QUACKENBOS on 16 Jun 1723.
103 F    vi Elisabet VAN O'LINDA, born in 1723; christened on 16 Jun 1723.

BAPTISM: Genealogies of First Settlers of Schenectday by Pearson


18 William Claessen VAN COPPERNOL, born in Mar 1688 at Schenectady, NY; christened on 22 May 1691 at Schenectady, NY; died on 29 Dec 1787 at Stone Arabia, NY.

SOURCE: The Van Coppernol Family in America

William Claessen VAN COPPERNOL married (1) Engeltien (Angelica) LANTGRAEF abt 1712.

Her parents were George and Elisabeth Catharine Lantgraaf, Palatines to West Camp New York in 1709.

Children:
104 M     i Claes Willemse VAN COPPERNOL, christened on 18 Dec 1714 at NY.
105 M    ii George Willemse VAN COPPERNOL, christened on 14 Apr 1716 at NY.

19 Annatje aka Anna STEVENS, christened on 27 Mar 1695 at Schenectady NY.

CHRISTENING: Parents at bptsm listed as Jonathan Stevens, Lea Claese. SP:Maria Dirkse
Lea's name of Claese came from that of her deceased husband, Claes Willemse Van Coppernol. It was common for Dutch women to be given the patronymic of a husband as a surname.

Annatje aka Anna STEVENS married (1) Hendrick HAGEDORN. Hendrick, born abt 1695.

BIRTH: His year of birth comes from AF. It also states he was "of Aalplaats, NY"

Children:
106 F     i Maria HAGEDORN, christened on 31 Aug 1717 at Schenectady, NY.

CHRISTENING: From AF 1991

107 M    ii Harmanus HAGEDORN, christened on 25 Jul 1719 at Schenectady, NY.

CHRISTENING: From 1991 AF

108 M   iii Jonathan HAGEDORN, christened on 17 Sep 1721 at Schenectady, NY.

CHRISTENING: From 1991 AF

Jonathan HAGEDORN married (1) Lea HAGEN. Lea, born in 1721.
109 M    iv Nicolas HAGEDORN, christened on 23 Mar 1723 at Schenectady, NY.

BIRTH: 1991 AF

+ 110 F     v Lea HAGEDORN.
111 M    vi Samuel HAGEDORN, christened on 20 Sep 1726 at Schenectady, NY.

BIRTH: 1991 AF

112 F   vii Dina HAGEDORN, christened in 1729 at Schenectady, NY.

--------------------------------------------------------------------------------

             BIRTH: 1991 AF

             Dina HAGEDORN married (1) Samuel MURRAY. Samuel, born abt 1729 at NY.

113 M   viii Dirck HAGEDORN, christened on 10 Jun 1733 at Schenectady, NY.

             BIRTH: 1991 AF

114 M    ix Arent HAGEDORN, christened on 3 Aug 1735 at Schenectady, NY.

             BIRTH: 1991 AF

115 F     x Geertruy HAGEDORN, christened on 9 Jul 1737 at Schenectady, NY.

             BIRTH: 1991 AF

116 M    xi Robert HAGEDORN, born abt 1739 at Schenectady, NY.

             BIRTH: 1991 AF


20 Nicolas Hendricus STEVENS, born on 10 Nov 1697.

    FAMILY:

    All his children died young and unmarried except for Arent and Johannes

Nicolas Hendricus STEVENS married (1) Maria PHENIX on 29 May 1730. Maria, christened on 18 Apr 1705 at NYC, NY.

    CHRISTENING: 1991 AF

Children:
117 M     i Jonathan STEVENS, christened on 21 May 1732 at Schenectady, NY.

             DEATH: died young

118 M    ii Sander STEVENS, born on 2 Dec 1733 at Schenectady, NY.

             DEATH DATE young

119 M   iii Arent STEVENS, christened on 21 Sep 1735 at Schenectady, NY.
120 F    iv Hester STEVENS, born on 21 Dec 1737 at Schenectady, NY.

             DEATH DATE young

121 F     v Cornelia STEVENS, born on 14 Jun 1741 at Schenectady, NY.

             DEATH DATE young

122 F    vi Lea STEVENS, born on 3 Jul 1743 at Schenectady, NY.

             DEATH DATE young

123 M   vii Johannes STEVENS, born on 31 Mar 1745 at Schenectady, NY.
             He married (1) Catalyntje VAN SCHAICK bef 1773. Catalyntje, christened on 13 Jan 1751 at Albany, NY.

             NAME: Her name as spouse of Johannes Stevens comes from 1991 AF


--------------------------------------------------------------------------------

Third Generation

124 F   viii Annatje STEVENS, born on 6 May 1748 at Schenectady, NY.

          DEATH DATE young

125 F    ix Maria STEVENS, born on 5 Apr 1752.

          DEATH DATE young

126 F     x Diana STEVENS, died aft 1747.

22 Arent STEVENS, born on 26 Jul 1702; died on 17 May 1758.

      OCCUPATION:  Indian Interpreter circa 1738-1758 employed by Sir William Johnson
in negotiations with various tribes

      NOTE:
Maria m. John STUART/STEWARD and had her first child in 1773.

      BAPTISM:
Sp:Manus VEDDER; Susanna VAN SLYK [sic]"Jonothan STEVENS oud 27 Jare syn
belydenisse gedaen en daer op gedoopt Jonothan"

Arent STEVENS married (1) Maritje HALL on 3 Feb 1726. Maritje, dau. of Willem HALL and x (____), born
abt 1697; died on 23 Dec 1739 at Schenectady, NY.

Children:
  127 M     i Jonathon STEVENS, born on 1 Dec 1726; died on 7 Sep 1755 at Ft. George, NY.

          MARRIAGE: He died unmarried

          Jonathon STEVENS married (1) (____).
  128 M    ii William STEVENS, born in 1732; christened on 10 Sep 1732 at Schenectady, NY.
  129 F   iii Catrina STEVENS, born in 1729; christened on 1 Aug 1729 at Schenectady, NY; died on 27
          Aug 1790.
  130 M    iv Nicolaas STEVENS, born in 1734; christened on 14 Nov 1734 at Schenectady, NY; died on
          19 Sep 1788.

          COMMENT: Nicholas Stevens is listed as a "Tory" during the American Revolution

          Nicolaas STEVENS married (1) Margareita MABIE. Margareita, died on 4 Aug 1764.
  131 M     v Johannes STEVENS, born in 1736; christened on 21 Jul 1736 at Schenectady, NY.
  132 M    vi Jacobus STEVENS, born on 13 Dec 1739 at Schenectady, NY.

He married (2) Mary GRIFFITHS on 4 Feb 1749. Mary, born abt 1721; died on 2 Jul 1794.

Children:
+  133 F   vii Maria STEVENS.
  134 M viii Richard STEVENS, born on 10 Dec 1752 at Schenectady, NY; died in 1800.
  135 F    ix Lea STEVENS, born on 22 Apr 1755 at Schenectady, NY; died on 11 Jul 1756.

          twin to Anna

  136 F     x Anna STEVENS, born on 22 Apr 1755 at Schenectady, NY.
          She married (1) Philip FRANSIKKEL.

Fourth Generation


23 Arent BRADT, born abt 1684 at NY.
    He married (1) Catrina MABIE on 4 Jun 1714 at Schenectady NY. Catrina, dau. of Jan Pieterse MEBIE and
    Anetjie Pieterse BOSBOOM, born in 1691; died in 1773.

        She died ae 82y 2m 17d
        She and Arent had 5 sons and 5 daus.
        Catrian was d/o Jan Pieterse MABIE & Annetje BOSBOOM

    Children:
        137 M       i  Samuel BRADT, christened on 16 Oct 1716; died on 3 Aug 1799.
                       He married (1) Catherine VAN GUYSLING. Catherine, dau. of Meyndert VAN GUYSLING and
                       Suster VIELE, born in 1722 at Schenectady, NY; christened on 3 Sep 1722 at Schenectady,
                       NY; died on 29 Dec 1803.
        138 M      ii  Johannes BRADT, christened on 15 Sep 1717; died in Jul 1748 at Buekendaal Massa,
                       Schenectady NY.

                       DEATH: Buekendaal Massacre, Schenectady NY
                       Killed by French Indians when he set out with a party of 60 volunteers to
                       avenge the murder of Daniel Toll.

    +   139 F     iii  Susanna BRADT.
    +   140 F      iv  Annetje BRADT.
        141 F       v  Margaret BRADT, christened on 6 Sep 1723; died on 30 May 1790.
        142 F      vi  Eve BRADT, born on 10 Mar 1726; christened on 27 Mar 1726.
                       She married (1) Simon VEEDER. Simon, son of Helmers VEEDER and Annetje MEBIE, born abt
                       1724.

                       NOTES: Rita Lancefield has him married to Elizabeth BANCKER on 25 Sept. 1755
                       Schenectady

        143 M     vii  Abram BRADT, born on 13 Dec 1727; died in 1816.
        144 M    viii  Jacob BRADT, christened on 9 Oct 1730; died on 26 Mar 1801.
    +   145 F      ix  Engeltie (Angelica) BRADT.

24 Margriet BRADT, born on 15 Apr 1686 at NY.

        NOTES:They had 2 sons and 5 daus.

    Margriet BRADT married (1) Daniel TOLL. Daniel, died on 18 Jul 1748 at Beukendaal, NY.

        OCCUPATION: Captain in the Militia

        DEATH: Beukendaal Massacre near Schenectady NY

        NOTES:
        Captn Daniel Toll was the first man killed when he and his servant Ryckert
        went in search of stray horses at Beukendahl, 3 mi. from Schenectady. He was
        killed by bullets from the guns of the French Indians, placed in a field by
        a fence and a crow attached to his propped-up body by a string so that his
        rescuers might be deceived into thinking him still alive.

    Children:

146 F      i ELizabeth TOLL, born on 14 Jan 1721 at Schenectady, NY.

          She was their second dau.

          ELizabeth TOLL married (1) Cornelius VAN SANTVOORD.

          OCCUPATION: Minister

147 F     ii Gertrude TOLL, born on 7 Aug 1729 at Schenectady, NY.

          youngest daughter

          Gertrude TOLL married (1) Jellis CLUTE.

26 Jacobus BRADT, christened on 3 Jan 1695 at Schenectady, NY.

    BAPTISM: RPDC extracts
    At his baptism his parents were listed as Samuel BRATT, Susanna VAN SLYK and
    sponsors were Harmen & Geertruy VAN SLYK

    Jacobus BRADT married (1) Margaret CLUTE. Margaret, dau. of Johannes CLUTE and .... (___).

    She was d/o Johannes CLUTE.

Children:
    148 M     i Samuel BRADT, christened on 2 Feb 1724 at Schenectady, NY.
    149 M    ii Johannes BRADT, christened on 2 Sep 1726 at Schenectady, NY.
    150 F   iii Elisabeth BRADT, christened on 24 Dec 1730 at Schenectady, NY.
    151 F    iv Bata BRADT, christened on 30 Jan 1731 at Schenectady, NY.
              She married (1) Abraham WATSON.
    152 M     v Harmanus BRADT, christened on 24 Feb 1734 at Schenectady, NY.
    153 M    vi Jacobus BRADT, christened on 27 Feb 1737 at Schenectady, NY.
    154 F   vii Susanna BRADT, christened in Jul 1739 at Schenectady, NY.
    155 M viii Arent BRADT.

29 Cataleintje BRADT, christened on 21 Dec 1701 at Schenectady, NY.

    BAPTISM:
    RPDC extracts in New England Historical & Genealogical Register Vol. 18
    SP: Kornelia Van SLYK, Diver Van PETTEN

    Cataleintje BRADT married (1) Jacobus (James) VAN SLYKE on 2 Sep 1732. Jacobus, son of Harmen VAN SLYKE
    and Jannetie VROOMAN, born on 28 May 1704 at Schenectady, NY.

    COMMENT: He was commanding officer at Schenectady in 1754, member of the
    assembly 1750 and 1771.

    CHILDREN:
    I believe he had a dau. Jannetie who was b. ca 1735 and md Philip
    RYLEY, then died 1 Aug. 1824 age 89. Jannetie md. 11 Oct. 1755 and had 3 sons
    Phillipus b & d Sept. 1756, Philippus b 7 Jan. 1759 and Jacobus Van Slyke b 22
    Oct. 1761 Albany who md. Jannetie Swits in 1792.

Children:
    156 M     i Harmanus VAN SLYKE, born on 3 Aug 1733.
              He married (1) Anna GLENN on 26 Sep 1767.

              d/o Alexander GLEN

```
        157 F    ii Geertruid VAN SLYCK, born in 1734; christened on 1 Nov 1734.
  +     158 F   iii Annatje VAN SLYKE.
        159 M    iv Samuel VAN SLYCK, born at Schenectady NY; christened on 17 Mar 1738 at Schenectady NY.

                    MILITARY: Samuel's name appears on the rolls of the 2d. Albany County Militia,
                    Land Bounty Rights [HSDR:248]
```

33 Samuel BRADT, christened on 30 Apr 1707 at Schenectady NY U.
He married (1) Catharine VAN PATTEN in 1732. Catharine, dau. of Arent VAN PATTEN and .. (___).

        Catharine d/o Arent VAN PATTEN

    Children:
```
        160 F     i Susanna BRADT, christened on 3 Jun 1733 at Schenectady, NY.
        161 M    ii Arent BRADT, christened in 1738 at Schenectady, NY.
                    He married (1) Maria VAN SLYKE on 10 May 1764 at Schenectady, NY.
```

34 Ephraim BRADT, christened on 13 Feb 1712 at Schenectady, NY.

        BAPTISM: Schenectady Reformed Church Baptism Record
        SP: Johannes WEMP; Annetjen VEEDERS

Ephraim BRADT married (1) Clara BORSIE in 1751. Clara, dau. of Philip BOSIE and Margarita BRADT, born on
23 Nov 1717 at Schenectady NY.

        Clara d/o Philip BORSIE, widow of Cornelius VIELE Jr.

    Children:
```
        162 F     i Susanna BRADT.
        163 F    ii Cornelia BRADT.
        164 F   iii Margaret BRADT.
```

35 Arent A. BRADT, born in 1680 at NY USA; died in 1767.
He married (1) Jannetje VROOMAN on 14 Oct 1704. Jannetje, dau. of Johannes (Jan?) VROOMAN and Grietje
Symonse VEEDER, born on 23 Jul 1682.

        COMMENT: Burke states that Jannetie and Harmen van Slyke had 11 children
        between 1704 and 1724 and that Harmen married in 1726 [after Jannetie's death]

    Children:
```
  +     165 M     i Andries BRADT.
        166 F    ii Catharina BRADT, born in 1706.
        167 F   iii Gezena BRADT, born in 1707.
  +     168 M    iv Johannes A. BRADT.
  +     169 F     v Margrietje BRADT.
        170 F    vi Magdalena (Helena) BRADT, born in 1716.
        171 F   vii Ariaantje BRADT, born in 1718.
        172 M  viii Harmanus BRADT, born in 1721; died in 1801.
        173 M    ix Simon Petrus BRADT, born in 1723.
        174 F     x Susanna BRADT, born in 1729.
```

37 Margarita BRADT, born in 1686.
She married (1) Philip BOSIE on 2 Sep 1704.

    Children:
```
  +     175 F     i Clara BORSIE.
```

44 Lydia VEDDER, died bef 1737.
     She married (1) Harmanus (Harme) VAN SLYCK on 16 Aug 1729. Harmanus, son of Cornelis VAN SLYKE and
     Claartje Janse BRADT, christened on 19 Apr 1702 at Schenectady NY; died aft Dec 1751.

          OCCUPATION: Indian Trader

          CHRISTENING: RPDC extracts in New England Historical & Genealogical Register
          Vol. 18
          SP: Kornelis FIELE [VIELE] & Fydye BOSBOOM

          NOTE:
          Harmanus was an Indian trader. He left 4 sons and 6 daughters when he died.

          He is in his brother Johannes' will dated Dec. 10 1751

     Children:
          176 F      i Margarita VAN SLYKE, born in 1731 at Schenectady NY.

                        Margaret is listed in the will of her uncle Jacobus Vedder of 1 July 1762 as
                        "daughter of deceased sister Lydia, Margariet van Sleyck."

      +  177 M     ii Anthony VAN SLYKE.
         178 F    iii Clara VAN SLYKE, born in 1735 at Schenectady, NY; christened on 27 Jul 1735 at
                        Schenectady, NY.

47 Jacobus (James) VAN SLYKE.
     ***** This individual's information has already been printed. *****.
     He married (1) Cataleintje BRADT on 2 Sep 1732.
     ***** This individual's information has already been printed. *****.

     ***** Descendants of this couple have already been printed. *****.

49 Margarieta VAN SLYKE, born on 9 Nov 1707 at Schenectady NY; died on 12 Mar 1787.
     She married (1) Antony VAN SLYCK on 19 Nov 1730 at Schenectady, NY. Antony, son of Cornelis VAN SLYKE
     and Claartje Janse BRADT, christened on 15 Dec 1706 at Albany, NY.

     Children:
          179 M      i Cornelius Antone VAN SLYCK, born on 12 Apr 1731 at Schenectady, NY; died aft 1751.

                        He is listed as Cornelis Antone, son of Antone, in his uncle Johannes Van
                        Slyke's will of Dec. 10 1751

50 Helena aka Lena VAN SLYCK, christened on 15 Jan 1710 at Schenectady NY; died bef Dec 1751.

          DEATH:
          Mentioned in husband's will written 10 Dec. 1751 as "Lena, d/o Harman Van
          Slyck, then deceased"

     Helena aka Lena VAN SLYCK married (1) Johannes VAN SLYCK on 4 Feb 1742 at Schenectady NY. Johannes, son
     of Cornelis VAN SLYKE and Claartje Janse BRADT, christened on 9 Jan 1700 at Schenectady NY; died in Nov
     1752.

          CHRISTENING: Reformed Protestant Dutch Church extracts in New England
          Historical & Genealogical Register Vol. 18
          SP: Gerrit SYMONSEN [VEEDER] & Hilletje VAN d'LINDE [sister to Cornelis VAN
          SLYKE] Mother listed as Claartje BRAT.

DEATH:
He left his property to his brothers and sisters, his wife having died before him, and to his nieces and nephews. No children are mentioned in his will of 1751 which was proved 14 Nov. 1752. He left land in Schenectady Tp. Albany Co. between Stene Kil and Plate Kil on the south side of the Mohawk River. The executors were his brothers Cornelius and Harme Van Slyck. The witnesses were Joseph Yates, Arent van Antwerpen and Jacob Peeck.

Bequests to: brothers Harme and Cornelis; sisters Margaret Peeck and Lena Van Antwerpe; nephews Cornelis s/o deceased brother Adreejan, Cornelis Petrus s/o brother Petrus, Conrelis Antone s/o brother Antone; nieces Clara d/o deceased brother Hendrick, Margret and Elisabeth daughters of brother Harme, Margaret d/o brother Albert, Gertruy d/o brother Cornelis, Elizabeth d/o Johannes Visger. His deceased wife Lena is mentioned as being the d/o Harme van Slyck.

Children:
    180 M     i Jacobus VAN SLYKE, born in 1741 at Schenectady NY; christened on 5 Jul 1741 at Schenectady NY.

               Not in father's will written 10 Dec. 1751

    181 M    ii Cornelis VAN SLYKE, born in 1744 at Schenectady NY; christened on 8 Jul 1744 at Schenectady NY.

               NOTES: He was not in father's will written 10 Dec. 1751.


56 Adam VAN SLYKE, born on 3 Mar 1721.
He married (1) Catarina VAN EPS on 19 Sep 1747. Catarina, dau. of Johannes Baptist VAN EPS and Helena GLEN, born on 16 Nov 1723 at Schenectady, NY.

    she was d/o Jan Baptist van Eps

Children:
+  182 M     i Harmanus VAN SLYKE.
   183 F    ii Helena VAN SLYKE, born abt 1754.
   184 F   iii Helena VAN SLYKE, born in 1759 at Schenectady NY; christened on 5 Aug 1759 at Schenectady NY.
             She married (1) Samuel THORN.

57 Harmanus VAN SLYKE, christened on 14 Jun 1724 at Schenectady NY; died aft Apr 1776.

    CONFLICT: There may be another child, Harme bp 21 June 1752, pa:Hermanes Van Slyke, ma:Elisabeth. Hi & Low Dutch Reformed Church, Schoharie

    CHRISTENING: Sp. Jacob Vedder, Lidia Van Sleyck.

    DEATH: His will of 20 April 1776 lists wife Elisabeth, son Nicholas and daughters Rebecca and Engeltje

    RESIDENCES: 1753 appears on Burnetsfield Church Collectionlist

  Harmanus VAN SLYKE married (1) Elisabeth VAN PETTEN on 27 Jan 1749 at Schenectady NY. Elisabeth, dau. of Nicholas VAN PETTEN and Rebecca GROOT.

    d/o Nicolaas Van Petten

Children:
185 M      i Harme VAN SLYKE, christened on 12 Jun 1752 at Schenectady, NY.

          CHRISTENING: Sponsors: Harme Browe, Sara Brower

+   186 M      ii Nicolaas VAN SLYKE.
    187 F     iii Jannetje VAN SLYKE, christened on 11 Dec 1757 at Schenectady, NY.
    188 M      iv Harmen VAN SLYKE, christened on 3 Jul 1760 at Schenectady, NY.

          CHRISTENING: Sponsors: Harme Brower & Sartie

    189 F       v Rebecca VAN SLYKE, christened on 17 Dec 1762 at Schenectady, NY.
               She married (1) Jacob H. WALLRATH in 1785.
    190 F      vi Engeltie VAN SLYKE, christened on 20 Sep 1766 at Schenectady, NY.
               She married (1) Jacob SCHAFER in 1782.
    191 M     vii Hermanus VAN SLYKE, christened on 1 Dec 1769 at Schenectady, NY.

          CHRISTENING: Sponsors: Harme Brower and wife Itie

58 Jacques (Akers) VAN SLYKE, christened on 7 Jan 1727 at Schenectady NY; died bef 1762.

    FATHER: There is a possibility that his father is Marten Van Slyke and not
    Harmen, Marten's brother.

    BAPTISM: Sponsors: Cornelius Van Sleyck [sic]; Jannetje Vrooman

Jacques (Akers) VAN SLYKE married (1) Maria PETRIE in 1748.

Children:
192 M      i Jacob VAN SLYKE, born abt 1756.

60 Margariet VAN SLYKE, christened on 12 Feb 1696 at Albany, NY; died aft Dec 1751.

    CHRISTENING: Sponsors Albert Rykman, Antoni Bries, Elsje Rutgers

    She is in her brother Johannes' will dated Dec. 10, 1751 of Schenectady Tp.
    Albany Co.

Margariet VAN SLYKE married (1) Jacobus PEECK on 1 Jan 1721. Jacobus, son of Jacobus PEEK and ELizabeth
TEUNISE, christened on 28 Dec 1698 at Schenectady NY.

    BAPTISM: RPDC extracts in New England Historical & Genealogical
    Register Vol. 18
    s/o Jacobus PEECK bp New Amsterdam 6 Mar 1658 & Elisabeth TEUNISE
    SP: Esias SWART, Maria GLENN

Children:
+   193 M      i Jacques PEEK.
+   194 F     ii ELizabeth PEEK.

61 Maria VAN SLYCK, christened on 23 May 1697 at Albany, NY.

    CHRISTENING: Sp: Jan Bratt, Dirk Wessel Ten Broek, Geertruy Van Slyk

Maria VAN SLYCK married (1) Johannes RYCKMAN on 13 Jun 1729 at Schenectady NY. Johannes, son of Johannes
RYCKMAN and Catharina KIP, born in 1705.

---

Fourth Generation

------------------------------------------------------------------------------------


        OCCUPATION: barber, perukemaker

     Children:
   +  195 M      i Johannes (John) RYCKMAN.
      196 M     ii Cornelis RYCKMAN, born in 1732 at Schenectady, NY; christened on 26 Mar 1732 at
                   Schenectady, NY.
      197 F    iii Cathrina RYCKMAN, born in 1733 at Schenectady, NY; christened on 23 Sep 1733 at
                   Schenectady, NY.
      198 F     iv Clara RYCKMAN, born in 1735 at Schenectady, NY; christened on 23 Mar 1735 at
                   Schenectady, NY.
      199 F      v Cathrina RYCKMAN, born in 1737 at Schenectady, NY; christened on 29 Mar 1737 at
                   Schenectady, NY.
      200 F     vi Susanna RYCKMAN, born in 1739 at Schenectady, NY; christened on 14 Feb 1739 at
                   Schenectady, NY.
      201 F    vii Maria RYCKMAN, born in 1741 at Schenectady, NY; christened on 8 Mar 1741 at
                   Schenectady, NY.

 64 Johannes VAN SLYCK.
    ***** This individual's information has already been printed. *****.
    He married (1) Helena aka Lena VAN SLYCK on 4 Feb 1742 at Schenectady NY.
    ***** This individual's information has already been printed. *****.

    ***** Descendants of this couple have already been printed. *****.

 65 Adriaen VAN SLYKE, christened on 9 Feb 1701 at Schenectady NY; died on 18 Jul 1748 at Beukendahl, NY.

        CHRISTENING:  Reformed Protestant Dutch Church extracts in New England
        Historical & Genealogical Register Vol. 18

        DEATH: Beukendahl Massacre, NY
        !SOURCE: History of Schenectady County, New York by Austin YATES, 1902

        PARENTS:
        Parents listed as Kornelis V. Slyk & Klaertje Brat. SP: Manus Vedder &
        Jannetje Vroman

    Adriaen VAN SLYKE married (1) Jannetje VIELE on 17 Oct 1736. Jannetje, died bef 1741 at Schenectady NY.

     Children:
      202 F      i Jannetje VAN SLYKE, born in 1738 at Schenectady NY; christened on 14 May 1738 at
                   Schenectady NY.

    He married (2) Bregie TOLL on 26 Nov 1741.

        She was d/o Carl Hansen Toll

     Children:
   +  203 F     ii Claartje VAN SLYKE.
      204 M    iii Cornelis VAN SLYKE, born on 3 Jun 1744 at Schenectady NY; christened on 10 Jun 1744 at
                   Schenectady NY; died on 27 Jan 1799.

                   DEATH: HSDR - Hanson  p. 246

                   He is the only child of Adrian listed in his uncle Johannes Van Slyke's will
                   dated Dec 10 1751. He was 7 years old when the will was written.

                   MILITARY: Cornelius or Cornelis Van Slyke was appointed, on 28 July 1778, a
                   second lieutenant in a company of Exempts fromed in Schenectady under Captain


------------------------------------------------------------------------------------
                                   Fourth Generation

Jacob SCHERMERHORN. [HSDR:246]

205 M      iv Carel Hansen VAN SLYKE, born in 1746 at Schenectady NY; christened on 2 Mar 1746 at
              Schenectady NY.

66 Harmanus (Harme) VAN SLYCK.
***** This individual's information has already been printed. *****.
He married (1) Lydia VEDDER on 16 Aug 1729.
***** This individual's information has already been printed. *****.

***** Descendants of this couple have already been printed. *****.

He married (2) Sarah VISSCHER in 1737. Sarah, born in 1711.

Children:
206 M       i Jacobus Visscher (Cobus) VAN SLYKE, born on 17 Jul 1739 at NY.
              He married (1) (___) bef 1783.
207 F      ii Maria VAN SLYKE, born in 1740 at Schenectady, NY; christened on 21 Sep 1740 at
              Schenectady, NY.
208 M     iii Johannes VAN SLYKE, born in 1742 at Schenectady, NY; christened on 9 May 1742 at
              Schenectady, NY.
209 F      iv Elizabeth VAN SLYKE, born in 1744; christened on 10 Jun 1744 at Schenectady, NY.

              She and her sister Margret are the only two children of Harme listed in their
              uncle Johannes Van Slyke's will of Dec. 10 1751

              Elizabeth VAN SLYKE married (1) Gerrit VAN SLYKE.

              NOTES: They quite likely had dau. Catlyntje who md. Hendrick BARHYDT s/o
              Johannes Barhydt & Helena PEEK. Catlyntje & Hendrick had ch:Johannes b 1798,
              Elisabeth, John, Lena, John, John. Catlyntje in her will called Sarah with a
              brother Harmanus VAN SLYKE. Her will was proved 3 Aug. 1809.

210 F       v Annatje VAN SLYKE, born in 1746 at Schenectady, NY; christened on 9 Nov 1746 at
              Schenectady, NY.
211 M      vi Johannes VAN SLYKE, born in 1748 at Schenectady, NY; christened on 18 Sep 1748 at
              Schenectady, NY.
212 F     vii Maria VAN SLYKE, christened on 8 Jan 1752 at Schenectady, NY.

              CHRISTENING: Sponsors: Joh. Fisher (Visscher), Caetje van Slyck

              Maria VAN SLYKE married (1) Pieter Symonse VEEDER. Pieter, son of Simon Volkertse
              VEEDER and Engeltie (___).
  +  213 M  viii Harmen VAN SLYKE.

67 Hendrick VAN SLYCK, born on 24 Oct 1703; christened on 24 Oct 1703 at Schenectady NY; died bef Dec 1751.

      CHRISTENING: RPDC extracts in New England Historical & Genealogical Register
      Vol. 18
      He is listed as Henderik at his bptsm with parents Kornelis Van Slyk &
      Klaertye Bratt. SP: Marten [VAN] BENTHUYSE & Grietye VAN SLIJK

      He is listed as deceased in his brother Johannes' will of Dec. 10 1751

  Hendrick VAN SLYCK married (1) Catharina SLINGERLAND on 6 Jun 1729. Catharina, dau. of Cornelis
  SLINGERLAND and Eva MABIE, christened in 1710.

      Catharina and Hendrick were first cousins. She was a BRADT descendant too

-------------------------------------------------------------------------------------------------

----------------------------------------------------------------------------------------------------

and the d/o Cornelius SLINGERLAND>

    Children:
    +   214 F      i Catrina (Clara) VAN SLYCK.

68 Helena (Lena) VAN SLYCK, christened on 6 May 1705 at Schenectady NY; died in Feb 1794.

    She is in her brother Johannes' will of Dec. 10 1751

    Helena (Lena) VAN SLYCK married (1) Daniel VAN ANTWERPEN on 17 Oct 1736 at Schenectady, NY. Daniel, son
    of Jan Danielse VAN ANTWERPEN and Angiente VEEDERS.

    Children:
        215 M      i Johannes VAN ANTWERPEN, born in 1743; christened on 29 May 1743 at Schenectady, NY.

69 Antony VAN SLYCK.
    ***** This individual's information has already been printed. *****.
    He married (1) Margarieta VAN SLYKE on 19 Nov 1730 at Schenectady, NY.
    ***** This individual's information has already been printed. *****.

    ***** Descendants of this couple have already been printed. *****.

70 Albert VAN SLYKE, christened on 26 May 1708 at Schenectady NY.

        BIOGRAPHY: Albert Van Slyke wrote to Col. William Johnson 21 July 1748,
        three days after the Beukendaal Massacre near Schenectady, and his is
        the only semi-official narrative from one who was there.
        A party of men from Schenectady, with Daniel Toll as leader, had
        gone to bring in several horses. They were surprised by the enemy and a
        fight began. Adrian Van Slyke, brother of Albert, heard the firing and
        sent a slave to Schenectady to give the alarm and bring reinforcements.
        Four parties of armed men were sent out, the first party consisting of 5
        or 6 young men, among them Daniel Van Slyke, brother to Adrian and
        Albert. The second party was led by Ackes Van Slyke, another brother.
        Akes Van Slyke led the third party of New York levies, but on
        reaching the fight where Adrian Van Slyke was holding the enemy off, the
        levies fled. Akes was forced to flee, and his brother Adrian, left on his
        own, was killed. Albert and his men, including Jacob Glen, rode out as
        the fourth party but when they arrived, Adrian was dead. Albert speaks
        of the other dead being stripped but Adrian being left as the Indians
        had to flee at Albert's approach. Albert complains that Garret Van
        Antwerpen would allow no more men to leave Schenectady to assist for if
        they had more men Albert believed they would have overrun and captured
        the Indians responsible.
        To CoLLo JOHNSON
        FROM ALBERT VAN SLYCK
        --      A. L. S.
        <Schonactenda.V Jul_v 21 1748>
        COLL JOHNSON
        I Cant but must acquaint you to my <great grief> Concerning this Last Cruall
        and most Barbarous <Slauter> wee had by the Enemey. Daniall Toll left the
        Company att Malewyck' to fetch <horses> from that Company
        and Shortly after they heard Severall guns fired and then my Brother adrian Sent
        his negro to Schonactenday to aqt. the people thereof - also Desired to the
        people to go to the House of abraham Degroft where he would meat them -firstly
        the New England Leut with Some of his men & 5 or 6 of our young Lead and my Br.
        Danial Van Aantwerpen went there to See if they Could See or find Daniall Toll
        also Aukas Van Slyck was there with some men and the New England with his

----------------------------------------------------------------------------------------------------

Company went further and aukas stayed by the House, then my Brother adrian Came
to Aukaskes as'd Dont you Hear <           > 'ting Go for gods Say[k] along then
my Brother with <     > men went allong and Aukas Saffely followed him my Brother
mett the enemy only with 5 of <     > an told them to and fight Expecting aukas
with his Company Every minite and when Aukas Came up he Look about and had no
men he had only Some of our People and the Rest of the New Levys all Left him,
So that Aukas was obliged to Run & my brother was only 3 of em and So Losst
their Lives.
Wee after hear In Schody that they were In Battle. wee Jacob glen & Self and
Severall more went to assist them but as Soon as they heard our Coming they all
Left the place as Doth appear for they where all Stripped Except my Brother
Adrian.
Wee where to Close on their heles made them not Strip Adrian.  It grieved me I
was
No Comander when wee went for garret Van antwerpen would Suffer no more men to
quit out of the place or Else I think wee would have overuned them & Concured
and over Runded em for the Day was but 1/2 Spent.   So I Conclude and am your
Sorrofull and Revengfull friend on those Bararous
Eneys and am att all Times on your Comand.
ALBERT V: SLYCK
I Need not to mention of the Number of Dead & prisoners for I Suppose you have
an  acct thereof.
ADDRESSED:To Coll.  William Johnson
att Albany

SOURCE: Sir William Johnson Papers Vol I, Albany, The University of the State
of New York, 1921:pp173,174]

COMMENT:
Albert's mention of Daniel Van Antwerpen as his brother refers to the marriage
of Daniel to his sister Jannetie Van Slyke

COMMENT:
Another account of the massacre is given by Giles F. Yates and
was published in the Schenectady Democrat and Reflector on 22 April
1836.
The official list of killed and missing at Buekendaal is:
KILLED
John A. Bradt
Johannes Marinus
Peter Vrooman
Daniel Van Antwerpeten
Cornelius Viele, Jr.
Nicholas DeGaaf
Adrian Van Slyck,
Jacob Glen, Jr.,
Adam Conde
J.. P. Van Antwerpen
Frans Van der Bogart
Capt. Daniel Toll was standing by a tree when the fatal bullet struck him.
WOUNDED
Ryer Wemp
---- Robinson
Dirck Van Vorst
---- Wilson
possibly more
MISSING AND PRISONERS
John Phelphs

------------------------------------------------------------------------------------------------

         Lewis Groot
         Johannes Seyer Vrooman
         Frank Connor
         Harman Veeder
         Isaac Truax
         Albert John Veeder
         and six soldiers

         SOURCE: Schenectady County New York Its History To the Close of the Nineteenth
         Century by Austin A. Yates

         In his brother Johannes' will of Dec. 10 1751 Albert's daughter Margaret is
         listed but I have no record of her.

    Albert VAN SLYKE married (1) Sarah Janse VAN ANTWERPEN on 17 Sep 1733. Sarah, dau. of Jan Danielse VAN
    ANTWERPEN and Angiente VEEDERS, born in 1712 at Schenectady NY; christened on 21 Jun 1712 at Schenectady
    NY.

         SP: Marytie GOELENT; Arenty VUYLER. Parents: Jan DANIELSE; Agnietie VELLERS

    Children:
      216 F      i Clara VAN SLYKE, born in 1734 at Schenectady, NY; christened on 16 Jun 1734 at
                   Schenectady, NY.
      217 F     ii Agnes VAN SLYKE, born in 1737 at Schenectady, NY; christened on 9 Jul 1737 at
                   Schenectady, NY.

                   Agnes=Agnietje

      218 F    iii Annatje VAN SLYKE, born in 1741 at Schenectady, NY; christened on 27 Dec 1741 at
                   Schenectady, NY.

                   DEATH DATE young?

      219 F     iv Annatje VAN SLYKE, born in 1743 at Schenectady, NY; christened on 27 Nov 1743 at
                   Schenectady, NY.
      220 F      v Lena VAN SLYKE, born in 1747 at Schenectady, NY; christened on 18 Oct 1747 at
                   Schenectady, NY.

    73 Cornelius VAN SLYKE, born in 1711 at Albany, NY; christened on 6 Mar 1711; died aft 1753.

         OCCUPATION: Trader

         BIRTH:  Manuscript of Truax/du Triuex family states this bptsm date but it
         is not in records of Albany

         DEATH: post 1753
         Made his will 30 May 1753: wife Jannetje, daus. Christina, Geertruy, Klaartje,
         Susanna

         MARRIAGE: The House of Truax in NYG&BR, Voll LVIII, 1927

    Cornelius VAN SLYKE married (1) Jannetie TRUAX on 11 Mar 1733 at Schenectady NY. Jannetie, dau. of
    Abraham TRUAX and Christina de la GRANGE, born on 17 Aug 1713 at Albany, NY.

         Albany church records show Joanna TRUAX bpt.7 Aug. 1713 but the Truax bible
         shows Jannetje b. 17 Aug. 1713

    Children:

------------------------------------------------------------------------------------------------

```
      221 M     i Abraham VAN SLYKE, born on 15 Jun 1736 at Schenectady, NY.
      222 F    ii Clara VAN SLYKE, born on 1 Sep 1737; died on 31 Oct 1745.
  +   223 F   iii Christina VAN SLYKE.
      224 F    iv Geertruy VAN SLYKE, born on 19 Jul 1743; died on 4 Nov 1745.
      225 M     v Abraham VAN SLYKE, born on 21 Jul 1745; christened on 29 Jul 1745; died on 12 Nov 1746.
      226 F    vi Clara VAN SLYKE, born on 27 Apr 1747; died on 4 Mar 1748.

                  twin to Geertruy

      227 F   vii Geertruy VAN SLYKE, born on 27 Apr 1747.

                  twin to Clara

                  She is in her uncle Johannes Van Slyke's will dated Dec. 10 1751. No other
                  children of her father Cornelis are listed.

                  Geertruy VAN SLYKE married (1) John LAMBERT.

                  OCCUPATION: Schoolteacher

  +   228 F  viii Clara Jean Clarissa VAN SLYKE.
      229 F    ix Susanna/Anna VAN SLYKE, born on 13 Oct 1751.
                  She married (1) Frans Pietersen VAN BUREN.
```

74 Peter (Petrus) VAN SLYKE, born in 1713 at Schenectady, NY; christened on 1 Feb 1713 at Schenectady, NY.

   BAPTISM: Schenectady Reformed Church, Schenectady

   He is not in his brother Johannes's will of 1751 but his son Cornelis Petrus is
   listed.

   Peter (Petrus) VAN SLYKE married (1) Angelica ERICKSON on 30 Aug 1734. Angelica, born on 30 Aug 1734 at
   Europe.

   Angelica d/o Dominie Reinhard Ericksen, pastor of the Dutch Reformed Church
   of Schenectady from 1728-1736. They had 3 sons and 4 daus.

```
   Children:
      230 F     i Clara VAN SLYKE, born on 15 Nov 1734 at Schenectady, NY; christened on 17 Nov 1734 at
                  Schenectady, NY.
                  She married (1) John STEERS.
  +   231 M    ii Cornelius Petrus VAN SLYKE.
      232 F   iii Claartje VAN SLYKE, born in Jul 1739 at Schenectady, NY.
      233 F    iv Annatje VAN SLYKE, born on 7 Aug 1741 at Schenectady, NY.
                  She married (1) Johannes BARHYDT bef 1765 at Schenectady?.
      234 M     v Willem VAN SLYKE, born on 4 Dec 1743 at Schenectady, NY.
      235 F    vi Geertruy VAN SLYKE, born on 30 Nov 1746 at Schenectady, NY.
      236 F   vii Geertruy VAN SLYKE, born on 8 Oct 1749 at Schenectady, NY.

                  NOTE: It is not known which Cornelis Van Slyke was her husband. There are at
                  least two possibilities: Cornelis b 1744 s/o Johannes Van Slyke and Lena/Helena
                  Van Slyke of Schenectady or Cornelis b 1744 s/o Adriaen Van Slyke and Bregie
                  Toll of Schenectady.

                  Geertruy VAN SLYKE married (1) Cornelis VAN SLYKE at Schenectady, NY.
  +   237 M  viii Adrian VAN SLYKE.
```

80 Margarita VAN SLYCK, christened on 16 Feb 1707 at Schenectady NY.

QUESTION: Did she m. Jacob Michael ITTIG aka EDICK 29 Dec. 1725? He md for a
second time Pearson's Genealogies of Schenectady p. 121 shows the following:
Jacob MICHELS from Maquaasland m. Margarieta VAN SLYCK, Dec. 29, 1725. Ch:
Johannes b 28 Apr 1726 More on p. 122 which I don't have!

Margarita VAN SLYCK married (1) Jacob Michael ITTIG on 29 Dec 1725 at Schenectady, NY. Jacob, born abt
1702/1708 at Germany.

Children:
    238 M      i Johannes ITTIG, christened on 28 Apr 1726 at Schenectady, NY.
    239 F     ii Margaret ITTIG, born abt 1729 at Schenectady, NY.
               She married (1) Nicholas LIGHTHALL on 14 Jan 1748.
    240 M    iii Jacob ITTIG, born abt 1729/1730 at Fort Herkimer, Herkimer Co, NY; died in 1770 at
               German Flatts, Herkimer Co, NY.

               DEATH: Jacob died from lockjaw after stubbing his toe in a jumping match.
               SOURCE: Mike Evans in a letter Nov. 1995

               Jacob ITTIG married (1) Catherine FRANK.

               FATHER:Stephen Frank.

               GRANDFATHER: Conrad Frank

  +  241 M     iv Christian ITTIG.

81 Petrus VAN SLYCK, christened on 30 Oct 1709 at Schenectady NY.

       CHRISTENING: Sponsors: Aldrik & Maria Van Franke (Van Vranken)

    Petrus VAN SLYCK married (1) Lysbetje DE GRAAF on 9 Apr 1738 at Schenectady, NY. Lysbetje, dau. of Jesse
    DE GRAAF.

       s/o Jesse De Graaf

    Children:
       242 F      i Marytje VAN SLYKE, christened on 14 Jun 1740 at Schenectady, NY.
  +    243 M     ii Jesse VAN SLYKE.
  +    244 M    iii Marten VAN SLYKE.

86 Eva VAN VALKENBURG, christened on 9 Oct 1708 at Schenectady NY.
    She married (1) Jochem VAN ALSTYNE on 12 Feb 1725. Jochem, son of Isaac Janse de Wever VAN ALSTYNE and
    Jannetje VAN VALKENBURG, christened on 8 Jan 1699 at Albany, NY.

       SOURCE: THE VAN VALKENBURG FAMILY IN AMERICA:Genealogy of the known descendants
       of Lambert and Annatje Van Valckenburgh who migrated to New Amsterdam (New York)
       in 1642-44 VOL. 1 by Paul I. Van Valkenburg Gateway Press, Inc. Baltimore 1981

       CHRISTENING:
       CONTRIBUTIONS FOR THE GENEALOGIES OF THE FIRST SETTLERS OF THE ANCIENT COUNTY
       OF ALBANY, FROM 1630 TO 1800 by Prof. Jonathan Pearson, 1984.

    Children:
  +    245 M      i Harmanus VAN ALSTYNE.
  +    246 F     ii Lydia VAN ALSTYNE.
       247 F    iii Dirckje VAN ALSTYNE, born on 10 May 1734/1735.
       248 F     iv Margaret VAN ALSTYNE, born on 13 Mar 1736/1737.

249 F        v Maria VAN ALSTYNE, born on 2 Feb 1744.

88 Isaac VAN VALKENBURG, born abt 1712 at Schenectady, NY, USA; christened on 13 Feb 1712 at RDC,
   Schenectady, NY; died in 1785 at Wysox, PA, USA.

        SOURCES: Reformed Dutch Church, Schenectady records
        Haldimand Papers, Add Mss 21, 843, Film A-765

        NOTES:
        Isaac and his second wife Jannetje and their 6 children were held captive by
        Seneca Indians for 6 years. From 1773 to 1776 he lived in Wyusling PA. From
        1776 to 1784 he lived in Wysox PA. According to the Haldimand Papers, a list of
        "Rebel Prisoners at Quebec, 1778-1783" has the following:
        Isaac Van Valkenburg, age 69, captured at Susquehana May 1780.

        There appears to be contradictory information over how long he was held
        prisoner. His illegitmate son, Isaac Vollick, the loyalist in Butler's Rangers,
        was at Quebec during those years, and must have been aware that his father was
        imprisoned.

        Isaac is a registered Patriot with the DAR

        !BAPTISM: At his baptism at Schenectady:
        His mother's name was given as Lidia Van Slyk, his father as Isaak Valkenburg.
        Sp:Cornelis van Slyk; Claartjen Brat.

   Isaac VAN VALKENBURG was not married to (1) Maria BRADT. Maria, dau. of Storm BRADT and Sophia UZIELE,
   born abt 1713 at Albany, NY; christened on 24 May 1713 at RDC, Albany, NY.

   Children:
   +   250 M        i Isaac VOLLICK, UEL.

   He married (2) Jannetje CLEMENT on 28 May 1737 at Albany NY USA. Jannetje, born in 1712; died in 1785.

        Children:
        251 F       ii Liddia VAN VALKENBURG, born at NY; christened on 21 Oct 1737 at Albany NY.
                       She married (1) Sebastian STROPE. Sebastian, born abt 1737.
   +    252 F      iii Annatie VAN VALKENBURG.
        253 F       iv Eva VAN VALKENBURG, born at NY; christened on 4 Oct 1741 at Albany NY.
        254 F        v Marytje VAN VALKENBURG, christened on 29 Jan 1744 at Schenectady NY.
                       She married (1) Johannes STROOP. Johannes, born abt 1744.
        255 F       vi Margareth VAN VALKENBURG, christened on 23 Feb 1746 at Schoharie NY.
        256 F      vii Jantjie VAN VALKENBURG, christened on 11 Jul 1752 at Schoharie NY.

89 Margarita VAN VALKENBURG, christened on 27 Sep 1713 at Albany NY USA.
   She married (1) Lammert VAN ALSTYNE on 29 Oct 1733 at Albany NY. Lammert, son of Isaac Janse de Wever
   VAN ALSTYNE and Jannetje VAN VALKENBURG, christened on 30 Apr 1710 at Albany, NY.

        CHRISTENING: CONTRIBUTIONS FOR THE GENEALOGIES OF THE FIRST SETTLERS OF THE
        ANCIENT COUNTY OF ALBANY, FROM 1630 TO 1800 by Prof. Jonathan Pearson, 1984.
        THE VAN VALKENBURG FAMILY IN AMERICA:Genealogy of the known descendants of
        Lambert and Annatje Van Valckenburgh who migrated to New Amsterdam (New York)
        in 1642-44 VOL. 1 by Paul I. Van Valkenburg Gateway Press, Inc. Baltimore 1981
        Sponsors: Johs [sic] & Catherina Vrooman

        Children:
        257 M        i Isaac Valk VAN ALSTYNE, christened on 1 Aug 1734 at Albany NY.
        258 F       ii Margritta VAN ALSTYNE, christened on 18 Jan 1758 at Schoharie, NY.

---------------------------------------------------------------------------------------

91 Jannetien VAN VALKENBURG, christened on 28 Oct 1716 at Schenectady, NY, USA.
   She married (1) Simeon LARRUA on 6 Dec 1744 at Schoharie NY. Simeon, son of Leonard Remi (Jonar) LE ROY
   and Maria UZIELE, born in 1711; christened on 15 Jul 1711 at Kingston, NY.

        CHRISTENING: Parents at baptism listed as Jona Lauroou, Marytjen Usile. SP;
        Jacobus Vand Bogaart; Sufyja Usile [This is my ancestor Sophia who md. Storm
        Bradt in 1712]

   Children:
     259 F      i Lidia LARUA, christened on 11 Nov 1745 at Schoharie NY.
     260 F     ii Jannetje LARUA, christened on 10 Jun 1753 at Schoharie NY.
     261 M    iii Isaac LARUA, christened on 21 Nov 1756 at Catskill NY.

94 Peter VAN O'LINDA, born in 1696; christened on 8 Nov 1696 at Albany, NY.

        BAPTISM: Genealogies of First Settlers of Schenectday by Pearson

   Peter VAN O'LINDA married (1) Susanna LEISCHER on 27 Jul 1736 at Albany, NY.

   Children:
     262 M      i Daniel VAN OLINDA, christened on 17 Jul 1737 at Albany, NY.
     263 M     ii Jacob VAN OLINDA, christened on 20 Feb 1739 at Albany, NY.

96 Martin VAN O'LINDA, born in 1702 at Schenectady, NY; christened on 25 Oct 1702 at Schenectady, NY.

        BAPTISM: He was baptised as Martinus. SP: Gysbert Van Brakel, Elisabit Lapate.
        Parents: Daniel Van olidne, Lisabit Krigier [sci]

   Martin VAN O'LINDA married (1) Jannetie VAN DER WERKEN on 8 Apr 1724 at NY.

   Children:
     264 F      i ELizabeth VAN OLINDA, christened on 24 Jan 1725 at Albany, NY; died in Mar 1756; buried
                  on 20 Mar 1756.
     265 M     ii Gerardus VAN OLINDA, christened on 5 Mar 1727 at Albany, NY.
     266 F    iii Maria VAN OLINDA, christened on 27 Apr 1729 at Albany, NY.
     267 F     iv Geertruy VAN OLINDA, christened on 2 Jul 1731 at Albany, NY.
   + 268 M      v Gerardus VAN OLINDA.
   + 269 M     vi Daniel VAN OLINDA.
     270 M    vii Martinus VAN OLINDA, christened on 16 Jan 1740 at Albany, NY.

100 Martin VAN O'LINDA, christened on 18 Jan 1718.

        BAPTISM: Genealogies of First Settlers of Schenectday by Pearson

        RESIDENCES:
        He lived in the Willigen

   Martin VAN O'LINDA married (1) Catharina CLUTE on 25 Jul 1741. Catharina, died bef 1754.

        FATHER: Frederic Clute

   Children:
     271 M      i Jacob VAN OLINDA, christened on 13 Jun 1742 at NY.
                  He married (1) Machtelt QUACKENBUSH on 12 Mar 1769 at Willigen, NY.
     272 F     ii Francyntje VAN OLINDA, christened on 15 Jan 1744 at NY.
     273 F    iii Eva VAN OLINDA, christened on 24 Nov 1745 at NY.
   + 274 M     iv Pieter VAN OLINDA.

-----------------------------------------------------------------------------------------


275 M        v Frederick VAN OLINDA, christened on 13 May 1750 at NY.

He married (2) Cornelia VAN VLECK on 7 Dec 1754.

     d/o Benjamin Van Vleck

Children:
     276 F       vi Catharina VAN OLINDA, christened on 19 Aug 1755 at NY.
+    277 M      vii Benjamin VAN OLINDA.
+    278 M     viii Willem VAN OLINDA.
     279 M       ix Johannes VAN OLINDA, christened on 3 Oct 1768.

110 Lea HAGEDORN, christened on 27 Dec 1724.

     BIRTH: 1991 AF

Lea HAGEDORN married (1) Petrus aka Peter CLUTE bef 1761. Petrus, christened on 12 Aug 1722 at
Onestounghjoone, NY.

     NAME: His name was also written as CLOET. This name as spouse of Lea Hagedorn
     comes from 1991 AF

     CHILDREN: I believe, but have no proof as yet, that Petrus Clute Jr. RIN 5147
     who married Engeltie Van Slyke, born 1764 Schenectady, was the son of this
     Petrus Clute.

Children:
     280 M        i Jacob CLUTE, christened on 12 Dec 1761 at Schenectady, NY.

               CHRISTENING: From 1991 AF

               Jacob CLUTE married (1) Maria OUDERKERK. Maria, christened on 3 Nov 1760 at
               Schenectady, NY.

               MARRIAGE: Her name as spouse of Jacob Clute comes from 1991 AF

     281 F       ii Geertruy CLUTE, christened on 25 Sep 1763 at Schenectady, NY.

               BIRTH: Her name comes from AF 1991


133 Maria STEVENS, born on 20 Oct 1750 at Schenectady, NY.
    She married (1) John STEWARD abt 1772.

       aka STUART

Children:
     282 M        i James STEWARD, born on 17 Jan 1773 at Schenectady, NY.
     283 F       ii Catarina STEWARD, born on 30 Oct 1774 at Schenectady, NY.
     284 M      iii Arent STEWARD, born on 31 Aug 1777 at Schenectady, NY.
     285 M       iv Abraham STEWARD, born on 16 Dec 1781 at Schenectady, NY.
     286 F        v Judith STEWARD, born on 9 Nov 1783 at Schenectady, NY.
     287 M       vi Nicolaas Stevens STEWARD, born on 25 Jan 1788 at Schenectady, NY.


                                   Fifth Generation


--------------------------------------------------------------------------------------------

---------------------------------------------------------------------------------

139 Susanna BRADT, christened on 29 Jul 1719.
    She married (1) Jacques PEEK on 24 Jun 1743. Jacques, son of Jacobus PEECK and Margariet VAN SLYKE,
    christened on 15 Apr 1721.

    Children:
       288 F      i Margrietje PEEK, christened on 15 Jan 1744.
       289 F     ii Eva PEEK, christened on 28 Jul 1745.

140 Annetje BRADT, christened on 3 Sep 1721; died on 1 Sep 1809.
    She married (1) Johannes VEEDER on 24 Nov 1750. Johannes, son of Helmers VEEDER and Annetje MEBIE, born
    on 2 Jun 1718 at Schenectady NY.

    Children:
       290 M      i Helmer VEEDER, christened on 22 Jul 1751.

                    died young

       291 M     ii Helmer VEEDER, christened on 29 Jul 1753; died on 16 Dec 1787.

145 Engeltie (Angelica) BRADT, born on 26 Aug 1733; died on 28 Sep 1812.

        She left most of her money to her nephew Daniel David Campbell Schermerhorn

    Engeltie (Angelica) BRADT married (1) Daniel CAMPBELL. Daniel, born abt 1731 at Ireland; died on 16 Aug
    1802 at Schenectady, NY.

    Children:
       292 M      i David CAMPBELL, born in 1768; christened on 15 Nov 1768 at Schenectady, NY.

158 Annatje VAN SLYKE, christened on 13 Jun 1736 at Schenectady NY; died on 1 Aug 1824.
    She married (1) Philip RYLEY on 11 Oct 1755 at Schenectady, NY. Philip, born on 29 Apr 1719 at NY.

    Children:
       293 M      i Phillipus RYLEY, born on 4 Sep 1756; died on 17 Sep 1756 at Schenectady, NY.
       294 M     ii Phillipus RYLEY, born on 7 Jan 1759.
       295 M    iii Jacobus Van Slyke RYLEY, born on 23 Oct 1761 at Albany, NY.

165 Andries BRADT, born in 1705 at NY USA; died in 1748.
    He married (1) Arriantje WEMPLE. Arriantje, born abt 1705.

        FATHER: Johannes WEMPLE
        d/o Johannes Wemple

    Children:
       296 F      i Catalina BRADT, born in 1729.

                    DEATH DATE young

    +  297 M     ii Arent (Aaron) BRADT.
    +  298 F    iii Catalina (Catherine) BRADT.

168 Johannes A. BRADT, born in 1709; christened on 1 Jan 1709 at Albany, NY; died on 15 Jul 1760.
    He married (1) Maria TRUAX on 19 Nov 1732 at Schenectady, NY. Maria, dau. of Abraham TRUAX and Christina
    de la GRANGE, born on 2 Apr 1712 at Normanskil, NY; christened at Albany NY; died on 15 Apr 1782.

----------------------------------------------------------------------------------

Fifth Generation

-------------------------------------------------------------------------------------------

Children:
    299 M      i Arent BRADT, born on 9 May 1734; died on 22 Jul 1752.

169 Margrietje BRADT, born in 1711; died aft 1762.

       She is provided for as the widow of Cornelis Van Dyke in the will of her
       uncle, Jacobus VEDDER who was the half-brother of her father Arent BRADT. Arent
       and Jacobus had the same mother, Margaret VAN SLYKE.

       Margrietje BRADT married (1) Cornelis VAN DYCK. Cornelis, born in 1698 at Schenectady, NY; christened on
       24 Aug 1698 at Schenectady, NY; died on 15 Feb 1759.

       Children:
       300 M      i Arent VAN DYCK, born on 14 Feb 1739 at Schenectady, NY.
       301 M     ii Cornelis VAN DYCK, born on 8 Oct 1740 at Schenectady, NY.
       302 M    iii Andries VAN DYCK, born on 22 Sep 1745 at Schenectady, NY.

175 Clara BORSIE.
    ***** This individual's information has already been printed. *****
    She married (1) Ephraim BRADT in 1751.
    ***** This individual's information has already been printed. *****

    ***** Descendants of this couple have already been printed. *****

    She married (2) Cornelise VIELE Jr..

177 Anthony VAN SLYKE, born in 1733 at Schenectady, NY; christened on 29 Apr 1733 at Schenectady, NY.

       Anthony's name is on the rolls of the 2d Albany County Militia during the
    American Revolution [HSDR:246]

    Anthony VAN SLYKE married (1) Claartje VAN SLYKE on 12 Apr 1767 at Schenectady, NY. Claartje, dau. of
    Adriaen VAN SLYKE and Bregie TOLL, born in 1742 at Schenectady NY; christened on 7 Nov 1742 at
    Schenectady NY.

    Children:
       303 M      i Harmanus VAN SLYKE, born on 21 Dec 1767 at Schenectady, NY; died on 12 Apr 1769 at
                 Schenectady, NY.
       304 M     ii Harmanus VAN SLYKE, born in 1770 at Schenectady, NY; christened on 14 Jan 1770 at
                 Schenectady, NY.
       305 M    iii Harmanus VAN SLYKE, born on 4 Feb 1777 at Schenectady, NY.

182 Harmanus VAN SLYKE, christened on 3 Jun 1750 at Schenectady NY; died on 2 Dec 1847 at Schenectady, NY.

       Harmanus A. Van Slyke appears on the rolls of the 2d Albany County Militia
    Land Bounty Rights, during the American Revolution. [HSDR:247]

    Harmanus VAN SLYKE married (1) Maria VROOMAN on 5 Dec 1771 at Schenectady, NY. Maria, dau. of Isaac
    VROOMAN and Dorothea VAN BOSKERKEN, born in 1747; died in 1789/1798 at Schenectady, NY.

    Children:
       306 M      i Adam VAN SLYKE, born in 1773 at Schenectady, NY; christened on 31 Oct 1773 at
                 Schenectady, NY.
       307 M     ii Adam VAN SLYKE, christened on 26 Mar 1775 at Schenectady, NY.

               NOTE: I believe he married Matilda Wentworth and had the following children:
               Maria Elisa bp 14 July 1804

------------------------------------------------------------------------------------------
Fifth Generation

-----

```
                      Herman bp 30 Sept. 1810
                      Caroline Amatilda bp 23 May 1814
                      Paul bp 23 May 1814
                      Lorenzo bp 28 June 1819
                      Cornelia bp 11 June 1822
                      Lorenzo bp 16 Aug 1824
                      Lorenzo bp 27 Apr. 1826
                      Isabella Cornelia bp 1829
                      Caroline Matilda bp 1831

      308 M     iii Jacobus VAN SLYKE, christened on 23 Mar 1777 at Schenectady, NY.
      309 F      iv Dorothea VAN SLYKE, christened on 18 Jul 1779 at Schenectady, NY.
      310 F       v Caterina VAN SLYKE, christened on 31 Mar 1782 at Schenectady, NY.
      311 F      vi Rachel VAN SLYKE, born in Dec 1784 at Schenectady, NY.
                      She married (1) Walter GROESBECK.
      312 F     vii Catharina VAN SLYKE, born on 20 Jul 1787 at Schenectady, NY.
      313 F    viii Christina Vrooman VAN SLYKE, born on 17 Dec 1789 at Schenectady, NY.
```

He married (2) Annatje HAVERLY on 28 Oct 1798 at Schenectady, NY. Annatje, born in 1781; died on 3 Jun 1855 at Schenectady, NY.

```
Children:
      314 M      ix Anthony VAN SLYKE, born in Jul 1800 at Schenectady, NY.
      315 M       x John Haverly VAN SLYKE, born on 20 Jan 1809 at Schenectady, NY; died on 30 Jan 1813 at
                      Schenectady, NY.
      316 F      xi Clarissa VAN SLYKE, born on 27 Sep 1810 at Schenectady, NY.
```

186 Nicolaas VAN SLYKE, born abt 1754 at Schenectady?.
    He married (1) Geertruy VISSCHER abt 1781.

```
Children:
      317 F       i Jannetje VAN SLYKE, christened on 2 May 1779 at Caughnawaga, Fonda, Montgomery Co., NY.

                      BAPTISM: Sponsors were Joh. Van Slyck & wife Margaret

   +  318 M      ii Harmanus VAN SLYKE.
```

193 Jacques PEEK.
    ***** This individual's information has already been printed. *****.
    Jacques PEEK married (1) Susanna BRADT on 24 Jun 1743.
    ***** This individual's information has already been printed. *****.

    ***** Descendants of this couple have already been printed. *****.

194 ELizabeth PEEK married (1) Arent PUTMAN.

```
Children:
      319 M       i Victor Arent PUTMAN married (1) Maria SCHULTHEIS.
```

195 Johannes (John) RYCKMAN, born on 14 Dec 1730; christened on 20 Dec 1730; died in 1795.
    He married (1) Eunice WARD on 30 May 1754 at New York, NY. Eunice, died in 1801.

```
Children:
   +  320 M       i John RYCKMAN.
   +  321 F      ii Rachel RYCKMAN.
      322 M     iii Cornelis RYCKMAN, born on 19 Oct 1760.
   +  323 M      iv Cornelis RYCKMAN.
   +  324 M       v Albert RYCKMAN, UEL.
```

-----

------------------------------------------------------------------------------------------

```
      325 F       vi Sarah RYCKMAN, born on 20 Nov 1768.
      326 M      vii Harmanus RYCKMAN, born on 19 May 1771.
      327 F     viii Clara RYCKMAN, born on 18 Sep 1774.
  +   328 M       ix Samuel RYCKMAN.
```

203 Claartje VAN SLYKE.
    ***** This individual's information has already been printed. *****.
    She married (1) Anthony VAN SLYKE on 12 Apr 1767 at Schenectady, NY.
    ***** This individual's information has already been printed. *****.

    ***** Descendants of this couple have already been printed. *****.

213 Harmen VAN SLYKE, born in 1755 at Schenectady, NY; christened on 13 Jul 1755 at Schenectady, NY.
    He married (1) Engeltje MARSELIS on 11 Jun 1775 at Schenectady, NY.

         d/o Ahasuerus Marselis

    Children:
```
      329 M        i Harmanus VAN SLYKE, born in 1775 at Schenectady, NY; christened on 10 Dec 1775 at
                     Schenectady, NY.
      330 M       ii Asehuerus VAN SLYKE, born in 1777 at Schenectady, NY; christened on 19 Oct 1777 at
                     Schenectady, NY.
      331 M      iii Ahasuerus VAN SLYKE, born in 1779 at Schenectady, NY; christened on 18 Sep 1779 at
                     Schenectady, NY.
      332 M       iv Johannes VAN SLYKE, born in 1781 at Schenectady, NY; christened on 1 Jan 1782 at
                     Schenectady, NY.
      333 M        v Hendrick VAN SLYKE, born on 3 Jul 1784 at Schenectady, NY.
      334 F       vi Sarah VAN SLYKE, born on 28 Jun 1787 at Schenectady, NY.
      335 M      vii Cornelius VAN SLYKE, born on 10 Nov 1789 at Schenectady, NY.
      336 M     viii Nicolaas VAN SLYKE, born on 19 May 1791 at Schenectady, NY; died on 11 Nov 1864 at
                     Schenectady, NY?.
      337 M       ix Anthony VAN SLYKE, born on 8 Dec 1793 at Schenectady, NY.
      338 F        x Maria VAN SLYKE, born on 16 Nov 1800 at Schenectady, NY.
```

214 Catrina (Clara) VAN SLYCK, born in 1730; died aft 1751.

    She is listed as Clara d/o Hendrick in her uncle Johannes Van Slyke's will of
    Dec 10 1751

    Catrina (Clara) VAN SLYCK married (1) Johannes Jacob VROOMAN. Johannes, son of Jacob VROOMAN and Maria
    GROOT, born on 8 Jan 1726 at Schenectady, NY.

    Children:
```
      339 M        i Jacob VROOMAN, christened on 17 Jun 1752 at Schenectady, NY.
      340 F       ii Catrina VROOMAN, christened on 4 Nov 1753 at Schenectady.
      341 M      iii Jacob Johannes VROOMAN, born on 29 Mar 1755; died on 4 Jan 1829.
```

             Jacob J. Vrooman, bp. 30 March 1755 according to HSDR, inherited his
          father's farm 3.5 miles south of Schenectady. His name appears on the rolls of
          the 2d. Albany County Militia during the American Revolution [HSDR:262]

```
      342 M       iv Hendericus VROOMAN, christened on 27 Oct 1757 at Schenectady, NY.
      343 M        v Abraham VROOMAN, christened on 10 Feb 1760 at Schenectady, NY.
      344 F       vi Catarina VROOMAN, christened on 15 Jul 1764 at Schenectady, NY.
      345 M      vii Johannes VROOMAN, christened on 1 Feb 1767 at Schenectady, NY.
      346 F     viii Maria VROOMAN, christened on 6 Aug 1769 at Schenectady, NY.
      347 F       ix Engeltie VROOMAN, christened on 15 Dec 1771 at Schenectady, NY.
      348 M        x Bartholomeus VROOMAN, christened on 13 Mar 1774 at Schenectady, NY.
```

------------------------------------------------------------------------------------------

223 Christina VAN SLYKE, born on 21 Sep 1739 at Ft. Hunter, NY; christened on 27 Sep 1739 at Queen Anne
    Chape, Ft. Hunter, NY.

        BAPTISM: Queen Anne Chapel Records by Maryly B. Penrose
        Sponsors at bpts: Abraham TRUAX, Christina TRUAX
        She kept an inn at Niagara ON after Gilbert died.

    Christina VAN SLYKE married (1) Gilbert TICE on 30 May 1761 at Schenectady NY. Gilbert, died in 1791 at
    Niagara, ON.

        Gilbert Tice, aka Geysbert Tyce or Thys, was a Royalist officer who came
        to Upper Canada with his brother-in-law, Jacob Bastedo during the American
        Revolution. He was an officer with the Indian Department at Niagara. In 1775
        he was a guide for Joseph Brant, the Mohawk leader, on his trip to England.
        Tice was an American of English extraction and a veteran of the French
        Wars under Col. Daniel Claus. He was a householder in the Mohawk Valley until
        financial problems arose, then he was imprisoned for debt and had his land
        sold. Sir William Johnson put Tice in charge of a tavern at Johnstown, and
        Tice's account books from that period are at Johnson Hall. [Ref: _The Mark of
        Honour_ Hazel C. Matthews. University of Toronto Press, 1965]

        MARRIAGE Genealogies of First Settlers of Schenectday by Pearson

    Children:
        349 F      i Jannetje TICE, christened on 21 Mar 1762 at Schenectady NY.
        350 M     ii David TICE, born on 6 May 1764 at Schenectady NY.

228 Clara Jean Clarissa VAN SLYKE, born on 27 Aug 1749 at Schenectady, NY; died in 1808 at Halton Co. ON.

            In the year 1743 the American Ancestor Jacob Bastedo was
        born and there he lived until 1783, when having refused to join
        in the rebellion of the Thirteen Colonies against Great Britain in
        1775-6 and in 1783, to take the oath required of his renouncing his
        former allegiance to the crown of England, he abandoned his lands and
        other possessions, except as he could bring with him by
        teams, and came to'Canada in 1784 with his wife and fours sons, three
        of whom the records of the Archives Department at Ottawa state were
        over the age of ten years - He was given a grant of lot No 5 in the
        sixth concession of Kingston, 200 acres and another lot of the, same
        size in concession No 1 of the Township near Cataraqtui. His name
        appears in the bound volume containing the certified list of U.E.
        Loyalists which is in the Archives Department. Jacob was married in
        Schenectady in 1767 to Clariassa Jean Van Slyke, a great grand
        daughter of Cornelius Van Slyke "The trader", who Was a grandson of
        Cornelius Antonissen Van Slyke a Hollander, and the first patentee
        of the Katskill (1746). '
            It is understood that members of the two families emigrated to
        America from Holland in or about the same year 1628. Some of the
        Van Slyke silver bearing the crest, a rising sun, is among the
        treasures of the Bastedo family.
            Clara Jean Van Slyke died in the county of Halton in 1828 in the
        at the home of her son Gilbert who settled in that
        County in the year 1808. Christiana Van Slyke, an elder sister of
        Mrs. Bastedo. married Col. Tice a Royalist officer, who also came to
        Canada with or soon after Jacob Bastedo, and who also subsequently
        removed to Niagara where'he became an officer of the Indian Dept.;
        and still another sister was the grandmother of Martin Van Buren 8th

President of the United States.

Clara Jean Clarissa VAN SLYKE married (1) Jacob BASTEDO on 31 Jan 1767/1769 at Schenectady NY. Jacob, born in 1743 at Schenectady NY; died in 1829 at Stamford Twp. ON.

   NOTES: One of the Gilberts/Gysberts listed as a son to Jacob & Clarissa was
   actually a nephew, and son to Jacob's brother, whose name is unknown to me. I do
   not know which Gilbert is the son and which the nephew.  However the fact that
   Louis and Gilbert the first were twins, would make me tend to think that
   Gilbert Tice b 1777 was the nephew.

   MARRIAGE SOURCE: Sketch of Bastedo Family by Laurabelle Lamb; 10 July 1947 in
   Miscellaneous

Children:
+   351 M     i David Tice BASTEDO.
    352 F    ii Elisabeth BASTEDO, born on 23 Dec 1770 at Schenectady NY.
    353 M   iii Ackus BASTEDO, born on 12 Sep 1772 at Schenectady NY.
    354 M    iv Louis BASTEDO, born on 3 Oct 1775 at Schenectady NY.
    355 M     v Gysbert BASTEDO, born on 3 Oct 1775 at Schenectady NY.

                  aka Gilbert

+   356 M    vi Gysbert BASTEDO.
+   357 M   vii Joseph BASTEDO.
    358 M  viii Cornelius BASTEDO, died on 14 Jul 1814 at Chippewa, ON.
    359 M    ix Abraham BASTEDO.

                  with 2nd. York Regiment Dundas Valley, 1812-1814

+   360 M     x John BASTEDO.

231 Cornelius Petrus VAN SLYKE, born on 1 Dec 1736 at Schenectady, NY.

   NOTES: Cornelius P. Van Slyke was elected first lieutenant in Captain John
   VAN PATTEN's company, 2d Albany County Militia, on 27 May 1775. On May 29 he was
   appointed ensign in a company in the Continental Service under Captain
   Cornelius VAN DYCK, for duty at Ticonderoga. On June 23 he was promoted to the
   rank of lieutenant and in this capacity served in the Canadian campaign, his
   company taking part in the siege of St. John's and forming part of the
   detachment that reduced Chamblee. On 1 March 1776, he signed an agreement with
   Philip SCHUYLER for service at Lake George and Ticonderoga, and on 24 April
   1777, was in command of a detail of 45 men for duty between Albany and Lake
   George. On 7 May he was elected a member of the third Committee of Safety.
   [HSDR:246,247]

   He is in his uncle Johannes Van Slyke's will of Dec. 10 1751

Cornelius Petrus VAN SLYKE married (1) Catarina VEEDER on 30 Mar 1764.

   d/o Peter Veeder

Children:
    361 F     i Engelina (Angelica) VAN SLYKE, born in 1764 at Schenectady, NY; christened on 2 Sep
              1764 at Schenectady, NY.
              She married (1) Petrus CLUTE Jr..
    362 M    ii Pieter VAN SLYKE, born in 1767 at Schenectady, NY; christened on 12 Apr 1767 at
              Schenectady, NY.

--------------------------------------------------------------------------------
                                Fifth Generation

------------------------------------------------------------------------------------------------

He married (1) Margarita LIGHTHALL on 28 Feb 1790 at Schenectady, NY.

363 F       iii Maria VAN SLYKE, born in 1769 at Schenectady, NY; christened on 8 Oct 1769 at
                Schenectady, NY; died on 12 Jul 1846.
                She married (1) Johannes C. BARHEYT on 24 Jan 1790 at Schenectady, NY. Johannes, born
                abt 1767; died in Feb 1830.

                MARRIAGE SOURCE: Genealogies of First Settlers of Schenectday by Pearson

+   364 F      iv Clara VAN SLYKE.
    365 F       v Annatje VAN SLYKE, born in 1774 at Schenectady, NY; christened on 23 Oct 1774 at
                Schenectady, NY.
                She married (1) Johannes LIGHTHALL.
    366 F      vi Geertruy VAN SLYKE, born in 1777 at Schenectady, NY; christened on 12 Oct 1777 at
                Schenectady, NY.
                She married (1) Peter BATH.
    367 F     vii Neeltje VAN SLYKE, born in 1780 at Schenectady, NY; christened on 22 Oct 1780 at
                Schenectady, NY.
                She married (1) Laurens VAN EPS.
    368 F    viii Margarita VAN SLYKE, born in 1783 at Schenectady, NY; christened on 26 Jul 1783 at
                Schenectady, NY.

                DEATH DATE young?

    369 F      ix Margarieta VAN SLYKE, born on 29 May 1786 at Schenectady, NY.
                She married (1) Robert BATH.
    370 M       x Adriaan VAN SLYKE, born in 1789 at Schenectady, NY; christened on 20 Oct 1789 at
                Schenectady, NY.

237 Adrian VAN SLYKE, born in 1751 at Schenectady, NY; christened on 23 Jun 1751 at Schenectady, NY.

    MILITARY:  Adrian served as a corporal and sergeant under Captain Jellis J.
    FONDA. Albany County Militia, and as a sergeant under Captain John MYNDERSE.
    In 1778 he enrolled under Captain Jesse VAN SLYCK. [HSDR:246]

    Adrian VAN SLYKE married (1) Annatje LIGHTHALL.

    FATHER: William LIGHTHALL

Children:
    371 F       i Engelina VAN SLYKE, born in 1772; christened on 12 Jun 1772.

                DEATH DATE young?

    372 F      ii Engelina VAN SLYKE, born in 1777 at Schenectady, NY; christened on 12 Jan 1777 at
                Schenectady, NY.
    373 M     iii Willem VAN SLYKE, born on 10 Oct 1778 at Schenectady, NY; christened on 18 Oct 1778 at
                Schenectady, NY.
    374 F      iv Elisabeth VAN SLYKE, born in 1781 at Schenectady, NY; christened on 25 Mar 1781 at
                Schenectady, NY.
    375 M       v Petrus VAN SLYKE, born in 1783 at Schenectady, NY; christened on 1 Jun 1783 at
                Schenectady, NY.

                twin to Abraham

    376 M      vi Abraham VAN SLYKE, born in 1783 at Schenectady, NY; christened on 1 Jun 1783 at
                Schenectady, NY.

                twin to Petrus

-------------------------------------------------------------------------------------------
Fifth Generation

```
      377 F    vii Elisabeth VAN SLYKE, born on 26 Aug 1785 at Schenectady, NY.
      378 F   viii Geertruy VAN SLYKE, born on 13 Sep 1787 at Schenectady, NY.
      379 M     ix Cornelius VAN SLYKE, born on 6 Aug 1790 at Schenectady, NY.
      380 F      x Elisabeth VAN SLYKE, born on 19 Aug 1792 at Schenectady, NY.
      381 F     xi Maria VAN SLYKE, born on 26 Jun 1795 at Schenectady, NY.
      382 M    xii Albert VAN SLYKE, born on 8 Jan 1798 at Schenectady, NY.
      383 M   xiii Ahasuerus VAN SLYKE, born on 21 Nov 1799 at Schenectady, NY.
```

241 Christian ITTIG, born in 1736 at Fort Herkimer, NY; died bef 1792 at German Flats, Herkimer, NY.
    He married (1) Margaret WEAVER bef 1758. Margaret, born in 1734; died bef 1776 at NY.

        CONFLICT: Parson's Edick Book lists Margaret as WEAVER, but Mike Evans submits
        evidence in Nov. 1995 that she is more likely a FRANK and cites EARLY FAMILIES
        OF HERKIMER COUNTY NY as his source.

    Children:
        384 F      i ELizabeth ITTIG, born in 1758; died in 1846.
                     She married (1) Christopher SHOEMAKER.
        385 M     ii George C. ITTIG, born abt 1760.

                     FAMILY: He had 5 children.

                     RESIDENCES:
                     1790 Herkimer Co. Census

                     George C. ITTIG married (1) Delia PETRIE on 9 Jan 1783 at German Flats, NY.
        386 M    iii Conrad ITTIG, born on 1 Feb 1762 at German Flatts, Tyron Co, NY; died on 12 Sep 1846 at
                     W. Frankfort, NY.

                     FAMILY: Conrad was married twice. The name of his first wife is unknown. He
                     had at least one child born ca 1785 by this first wife.

                     MILITARY: Conrad testified in Oct. 1832 that he served in the Revolutionary
                     War on the Patriot side. He may have been the Conrad listed in 4th Tryon Co.
                     Regiment. He enlisted Spring 1781 as a private in Capt. Andrew Moody's Co.,
                     Col. John Lamb's Regiment of Artillery until the War ended.

                     Conrad ITTIG married (1) Nancy Hannah FIKES on 30 Oct 1810 at Johnston, NY.

                     NOTES: She was the widow of John Coughnut at her marriage in 1810 to Conrad
                     Ittig.

                     CHILDREN: She had 4 children by Conrad Ittig

    +   387 M     iv Johan Jacob Christian ITTIG.
        388 M      v Christian ITTIG, born on 22 Nov 1766 at Stone Arabia, Herkimer Co, NY; died on 16 Apr
                     1814.
                     He married (1) ELizabeth EMPIE on 6 Jul 1794.
        389 F     vi Maria Catharina ITTIG, born on 22 Nov 1770 at Stone Arabia, Herkimer Co, NY.
                     She married (1) Henrich WERNER in 1789.
        390 F    vii Anna ITTIG, born abt 1772.
                     She married (1) George FRIBA on 29 Jan 1793.
        391 M   viii Johannes ITTIG, born on 27 Mar 1776 at German Flats, Herkimer Co., NY.
        392 F     ix Margaretha ITTIG, born on 5 Jan 1778 at German Flats, Herkimer Co., NY.
        393 M      x Johan Jost ITTIG, born on 5 Jan 1781 at German Flats, Herkimer Co., NY.
        394 M     xi Johann Dieterich ITTIG, born on 29 Sep 1783 at German Flats, Herkimer Co., NY.
        395 M    xii Marcus ITTIG, born on 10 Aug 1785 at German Flats, Herkimer Co., NY.
```

-----------------------------------------------------------------------------------------------

                                    Fifth Generation
```

------------------------------------------------------------------------------------------------

        396 M    xiii Johan Jost ITTIG, born on 14 Oct 1787 at German Flats, Herkimer Co., NY.
        397 F    xiv  Anna Eva ITTIG, born on 6 Mar 1790 at German Flats, Herkimer Co., NY.

243 Jesse VAN SLYKE, christened on 29 Jan 1744 at Schenectady, NY; died in Sep 1815 at Schenectady, NY.

        MILITARY: Captain in The American Revolutionary War

        Jesse VAN SLYKE married (1) Jacomyntje GROOT on 4 Dec 1762 at Schenectady, NY. Jacomyntje, born in Oct
        1742 at Schenectady, NY?; died on 28 Dec 1809.

            d/o Cornelis Groot

        Children:
        398 M     i  Pieter VAN SLYKE, born in 1763 at Schenectady, NY; christened on 20 Nov 1673 at
                     Schenectady, NY.
      + 399 M     ii Cornelius VAN SLYKE.
      + 400 F    iii Margarita VAN SLYKE.
        401 F     iv Elisabeth VAN SLYKE, born in 1772 at Schenectady, NY; christened on 26 Apr 1772 at
                     Schenectady, NY.
      + 402 M      v Marten VAN SLYKE.
      + 403 M     vi Abraham VAN SLYKE.
        404 M    vii Simon VAN SLYKE, born in 1781 at Schenectady, NY; christened on 8 Jul 1781 at
                     Schenectady, NY; died bef 1783 at Schenectady, NY.
        405 M   viii Simon VAN SLYKE, born in 1783 at Schenectady, NY; christened on 1 Feb 1783 at
                     Schenectady, NY.
        406 F     ix Lena (Helen) VAN SLYKE, born in 1786 at Schenectady, NY; christened on 5 Aug 1786 at
                     Schenectady, NY.

244 Marten VAN SLYKE, christened on 20 Oct 1748 at Schenectady, NY.

            Martin aka Marten signed an agreement with philip SCHUYLER for service at
        Lake George and Ticonderoga on 1 March 1776. His name is on the rolls of the
        2d. Albany County Militia and the 2d. Albany County Militia, Land Bounty
        Rights. In 1778 he was enrolled under Captain Jesse VAN SLYCK [sic]. This
        Jesse is Martin's brother. [HSDR:248]

        Marten VAN SLYKE married (1) Helena (Lena) VROOMAN on 6 Jun 1773. Helena, dau. of Adam VROOMAN and
        Susanna SWITS, born in 1753.

        Children:
        407 M     i  Peter VAN SLYCK, born on 9 Aug 1774.
                     He married (1) Rebecca FAIRCHILD.
        408 F     ii Susanna VAN SLYCK, born on 25 Apr 1776; died on 1 Sep 1778.
        409 F    iii Elisabeth VAN SLYCK, born on 10 Mar 1778.
                     She married (1) Arent B. SCHERMERHORN.
        410 M     iv Adam VAN SLYCK, born on 2 Apr 1780.
        411 F      v Susanna VAN SLYCK, born on 4 Jul 1782.
        412 F     vi Alida VAN SLYCK, born on 2 Jan 1785.
        413 M    vii Jacob VAN SLYCK, born on 25 Jan 1787.
        414 F   viii Margarietje VAN SLYCK, born on 11 Jun 1789.
        415 M     ix Jesse VAN SLYCK, born on 22 Nov 1791.
        416 M      x John VAN SLYCK, born on 6 Dec 1793.

245 Harmanus VAN ALSTYNE, christened on 6 Jan 1731.
    He married (1) Anna Catherina BESINGER. Anna, born abt 1732.

        Children:
        417 F     i  Eva VAN ALSTYNE, born in 1754; christened on 4 Jul 1754.



------------------------------------------------------------------------------------------------
                                      Fifth Generation

                    She married (1) Johannes Van den BURGH in 1774.
    418 M     ii Jochem VAN ALSTYNE, born in 1756; christened on 12 Apr 1756.
    419 M    iii Andries VAN ALSTYNE, born in 1757; christened on 18 Sep 1757.
    420 F     iv Anna Rosina VAN ALSTYNE, born in 1759; christened on 5 Jul 1759.
    421 F      v Jannetje VAN ALSTYNE, born in 1762; christened on 13 Jan 1762.
    422 F     vi ELizabeth VAN ALSTYNE, born in 1764; christened on 15 Nov 1764.
    423 F    vii Lydia VAN ALSTYNE, born in 1766; christened on 23 Oct 1766.
    424 M   viii Zeferinus VAN ALSTYNE, born in 1768; christened on 18 Sep 1768.
    425 F     ix Catherina VAN ALSTYNE, born in 1771; christened on 26 Dec 1771.
    426 F      x Dirckje VAN ALSTYNE, born in 1774; christened on 14 May 1774.
    427 M     xi Harmonious VAN ALSTINE, born in 1777.

246 Lydia VAN ALSTYNE, christened on 20 May 1732.

    It is possible that the Adrian Bradt she md. is Adrian b 1722 s/o Storm
    Bradt & Sophia Uziele

    Lydia VAN ALSTYNE married (1) Adrian BRADT on 15 Jan 1757.

    Children:
    428 F      i Celia BRADT, born in 1757; christened on 16 Oct 1757.
    429 F     ii Eva BRADT, born abt 1760.
    430 M    iii Geurt BRATT, born on 27 Feb 1762.
    431 M     iv Jocehm BRATT, born on 4 May 1765.
    432 M      v Andries BRATT, born on 29 Aug 1767.
    433 F     vi Wyntie BRATT, born on 8 Oct 1769.

250 Isaac VOLLICK, UEL, born in 1732 at Schoharie, NY, USA; christened on 17 Dec 1732 at Lutheran Church,
    Schoharie; died aft 1802 at ON.

    MILITARY: private in Butler's Rangers 1777-1782

    Isaac was a Loyalist who fought in Butler's Rangers in the American
    Revolution. It was during this time period that his surname was changed from
    VAN VALKENBURG to VALK, with the resulting phonetic spelling of VOLLICK or
    FOLLICK. As far as is known it is from Isaac VOLLICK that all VOLLICK and
    FOLLICK families in Ontario descend.

    TIMELINE:
    17 Dec. 1732:baptised Schoharie Co. NY
    28 Dec. 1756:married Schoharie Co. NY
    pre 1777:arrested three times by Americans in New York for British sympathies
    24 Dec. 1777:joined Butler's Rangers, 2nd. Co.
    1778: William Caldwell's Co. Butler's Rangers
    25 July 1779:Montreal, Quebec as impoverished Loyalist with family
    25 Sept. 1779:St. Claire, Quebec as impoverished Loyalist with family
    8 April 1784:settled with family west Side River Niagara, Niagara-on-Lake ON
    14 Dec. 1786:St. Catharine's, ON
    10 March 1797:free grant land C.6 Lots 6,7,8  E. Flamborough Twp. Wentworth Co.
    17 March 1797:free grant land C.3, L.1 & 3, Louth Twp. Lincoln Co. [between
    Port Dalhousie and St. Catharine's, ON]
    4 April 1797:free grant land C.4, L.22,23 Grantham Twp. Lincoln Co.
    17 Mar. 1804:in court over disputed land claim C.3, L.3 Louth Twp. Lincoln Co.
    ON
    7 Apr. 1804:disputed land claim C.3, L.1 Louth Tp.

    SOURCE:
    EARLY SETTLERS IN NIAGARA Including the First "Census" 1782, 1783, 1784, 1786,

--------------------------------------------------------------------------------

1787 Published by the Ontario Genealogical Society, Niagara Peninsula Branch,
1992. OGS NPB, Box 2224, Station B., St. Catharines, ON, Canada
THE VAN VALKENBURG FAMILY IN AMERICA:Genealogy of the known descendants of
Lambert and Annatje Van Valckenburgh who migrated to New Amsterdam (New York)
in 1642-44 VOL. 1 by Paul I. Van Valkenburg Gateway Press, Inc. Baltimore 1981
THE SONS AND DAUGHTERS OF AMERICAN LOYALISTS by William D. Reid
Corlene Taylor, Beamsville Ontario in letter dated 13 June 1993
Sheila Webb, Librarian,La Grangeville, NY: letter of 21 Sept. 1993
HALDIMAND LOYALIST LISTS OF 1777-1785 Microfilm C-1475, National Archives of
Canada
LIST OF LOYALISTS, Manuscript Group 21, Vol B 105, pp. 24, 64
HALDIMAND LOYALIST LISTS: Vol 105, pp 24, 64b, 76, 408. Vol 166 pp12, 24, 37
Vol. 168 p 38
THE STORY OF BUTLER'S RANGERS AND THE SETTLEMENT OF NIAGARA by Ernest
Cruikshank
UPPER CANADA LAND PETITIONS:UCLP U-V, 2/27 & 1/13 1792-1795, Reel #C2842 V.514;
1791-1867: Index on Reel C-10834 National Archives of Ontario
UPPER CANADA LAND BOOK B 1796-1797, pp255, 292, 298, 264 vol. 20 Reel C101
CROWN PATENTEES OF WENTWORTH COUNTY
CENTENNIAL OF SETTLEMENT OF UPPER CANADA BY UNITED EMPIRE LOYALISTS, 1784-1884
author unknown

Isaac VOLLICK, UEL married (1) Anna Maria (Mary) WARNER on 28 Oct 1757 at St. Paul's Evang, Schoharie,
NY. Anna, dau. of Johan Matthias (Matthias) WARNER and Anna BELLINGER, born on 28 Oct 1735 at Schoharie,
NY, USA; christened at Schoharie, NY, USA; died at ON.

     CHRISTENING: Schoharie Reformed Dutch Church. Sponsors: John Fridrich Bauch
and his wife Anna Magdalena.

     MARRIAGE: To Isaac Falck [sic] on 28 oct. 1757 Schoharie Lutheran Church.

     BIOGRAPHY: !Mary's husband, Isaac, was imprisoned three times by the Americans,
for his loyalty to the British King. After Isaac joined Butler's Rangers and
fled to Canada, Mary was left with ten children, six of them small.
Mary continued to aid the British, and in 1779 she and the children were taken
from their home at North River, New York, by American patriots. Their home was
burned, Mary and the children were marched 80 miles north through the forest and
left in destitute circumstances. Mary and family made their way to Canada
and reached Montreal by July of 1779.

     They received food rations, lodging and blankets until 1782 when they settled
in the Niagara area as impoverished Loyalists.

     Children:
      434 F      i   Maryetje VOLLICK, born at Albany, NY, USA; christened on 28 May 1758 at Albany RC, NY,
                         USA.
+   435 M     ii   Matthias VALCK.
+   436 M    iii   Cornelius VOLLICK, UEL.
+   437 F     iv   Annaje (Hannah) VOLLICK.
+   438 M      v   Storm FOLLICK, UEL.
+   439 F     vi   Sophia VOLLICK.
+   440 F    vii   Elizabeth VOLLICK.
+   441 F   viii   Catharina (Catherine) VOLLICK.
+   442 F     ix   Sarah VOLLOCK.
+   443 M      x   Jan (John) VOLLICK.
      444 F     xi   Maria VOLLICK, born in 1775 at USA.

252 Annatie VAN VALKENBURG, born at NY; christened on 5 Aug 1739 at Albany NY.

--------------------------------------------------------------------------------

She married (1) Isaak LARROWA. Isaak, son of Petrus (Peter) LEROY and Marytie (Marie) VAN ALSTEYN, christened on 21 Feb 1731 at Schoharie NY.

Children:
- 445 M      i Petrus LARROWAY, christened on 25 Jun 1758 at Schoharie NY.
- 446 M     ii Isaak LARROWAY, christened on 3 Apr 1760 at Schoharie NY.
- 447 M    iii Abraham LARROWAY, christened on 24 Jan 1762 at Catskille, NY.
           He married (1) Catherine DIES.

           Catherine was d/o Matthew Dies & Eva Van Valkenburg, 3rd. Branch

- 448 F     iv Jannitje LARROWAY, christened on 18 Jan 1764 at Catskill NY.
- 449 M      v Jonas LARROWAY, christened on 10 Feb 1766 at Catskill, NY.
- 450 F     vi Maria LARROWAY, christened on 23 Jan 1768 at Catskill NY.
- + 451 F  vii Lidia LARROWAY.

268 Gerardus VAN OLINDA, christened on 6 Mar 1734 at Albany, NY.
He married (1) Catharina OSTRANDER on 14 Mar 1770.

Children:
- 452 F      i Jannetie VAN OLINDA, christened on 5 Jan 1771 at Albany, NY.
- 453 M     ii Martinus VAN OLINDA, christened on 13 Dec 1775 at Albany, NY.

269 Daniel VAN OLINDA, christened on 30 Apr 1737 at Albany, NY.
He married (1) Marytje VAN DER WERKEN on 1 Dec 1764 at Albany, NY.

Children:
- 454 M      i Johannes VAN OLINDA, christened on 29 Nov 1771 at Albany, NY.
- 455 F     ii Elisabeth VAN OLINDA, christened on 5 Jan 1777 at Albany, NY.
- 456 M    iii Daniel VAN OLINDA, born in 1783 at Albany, NY; christened on 25 Apr 1783 at Schenectady, NY.

274 Pieter VAN OLINDA, christened on 17 Jan 1748 at NY.
He married (1) Eva SPOOR bef 1782.

Children:
- 457 M      i Nicolaas VAN OLINDA, christened on 9 Jun 1782.
- 458 F     ii Franceyntje VAN OLINDA, christened on 7 Mar 1784.
- 459 F    iii Maria VAN OLINDA, christened on 15 Sep 1786.
- 460 F     iv Cornelia VAN OLINDA, christened on 14 Dec 1788.
- 461 M      v Martinus VAN OLINDA, christened on 27 Oct 1791.
- 462 F     vi Judith VAN OLINDA, christened on 27 Sep 1793.
- 463 F    vii Eva VAN OLINDA, christened on 16 Jun 1796.

277 Benjamin VAN OLINDA, christened on 25 Dec 1757 at NY.
He married (1) Annatje GROOT on 28 Feb 1790 at Willigen, NY.

Children:
- 464 F      i Cornelia VAN OLINDA, christened on 31 Oct 1790.
- 465 F     ii Neeltje VAN OLINDA, christened on 27 Aug 1793 at NY.
- 466 M    iii Benjamin VAN OLINDA, christened on 13 Jun 1797 at NY.
- 467 M     iv Peter Groot VAN OLINDA, christened on 26 Jul 1805 at NY.

278 Willem VAN OLINDA, christened on 2 Feb 1766 at NY.
He married (1) Elisabeth TRUAX.

Children:
- 468 M      i Martinus VAN OLINDA, christened on 21 Jul 1789 at NY.

Fifth Generation

469 M   ii Jacob VAN OLINDA, christened on 13 Dec 1790 at NY.
470 M   iii Peter VAN OLINDA, christened on 9 Mar 1798 at NY.


                              Sixth Generation


297 Arent (Aaron) BRADT, born on 3 Sep 1732 at Schenectady, NY, USA; died in 1796; buried at C.6, L.13,
Louth Twp..

        OCCUPATION: Capt. Butler's Rangers, UEL

        BIRTH SOURCE: Annals of the Forty

        RESIDENCES
        Res:C.6, L.13, Louth Twp. ON

    Arent (Aaron) BRADT married (1) Eva VAN ANTWERP. Eva, dau. of Pieter Danielse VAN ANTWERPEN and Engeltie
MEBIE, born in 1730.

        BIRTH SOURCE: Annals of the Forty

    Children:
        471 M       i Andries (Andrew) BRADT, UEL, born on 27 Aug 1755; died on 6 Nov 1830 at Louth Twp.,
                      Niagara, ON.

                      MILITARY: UEL: Cpt. in  Butler's Rangers American Revolution
                      Col. 5th. Lincoln Militia War of 1812-14

                      BIOGRAPHY:
                      It was Andries' aunt, Catherine/Catalyntie BRADT b 1735 who md. Col. John
                      BUTLER, founder of Butler's Rangers, a fighting unit of Loyalists and Indians
                      in the American Revolution.

                      Andries (Andrew) BRADT, UEL married (1) Rachel RYCKMAN. Rachel, dau. of Johannes (John)
                      RYCKMAN and Eunice WARD, born in 1758 at Schenectady, NY; christened on 8 Oct 1758 at
                      Schenectady, NY.
        472 F      ii Margaret BRADT, born on 16 Apr 1758.
        473 M     iii John BRADT, born on 28 Jul 1761.
        474 M      iv Peter BRADT, born on 10 Aug 1763/1769; died in 1824 at Louth Twp?.


                      OCC  Indian Interpreter

                      During War of 1812, a company of Indians with U.S. army invaded Canada with in
                      tentions to march on Stoney Creek and massacre all families living there. Pete
                      r went to Indian encampment in valley of the Sixteen and speaking in their own
                      language, persuaded Indians to return to U.S. [A.of40]

                      Peter BRADT married (1) Mercy BURTCH in 1792. Mercy, born in 1776 at Fredericksburg,
                      NY.


                      BIRT SOUR Annals of the Forty

Line 19752 from GEDCOM File not recognizable or too long:
BIRT SOUR Annals of the Forty PAGE 64

475 M      v Reyer (Roger) BRADT, born on 28 Jul 1765.

           never married. He lived among the Indians and was remembered as an odd little
           man. [Annals of the 40:64]


298 Catalina (Catherine) BRADT, born in 1735 at NY USA; died on 29 May 1793 at Niagara, Ont. Canada.

       Obituary 29th. May, 1793: "Died, Catharine Butler, wife of John Butler, Esq.,
       first Judge of Common Pleas, Lieut.-Col of old Rangers and chief agent for the
       Indinas. Few in her station have been more useful, none more humble. She lived
       58 yrs. in the world without provoking envy or resentment and left the world a
       s a weary traveller leaves an inn to go to the land of his nativity." [H of N
       p.245]

    Catalina (Catherine) BRADT married (1) John BUTLER in 1752. John, born in 1725 at New London,
    Connecticut, USA; christened on 28 Apr 1728; died on 15 May 1796 at Niagara.

       OCCUPATION: Col. Butler's Rangers

       John Butler was the founder of Butler's Rangers, a fighting unit made up of
       Indians and whites, during the American Revolution. He settled at Niagara
       Ontario as a Loyalist after the war's end.

    Children:
    476 M      i Walter BUTLER, born in 1753 at Mohawk Valley, NY; christened on 26 Aug 1753 at NY; died
               on 30 Oct 1781 at W. Canada Creek, NY; buried in 1781 at Schenectady, NY.
    477 M     ii Thomas BUTLER, born in 1755 at Schenectady, NY; christened on 30 Nov 1755 at RDC,
               Schenectady, NY; died on 12 Dec 1812 at ON.
               He married (1) Ann HAMPTON. Ann, born on 30 Nov 1755; died on 15 Apr 1842 at ON.
    478 M    iii Andrew BUTLER, born in 1759 at Schenectady, NY; christened on 13 May 1759 at RDC,
               Schenectady NY; died on 21 May 1804 at ON.
               He married (1) Ann CLEMENT.

                   This may be Mary Anne aka Anne Clement, RIN 1596, d/o Lewis Cobes Clement and
               Catherine Putnam. More research is needed.

    479 M     iv William Johnson (Johnson) BUTLER, born in 1760; died in Dec 1812 at ON; buried on 17
               Dec 1812 at Niagara, ON.

                  William Johnson Butler was known as Johnson Butler.

               William Johnson (Johnson) BUTLER married (1) Eva YATES in 1794. Eva, born in 1765 at
               NY; christened on 13 Jan 1765 at NY; died on 6 Dec 1800 at Niagara, ON.
               He married (2) Susanna HATT on 15 Jul 1802 at Niagara, ON.
    480 F      v Deborah BUTLER, born in 1764 at Schenectady, NY; christened on 12 May 1764 at RDC,
               Schenectady, NY; died on 29 Jun 1844 at ON.
               She married (1) James MUIRHEAD on 19 May 1795 at Niagara, ON. James, born in 1764; died
               in 1834 at ON.

                  James Muirhead was a doctor at Niagara.

    481 M     vi John BUTLER, born in 1768 at Schenectady, NY; christened on 22 Apr 1768 at Schenectady,
               NY.

318 Harmanus VAN SLYKE, born in 1781 at Schenectady NY; christened on 28 Sep 1781 at Schenectady NY.

    SPOUSE: He may have md. Margaret ECKER 1 June 1782-1860.

   Harmanus VAN SLYKE married (1) Margaret ECKER? bef 1805. Margaret, born on 1 Jun 1782; died in 1860.

Children:
    482 M     i Nicholas VAN SLYKE, born on 17 Jul 1805.

               BAPTISM: Sponsors were Nicolas Van Slyck and wife Gertrude


320 John RYCKMAN, born in 1755/1762 at PA; died in 1842 at Barton?; buried at Hamilton, ONt..

    MILITARY:  Lieut. Butler's Rangers during American Revolution

    BIRTH: CONFLICT:  Annals of the Forty states d.o.b. 1762 but Early Census in
Niagara shows 1755

    BURIAL: Christ Church

    BIOGRAPHY:
John belonged to the Indian Dept. On July 5, 1778 he was captured by British but
escaped. In 1784 he was placed on half pay. He settled Saltfleet C.4, L 32, 33,
34. Later he settled in Barton Tp. Ontario on C.7, L.14,15,16. 1801:C.1
Saltfeet, L.28 Broken Front. The battle of Stoney Creek was fought near his
farm. In 1795 he joined the Barton Masonic Lodge. 1804:Cptn. West Lincoln
Regiment. Reid's Sons & Daugthers of American Loyalists states he d. prior 28
July 1820 and wife was Elizabeth!

  John RYCKMAN married (1) Sarah --. Sarah, born in 1761.

    BIRTH: Early Census in Niagara

Children:
    483 F     i Sarah RYCKMAN, born in 1779; died aft 1843 at Hamilton, ON.

               BIRTH: EARLY SETTLERS IN NIAGARA Including the First "Census" 1782, 1783, 1784,
               1786, 1787 Published by the Ontario Genealogical Society, Niagara Peninsula
               Branch, 1992. OGS NPB, Box 2224, Station B., St. Catharines, ON, Canada
               CONFLICT:  Early Census in Niagara conflicts with Loyalist Lineages states b.
               1770 PA [p.655]

               DEATH: Brian Gawne query Families V.32#4, 1993 PAGE 254

               Sarah RYCKMAN married (1) John SPRINGER.
    484 F    ii Mary RYCKMAN, died on 30 Aug 1834 at Blenheim Tp., Oxford Co., ON.

               DEATH: THE BIOGRAPHICAL HISTORY OF WATERLOO TOWNSHIP by Eby

               NOTE:
               Mary Ryckman/Rykeman was a prominent member of the Mennonite Church. She died
               of cholera 14 days after her husband's death of same disease.

               Mary RYCKMAN married (1) Benjamin SPRINGER. Benjamin, born abt 1773 at Albany, NY; died
               on 16 Aug 1834 at Blenheim Twp., Oxford Co., ON.

OCCUPATION: merchant & farmer

BIRTH: THE BIOGRAPHICAL HISTORY OF WATERLOO TOWNSHIP by Eby
!BIRTH: CONFLICT: Albany (Poughkeepsie?) NY

DEATH: THE BIOGRAPHICAL HISTORY OF WATERLOO TOWNSHIP by Eby

NOTE:
Benjamin, his brother Daniel and b-in-law Richard Beasley waas one of charter
members of Barton Lodge of Freemasons [A. of 40]

485 M     iii John RYCKMAN Jr., born in 1798.
486 F      iv Eunice RYCKMAN, born abt 1780.
              She married (1) Hugh BUCKBOROUGH.

              Res:Ancaster

487 M       v Albert RYCKMAN, born abt 1800.

              QUESTION: Did he m. 10 Sept. 1822 Margaret BASTEDO, widow of Joseph BASTEDO who
              was killed at the Battle of Chippewa 1815?

488 F      vi Nancy RYCKMAN, born abt 1800.
              She married (1) Phineas ALLEN.
489 F     vii Susan RYCKMAN, born abt 1805.
              She married (1) Isaac KERR.


              MARR DATE ca 1830s?

490 M    viii Cornelius RYCKMAN, born abt 1805.
491 M      ix Samuel J. RYCKMAN, born abt 1805.
              He married (1) Nancy MCCRIMMON on 25 Jan 1825 at ON.

321 Rachel RYCKMAN.
     ***** This individual's information has already been printed. *****.
     She married (1) Andries (Andrew) BRADT, UEL.
     ***** This individual's information has already been printed. *****.

     Children:
     492 M       i Arent butler BRADT, born abt 1778.
     493 F      ii Eve BRADT, born abt 1782.
                   She married (1) William SCHRAM. William, son of John SCHRAM and Ann DERBY.


                   BIRT DATE ca 1790?

                   William of Louth

     494 M     iii John S. BRADT, born in 1785; died in 1850.
                   He married (1) Ann HARE. Ann, dau. of Peter HARE and Catherine GREENWALT, born in 1790.


                   BIRT SOUR Annals of the Forty

     495 M      iv Thomas BRADT, born in 1786.
                   He married (1) Elizabeth HARE. Elizabeth, dau. of Peter HARE and Catherine GREENWALT,
                   born in 1788.

     BIRT SOUR Annals of the Forty

  496 M  v Simon Van Antwerp BRADT, born in 1788.

     RESIDENCES: Simon Bradt lived after 1832 C.8 L.13 and S.half L11, Barton Twp.
     148 acres.

     Simon Van Antwerp BRADT married (1) ELizabeth YOUNG. ELizabeth, dau. of Daniel YOUNG
     and ELizabeth WINDECKER, born in 1794; christened on 6 Mar 1794 at St. Mark's,
     Niagara-on-the-L, ON; died on 8 Feb 1883.

     CHR PLAC St. Mark's, Niagara-on-the-Lake, On

     CHR SOUR Papers & Records of a Family of Youngs of Grand River - Geo.
     Nunamaker

     CHR SOUR Papers & Records of a Family of Youngs of Grand River - Geo.
     Nunamaker PAGE 100

  497 F  vi Eunice BRADT, born in 1790.
       She married (1) Thomas KELLY.
  498 M  vii Walter BRADT, born in 1794.
  499 M  viii Andrew BRADT, born in 1797; died in 1854.
       He married (1) Charity HESS.

323 Cornelis RYCKMAN, born in 1763; christened on 6 Nov 1763 at Schenectady, NY.

  RESIDENCES: He was granted land in West Lincoln Co. before 1798.

 Cornelis RYCKMAN married (1) Margaret BRADT.

  NOTE: 7 July 1796 Petition by Margaret Ryckman reads:
  "Margaret Ryckman states that she is the daughter of a Loyalist and that her
  husband Cornelius Ryckman received two hundred acres in the 8th Township, that
  the late Land Board granted her 100 acres Family Lands. She has been separated
  from her husband for a length of time in consequence of ill usage and now
  understanding that he intends to dispose of said lot, prays to have it
  confirmed to her and her son, Cornelius C. Ryckman."

  FATHER: Captain Arent Bradt of Butler's Rangers

 Children:
  500 M  i Cornelis RYCKMAN, born in 1784; christened on 14 Nov 1784 at Schenectady, NY; died in
      1836 at Beamsville, ON.

     BURIAL: His gravestone is in Mount Osborne Cemetery, Beamsville with the dates
     1784-1836. He is buried there with his second wife, Catherine Money.

     Cornelis RYCKMAN married (1) Catherine MONEY. Catherine, born in 1809; died in 1873 at
     Beamsville, ON.

324 Albert RYCKMAN, UEL, born on 24 Aug 1766 at Schenectady, NY; died on 23 Apr 1850 at London, Middlesex
  Co., ON.

--------------------------------------------------------------------------------

MILITARY: Loyalist to Ontario in The American Revolution

SOURCE: The information on Albert's descendants comes from Dale T. Alexander
on Compuserve

Albert RYCKMAN, UEL married (1) Hanna Annatje VAN ETTEN on 25 Jan 1791 at Schenectady, NY. Hanna, dau.
of Jacobus VAN ETTEN and Annatje PANGBURN, died in 1821.

Children:
  501 F      i Marytje RYCKMAN, born on 14 Nov 1791.
  502 M     ii Peter RYCKMAN, born in 1799 at Hamilton, Wentworth Co., ON; died on 7 Apr 1876 at
              Cannington, Ontario Co., ON.
              He married (1) Catherine SHEWFELT in 1826 at Markham, York Co., ON. Catherine, born in
              1803; died in 1895.

328 Samuel RYCKMAN, born in Jul 1777; died in 1846 at Hamilton, ON.

   SOURCE: ANNALS OF THE FORTY by Grimsby Historical Association

Samuel RYCKMAN married (1) Rachel (____). Rachel, born in 1786; died in 1868.

Children:
  503 F      i Clarissa RYCKMAN, born in 1813 at ON; died in 1837 at ON.

             SOURCE: ANNALS OF THE FORTY by Grimsby Historical Association

             Clarissa RYCKMAN married (1) Richard TAYLOR.
  504 M     ii Samuel Ward RYCKMAN, born in 1814 at ON; died in 1854 at Hamilton, ON.

             SOURCE: ANNALS OF THE FORTY by Grimsby Historical Association

  505 M    iii George RYCKMAN, born in 1818; died in 1866 at ON.

             SOURCE: ANNALS OF THE FORTY by Grimsby Historical Association

  506 M     iv Hamilton RYCKMAN, born in 1821 at ON.
             He married (1) Alma GAGE bef 1851 at ON. Alma, born in 1823 at ON.

             PARENTS: William Gage and Catherine Pettit

  507 M      v R L RYCKMAN, born in 1827 at Hamilton, ON; died in 1854.
  508 F     vi Sarah RYCKMAN married (1) John CARR.

351 David Tice BASTEDO, born on 3 Dec 1769 at Schenectady NY; died in 1834.

   NOTES: He had 3 sons and 4 daughters. He died at the home of his youngest
   daughter Catherine STOCK.

David Tice BASTEDO married (1) Elizabeth MCMICKING.

   She was d/o Peter McMicking, UEL, of Queenston

Children:
  509 M      i Peter BASTEDO, born on 23 Mar 1794 at Stamford, ON; died on 14 Dec 1834 at Princeton,
              Blenheim Tp, Oxford Co., ON; buried at Lot 11, Oxford Co. ON.

              BURIAL: FAMILY PLOT

--------------------------------------------------------------------------------

Sixth Generation

--------------------------------------------------------------------------------

MILITARY: Private in Cptn. Rowe's Co. 2nd. Reg. Lincoln Militia in War of 1812.

RESIDENCES:
Came to Oxford Co. 1817 and lived Lot 11.
Resided 17 years in Blenheim Tp.

Peter BASTEDO married (1) Margaret GALBRAITH on 27 Jun 1820 at Princeton ON. Margaret, born on 8 Jul 1801 at Blenheim Tp.; died on 5 Jan 1882 at Princeton ON; buried at Princeton Cem., Princeton, Oxford Co., ON.

PARENTS:
She was d/o John Galbraith and Mary Cron. Mary was d/o James Cron of Augusta Tp., UEL.
John GALBRAITH a native of Parish of Belfron Scotland d. June 18, 1843 ae 71 y yrs, buried Princeton Cem. Mary wf of Jaohn ALBRAITH d. 3 July 1837 ae 70 yr buried Princeton Cem.

510 M       ii Gilbert BASTEDO.

            Was he Gilbert Tice Bastedo b 12 Oct. 1800 d 30 Apr. 1848 m. to Anne [RODGERS? b 24 FEb. 1806 d 26 June 1867. Kids Clarissa J. b 25 Oct. 1828 d 18 nov. 1848, Catherine M. b 31 Jan. 1840 d 1 Feb. 1917, Joseph Rogers b 1 Apr. 1830 d 21 Sept 1856,Agnes C. d 14 Apr. 1846 ae 22 y 24 d? All buried Princeton Cem, Oxford Co.

511 M      iii John McMicking BASTEDO.
512 M       iv Jacob BASTEDO.
513 F        v Catharine BASTEDO married (1) Thomas STOCK.

            Warden of Wentworth Co. 1874: Conservative MP for North Riding

514 F       vi Christina BASTEDO.

356 Gysbert BASTEDO, born on 19 Oct 1777 at Schenectady NY.

       NOTES: Is this the Gilbert Tice Bastedo who married Marion Thompson living in Nelson Twp. Halton Co. ON? Their son Jacob 1807-1878 m1 Margaret SINCLAIR and had Gilbert Tice 1833 -1868

Gysbert BASTEDO married (1) Marion THOMPSON.

Children:
515 M        i Jacob BASTEDO, born in 1807; died in 1878.

            He had 10 children, 3 of whom died young. Ref. Ernie Kerr

            Line 64406 from GEDCOM File not recognizable or too long:
             MARR PLAC Home District Marr. Register V.11

            Jacob BASTEDO married (1) Margaret SINCLAIR.
            He married (2) Hebzibah CHILVER on 24 Aug 1840 at Home District Ma. Hebzibah, born at Engl.
516 F       ii Margaret BASTEDO.

            Ref Ernie Kerr, 41 Hawk Crescent, Ottawa ON K1V 9G8

517 F      iii Marion C. BASTEDO.

--------------------------------------------------------------------------------

--------------------------------------------------------------------------------

Ref: Ernie Kerr, 41 Hawk Cresc. Ottawa ON K1V 9G8

357 Joseph BASTEDO, born on 30 Apr 1780 at Schenectady NY; died on 14 Jul 1814 at Chippawa, ON.
    He married (1) Margaret (___).

        She md. 10 Sept. 1822, Albert Ryckman of Barton

    Children:
        518 M       i David BASTEDO, born on 20 Jan 1812 at Stamford?; died on 5 May 1864 at Gowanda NY.

                    By 1855 he was in NY.

                    David BASTEDO married (1) Anjaline (Jane) WOODRUFF. Anjaline, died on 21 Aug 1871 at
                    Gowanda NY.


                        BIRT DATE ca 1817

        519 M      ii William BASTEDO.
        520 F     iii Rachel BASTEDO.

360 John BASTEDO.
    He married (1) Mary FLEWELLING.

    Children:
        521 M       i Maurice BASTEDO, born in 1816.
                      He married (1) Maria LAMBERT.
        522 M      ii William BASTEDO.
        523 M     iii Jacob BASTEDO.
        524 M      iv Gilbert BASTEDO.
        525 F       v ELizabeth BASTEDO.
        526 F      vi Katharine BASTEDO.

364 Clara VAN SLYKE, born in 1772 at Schenectady, NY; christened on 23 Aug 1772 at Schenectady, NY; died on
    18 May 1821.
    She married (1) Alexander VAN EPS on 30 Aug 1794. Alexander, son of Jacobus VAN EPS and Engeltie WENDEL,
    born on 9 Dec 1770.

        s/o Jacobus Van Eps

    Children:
        527 F       i Engeltie VAN EPS, born on 17 Jun 1796; died on 2 Sep 1825.
        528 F      ii Catharina VAN EPS, born on 24 Oct 1799.
        529 F     iii Neeltje VAN EPS, born on 4 Oct 1802.


                        DEAT DATE young?

                    twin to Maria

        530 F      iv Maria VAN EPS, born on 4 Oct 1802.

                    twin to Neeltje

        531 M       v Jacobus VAN EPS, born on 16 Jul 1807.



--------------------------------------------------------------------------------

twin to Neeltje

  532 F      vi Neeltje VAN EPS, born on 16 Jul 1807.

387 Johan Jacob Christian ITTIG, born on 30 Jun 1764 at German Flats, Herkimer, NY; died on 12 Oct 1844 at Spinnerville, Herkimer, NY.

    SOURCE: Information on this family comes from Rex Stevenson at Compuserve 75257,1074 and Mike Evans on Internet mevans@cyberportal.com, both of whom descend from this line. Information given Nov. 1995

    MILITARY:
    Jacob was a private in the Revolutionary War, Tyron co. Militia in Col. Bellinger Regt. He was wounded in the back by a tomahawk attack by natives in Sept. 1779. Jacob was an aide to General Herkimer and was on the roster at the Battle of oriskany. He served in 1779 under Capt. Frederick Getman at German Flats at Fort Herkimer and later under Capt. John Smith. His brother Conrad testified that he was in Capt. Smith's unit.

Johan Jacob Christian ITTIG married (1) Anna Eva Barbara FRANK in 1792. Anna Eva, born abt 1774.

    AKA: She was known as Eva Frank

    PARENTS: John Stephen Frank and Anna Eva Barbara

Children:
  533 M       i Jacob EDICK, died aft 1854.

              He testified his family name was spelled EDICK, ITTIG, ITTICK but in 1854 accepted as EDICK. According to Jacob, Catherine Christman was his father's second wife and they had had one child still alive. Jacob and Catherine had lived with this Jacob for 10 years prior to Jacob Sr.'s death.

Johan Jacob Christian ITTIG married (2) Catherine CHRISTMAN.

    SPOUSE: She was the second wife of Jacob Ittig according to a deposition made on 24 Apr. 1854 by Jacob Edick, son of Jacob Ittig by his first marriage to Eva Frank.

    CHILDREN: Catherine and Jacob Ittig had a child still living in 1854, but the name is unknown

Johan Jacob Christian ITTIG married (3) Susan WOHLEBEN on 5 Apr 1795 at German Flats, Herkimer, NY. Susan, born in 1771; died on 20 Dec 1820 at Spinnerville, NY.

    PARENTS: Peter Nicholas Wohleben & Catharina Flack/Flagg

Children:
  534 M      ii Jacob Henry EDICK, born on 6 Jul 1802; died on 16 Aug 1878.
             He married (1) Mary Margaret CRIM in 1823. Mary, born on 13 Aug 1803; died on 20 Nov 1892 at Spinnerville, Herkimer, NY.

             Line 47620 from GEDCOM File not recognizable or too long:
               DEAT SOUR Rex Stevenson at Compuserve 75257,1074

--------------------------------------------------------------------------------------

399 Cornelius VAN SLYKE, born in 1766 at Schenectady, NY; christened on 19 Oct 1766 at Schenectady, NY.

     He is not listed in his father's will of 1815

    Cornelius VAN SLYKE married (1) Ruth CLARK.

    Children:
       535 M     i Jesse VAN SLYKE, born in Oct 1794 at Schenectady, NY.
       536 M    ii William VAN SLYKE, born on 7 Jul 1801 at Schenectady, NY.

400 Margarita VAN SLYKE, born in 1769 at Schenectady, NY; christened on 11 Sep 1769 at Schenectady, NY.

     She is not listed in her father's will of 20 May 1815

    Margarita VAN SLYKE married (1) Cornelis VAN PETTEN.

    Children:
       537 M     i Jesse VAN PETTEN, born bef 1815.

402 Marten VAN SLYKE, born on 12 Feb 1775 at Schenectady, NY; christened on 19 Feb 1775 at Schenectady, NY; died on 12 May 1817 at Schenectady, NY.
He married (1) Margarietje OLSAVER on 4 Feb 1798 at Schenectady, NY. Margarietje, born on 26 Feb 1780; died on 1 Jun 1826.

    Children:
       538 F     i Jacomyntje VAN SLYKE, born on 27 Dec 1798 at Schenectady, NY.

               Not in her grandfather's will of 1815 but her two younger siblings Jesse and Jemima are.

       539 F    ii Jannetje VAN SLYKE, born on 2 May 1800 at Schenectady, NY.

               Not in her grandfather's will of 1815 but her two younger siblings Jesse and Jemina are

       540 M   iii Jesse VAN SLYKE, born on 4 Mar 1802 at Schenectady, NY.
       541 F    iv Jemima VAN SLYKE, born on 20 Dec 1803 at Schenectady, NY.
       542 F     v Sarah VAN SLYKE, born on 20 Sep 1805 at Schenectady, NY.
       543 F    vi Margaret VAN SLYKE, born on 22 Dec 1808 at Schenectady, NY.
       544 M  vii Henry M. VAN SLYKE, born on 28 Jul 1815 at Schenectady, NY; died on 27 Sep 1834.

403 Abraham VAN SLYKE, born in 1778 at Schenectady, NY; christened on 12 Apr 1778 at Schenectady, NY.
He married (1) unknown (____).

    Children:
       545 F     i Jemima VAN SLYKE, born bef 1815 at Schenectady, NY.

435 Matthias VALCK, born on 12 Jun 1759 at Schoharie, NY, USA; christened on 6 Dec 1759 at Schoharie, NY, USA; died at NY?.
He married (1) Bertha (Baertie) BRADT on 4 Jan 1786 at Albany RC Church, Albany, NY, USA. Bertha, dau. of David BRADT and Tryntje LANG, christened on 23 Apr 1758 at Albany RC Church, Albany, NY, USA; died at NY?.

    Children:
       546 F     i Maria VALCK, born abt 1785 at Albany, NY, USA; christened at Albany Lutheran.
       547 M    ii David VALCK, born on 21 Feb 1796 at New Salem, NY, USA; christened on 28 Mar 1796 at New Salem.
       548 F   iii Sarah VALCK, born on 17 Apr 1798 at New Salem, NY, USA; christened on 6 May 1798.

--------------------------------------------------------------------------------------

436 Cornelius VOLLICK, UEL, christened on 16 Aug 1761 at Albany, NY, USA; died aft 1814 at ON.

    MARRIAGE: Ontario Historical Society V.3 Weddings in Niagara 1792-1830

    TIMELINE:
    16 Aug. 1761:baptised Dutch Reformed Church Albany NY
    1782:listed as living at Niagara ON with disbanded Butler's Rangers and
    families. Although not on the roster for Butler's Rangers, a letter signed by
    an officer, John Bradt, states Cornelius was a soldier in this Loyalist unit
    during the American Revolution
    24 Mar. 1795:married at Niagara ON
    17 Aug. 1795:Newark ON
    10 Mar. 1797:free grant of land C.5, L.7 East Flamborough Tp. ON
    24 Oct. 1812:1st. Regiment Lincoln Militia where he is listed as ill.

  Cornelius VOLLICK, UEL married (1) Eve LARROWAY on 24 Mar 1795 at Niagara. Eve, dau. of Jonas LARRAWAY,
  UEL and ELizabeth (Betsy) MULLER, born in Sep 1776 at Niagara, ON.

    BIRTH: I believe Eve was a twin to her brother Jonas Larroway and born Sept.
    1776 at Niagara

Children:
  549 M     i Isaac VOLLICK, born on 24 Apr 1796 at Nelson Tp, Halton Co, ON; died on 30 Apr 1864 at
              Nelson Twp. Halt; buried at Nelson Twp. Halt, ONt..

              DEATH SOURCE Ruth Burkholder

              BURIED Salem Cemetery

              1861:Nelson Twp., Halton Co. [census Dist.5, p.11]Harriet & Jos. listed absent
              1864:Conc. 5, Lot 1, Nelson Twp., Halton Co.
              Isaac & Sophia lived under Bradt's Peak, Lowville, Ont.
              Isaac Vollock [sic] age 34 in 2nd. Regiment Gore Militia, Nelson Tp. as of 22
              Dec. 1828 [#92] Is this the Isaac VOLLOCK who is on the Muster Roll & Paylist
              of Cptn. George Law's Co. 1st. Reg. Lincoln Militia 19-24 Sept. 1813? He
              served 6 days for 3 shillings.Is he Cornelius or John's son??? More proof reqd

              Isaac VOLLICK married (1) Sophia BURKHOLDER. Sophia, dau. of David BURKHOLDER and
              ELizabeth GINGERICH, born abt 1810 at Hamilton, ON; died abt 1881 at Kilbride, Nelson
              Twp., Halton Co. Ont.; buried at Salem Cemetery, Kilbride, ON.

              BURIAL:Salem Cemetery has deeply cut stone: S.V.
              Bessie E. Vollick 1987 letter to Ruth Burkholder

  550 M    ii Matthias (Tice) FOLLICK, born in 1798 at St. Catharines, ON; died on 11 Jan 1870 at Hay
              Twp., Huron Co., ONt.; buried at Hay Twp., Huron Co., ONt..

              OCCUPATION farmer

              BURIED Hillsgreen Cem.

              1838:living Hespeler, Ont.
              1851:Puslinch Twp., Wellington Co. [census p.11]
              later:Hay Twp., Huron Co.
              Is he Cornelius or John's son? More proof required.
              Inscription reads"aged 70 yrs, a native of St. Catharins[sic]"

Matthias (Tice) FOLLICK married (1) Catharine BURKHOLDER. Catharine, dau. of David
BURKHOLDER and ELizabeth GINGERICH, born on 23 Mar 1812 at Hamilton, ON; died on 18 Jan
1864 at Hay Twp., Huron Co., ONt.; buried at Hay Twp., Huron Co., ONt..

BURIED Hillsgreen Cem.

Inscription reads "aged 52 y, 4 m, 5 d"

551 M     iii Richard VOLLICK, born in Oct 1809 at Upper Canada; died on 17 Jul 1891 at Hay Twp.,
              Huron Co., ONt..

OCCUPATION: Farmer

RESIDENCES:
1860: East Flamborough Twp.
1868-1881:Hay Twp., Huron Co.

COMMENT:
Richard is the  grandson of Isaac Van Valkenburg/Vollick, but it is not known
who his parents are: Cornelius & Eve or John & Sarah Vollick.

MILITARY:
22 Dec. 1828: Richard VOLICK ae 19 in 2nd. Reg. of Gore Militia for Nelson Tp.

DEATH: Richard died at age 81 y. 9 mo. of Dropsy. Death certificate.

RELIGION:
Trustee Bethel Church, Kilbride in 1853 along with Jonas Vollick

Richard VOLLICK married (1) ELizabeth (Betsy) BURKHOLDER bef 1832. ELizabeth, dau. of
David BURKHOLDER and ELizabeth GINGERICH, born abt 1816 at Hamilton, ON; died in 1879
at Hay Twp., Huron Co., ON.

552 F     iv Margaret VOLLICK, born in 1815; died in 1851.

It is possible that Margaret is d/o Cornelius Vollick and Eve Larroway.
She died of Black Fever and Consumption at Middleton Twp. Norfolk Co. and is
listed in the 1851 census under deaths.
She was married as Margaret Van Valenby aka Van Valkenburg.

Margaret VOLLICK married (1) David BURKHOLDER in 1831. David, son of David BURKHOLDER
and ELizabeth GINGERICH, born in 1808; died on 9 Jun 1882.

Norah was listed in the 1881 census as having a deaf and mute dau from a
previous marriage, aged 27, named Xanu GRISSON. It is possible that Norah is
really Laura and was married to Bramen/Raymond GREEN before m. David.

437 Annaje (Hannah) VOLLICK, christened on 26 Jun 1763 at Schoharie, NY, USA; died bef 1823 at Ontario
Canada.

BAPTISM: Schoharie Lutheran, NY, USA

Annaje (Hannah) VOLLICK married (1) Derrick (Richard) HAINER abt 1783 at Niagara, Ont. Canada. Derrick,
born abt 1759 at NY, USA; died in 1801 at Ontario Canada.

Children:
553 M      i unknown HAINER, born abt 1783 at Niagara, Ont. Canada; died bef 1812 at Ont. Canada.
554 F     ii Catherine HAINER, born abt 1783 at Niagara, Ont. Canada; died bef 1814 at Ont. Canada.

--------------------------------------------------------------------------------------------------
Sixth Generation

-------------------------------------------------------------------------------------------

She married (1) William Henry MAY Jr.. William, son of Peter MAY and Eve CLENDENNING,
born on 17 Apr 1789; died on 10 Feb 1862.

555 F      iii Dorothy HAINER, born on 26 Apr 1784 at Niagara, Ont. Canada; died on 2 May 1830 at Ont.
           Canada.
           She married (1) John MAY on 5 Aug 1802 at Niagara, Ont. Canada. John, son of Wilhelm
           WILLIAM   and Lena JANSSEN, born on 29 Feb 1776; died on 8 Nov 1812 at Lincoln Co.,
           Ont. Canada.
           She married (2) Columbus GILDEA bef Apr 1819 at Ont. Canada. Columbus, died bef 1838.

556 F      iv Mary HAINER, born abt 1785 at Niagara, Ont. Canada.
           She married (1) George GHASKY abt 1810 at Niagara, ON. George, born abt 1785.

557 F      v Cornelia HAINER, born abt 1790 at Ont. Canada; died on 10 Dec 1870 at Ont. Canada.
           She married (1) Frederick Augustus SCHRAM abt 1819 at Niagara. Frederick, son of
           Frederick SCHRAM and Angelica ---, born in 1792; christened on 13 Jul 1792; died on 13
           Sep 1872 at Ont. Canada.

558 F      vi Chloe Clarinda HAINER, born on 1 Feb 1792 at Niagara, Ont. Canada; died on 1 Aug 1850
           at Ont. Canada.
           She married (1) John PATTERSON. John, born abt 1784; died abt 1852.

559 F      vii ELizabeth HAINER, born abt 1792 at Niagara, Ont. Canada; died on 14 May 1862 at Ont.
           Canada; buried at Port Dalhousie, ONt..
           She married (1) Jacob GOULD aft 1816. Jacob, born on 6 Mar 1785; died on 6 Jan 1859.

560 F      viii Eve HAINER, born abt 1799 at Ont. Canada.
           She married (1) George YOCUM in 1816/1823 at Gainsborough?.

561 F      ix Margaret (Peggy) HAINER, born abt 1800 at Ont. Canada; died on 27 Jun 1864 at Ont.
           Canada; buried at Pelham-Louth Bor, Niagara.

           BURIED Rockway Presb.
           Pelham-Louth Border, Niagara

           Margaret (Peggy) HAINER married (1) John Frederick SCHRAM. John, son of John William
           SCHRAM and Margaret BEAMER, died on 21 Nov 1879 at Niagara area; buried at Pelham Louth
           bor, Niagara.

           BURIED Rockway Presb.

           Known as "Mountain Frederick" to distinguish him from cousin John Frederick,
           or "Monney" who marr. Peggy's sister, Cornelia Hainer.

562 F      x Sarah HAINER, born on 22 Nov 1801 at Ont. Canada; died on 3 Oct 1866 at Ont. Canda.
           She married (1) John TINLINE at Ont. Canada. John, born on 7 Nov 1800; died on 10 Nov
           1879 at Ont. Canada.

438 Storm FOLLICK, UEL, born on 17 Feb 1765 at Schoharie, NY, USA; christened on 19 Feb 1765 at Schoharie,
NY, USA; died at ON.

   BAPTISM: Schoharie Lutheran, NY, USA

Storm FOLLICK, UEL married (1) Esther SPIRBECK? aft Sep 1787 at Niagara, Ont. Canada. Esther, born abt
1770.

Children:
   563 M      i Isaac VOLLICK, born abt 1801 at ON.

              I believe this is the Isaac Vollick, age 27, listed with Jacob and Mathias in
              1828 list for 1st. Haldimand Militia. This gives us a d.o.b. for Isaac as ca
              1801

   564 M      ii Jacob VOLLICK, born in Oct 1800 at Canboro, Haldimand Co. ON.

-------------------------------------------------------------------------------------------
                                    Sixth Generation

RESIDENCES:
1851:Canboro Tp. Haldimand Co. Census
1871:S. Cayuga Tp. Haldimand Co. Census
I believe this is the Jacob Vollick, age 26 in First Haldimand Militia 1828.

Jacob VOLLICK married (1) Rachael (___) abt 1823. Rachael, born on 17 May 1809; died on 26 Jul 1865 at Canboro Tp. Hald; buried at Canboro, ON.

DEATH  SOURCE Keith Topp 1994
Rachel's age at death:56 y, 2 m, 9d
BURIED Melick Cemetery

I believe it is possible she is a SMITH - note the name of her son Smith Frederick

Jacob VOLLICK married (2) Christian CRAMER in 1866.

Christian was a widow Mrs. WRAY when she md. Jacob, who may have been a widower.

565 M   iii Peter VOLLICK, born abt 1805 at Upper Canada; died bef 1871.
            He married (1) Helen (Ellen) (___) bef 1851. Helen, born abt 1819 at Ireland.
566 M    iv Matthias (Tice) FOLLICK, born on 12 Oct 1810 at Canboro, Haldimand Co. ON; died on 23 Oct 1879 at Canboro, Haldimand Co. ON.

DEATH SOURCE Ancestral File, LDS Library, Salt Lake City, Utah:1879
is date in petition filed by widow Gittie Vollick

Information this family from LDS library Ancestral File

Is he the Matthias Vollick b. 1813 in 1871 S. Cayuga Tp. Haldimand Co. census?

1851:Canboro, Haldimand Co. census with second wife Gittie

I believe he is the Mathias VOLLICK age 19 in 1828 list for 1st. Haldimand Militia. His brother Jacob is also there, as is an Isaac Vollick age 27.

Matthias (Tice) FOLLICK married (1) Rachel MCLAUGLIN in 1830 at Canboro, ONt.. Rachel, born on 26 Dec 1814 at Canboro, Haldimand Co. ON; died abt 1833/1834.

BIRTH SOURCE Ancestral File at LDS in Salt Lake City

Matthias (Tice) FOLLICK married (2) Gittie MCLAUGHLIN in 1834. Gittie, born on 26 Apr 1819 at Canboro, Haldimand Tp., Ont; died on 2 Jun 1900 at Canborough Twp..

DEATH SOURCE Reel #96 ARchives Death Indexes      under VOLLICK

Gittie is another name for Gertrude and it is possible her name was indeed Gertrude. She died of old age. She was a Baptist.
Gittie filed, in conjunction with Joel Vollick a carpenter and Henry Harvey Vollick, a farmer, a petition after her husband Matthias died without a will. The date was Jan. 1880

567 F    v Catherine VOLLICK, born bef 1813 at Canboro, Haldimand Co. ON.
568 M   vi George VOLLICK, born abt 1813 at Canboro, Haldimand Co. ON.

1871 census S. Cayuga Tp. Haldimand Co. along with Ellen b. 1816 Ire., Jacob b. 1802, Jacob b. 1843, Jesse b. 1844, Mary b. 1826 and Matthias b. 1813

---------------------------------------------------------------------------------------

1851:Canboro, Haldimand Co. with wife Mary and Isaac BRADT, single, b. 1795
who has stated he is not a family member

George VOLLICK married (1) Mary UNKNOWN bef 1851. Mary, born abt 1817 at Upper Canada.

569 F      vii Sophia VOLLICK, born bef 1813 at Canboro, Haldimand Co. ON.
               She married (1) John SPERBACK.
570 F     viii Nancy VOLLICK, born bef 1813 at Canboro, ONt..
               She married (1) James WHITE.
571 M       ix Daniel Peter VOLLICK, born bef 1813 at Canboro, ONt..

               There may be two individuals, one named Peter Vollick and one named Daniel
               Vollick, each of them md. to a Nancy. However due to strong evidence in favour
               of one man named Peter Daniel/Daniel Peter, I am listing him this way for now.
               More proof is needed however on this family to be certain the lineage is
               correct. Is Sophia FOLLICK b ca 1851 d/o Peter & Ellen who md. 4 June 1874 Ca
               nboro, to Robert CAMPBELL of N. Cayuga, their dau?
               Is this Peter FOLACK ae 28 in Gore Militia, Nelson Tp. 1828?

               Daniel Peter VOLLICK married (1) Nancy HANART. Nancy, born abt 1818 at Port Credit, ON.

439 Sophia VOLLICK, christened on 11 Apr 1766 at Schoharie, NY, USA.
    She married (1) Adrian (Arent) BRADT bef 1784 at Niagara, Ont. Canada. Adrian, son of Albert BRADT and
    Magdelena LANG, born on 14 Aug 1765 at NY, USA; christened on 6 Sep 1765 at NY, USA; died at Canada.

    Children:
    572 F       i Mary BRADT, born abt 1789 at Niagara, Ont. Canada.
    573 M      ii Albert BRADT, born in Apr 1791 at Niagara, Ont. Canada; died in 1878 at Canada.
               He married (1) Mary VOLLICK. Mary, born abt 1791.
    574 M     iii Walter BRADT, born abt 1793 at Niagara, Ont. Canada; died at Canada.
               He married (1) Abigail GUIRE?.
    575 M      iv Peter BRADT, born abt 1799 at Niagara, Ont. Canada.
               He married (1) Lucinda UNKNOWN.
    576 M       v Isaac BRADT, born in 1795 at Niagara, Ont. Canada; died on 18 Oct 1829.
               He married (1) Martha MCWILLIAMS on 11 Oct 1818. Martha, born abt 1798; died on 18 Oct
               1829.
    577 M      vi Storm BRADT, born abt 1798 at Niagara, Ont. Canada.
               He married (1) Sarah UNKNOWN. Sarah, born abt 1800.
    578 F     vii Leona BRADT, born abt 1801 at Ont. Canada.
               She married (1) Francis (Wm.?) POWERS abt 1840 at Malahide, Ont.?. Francis, born abt
               1800.
    579 F    viii Christiana BRADT, born abt 1803 at Ont. Canada.
               She married (1) Elisha R. SMITH abt 1835 at Malahide, Ont.?. Elisha, born abt 1800.
    580 M      ix William BRADT, born abt 1802 at Ont. Canada.
               He married (1) ELizabeth UNKNOWN.
    581 M       x Christopher BRADT, born abt 1809 at Ont. Canada.

440 ELizabeth VOLLICK, born in Feb 1767 at Schoharie NY USA; christened in Dec 1767 at Schoharie, NY, USA.

    BAPTISM: Schoharie Lutheran, NY, USA

    ELizabeth VOLLICK married (1) Christian BRADT bef 1784 at Niagara, Ont. Canada. Christian, son of Albert
    BRADT and Magdelena LANG, born on 28 Jan 1763 at NY, USA; christened on 27 Feb 1763 at Albany RC, NY,
    USA; died at ON.

    NOTES: 11 March 1797: praying for family lands and land in addition to 100 A
    which he had already received. Ordered 100 acres extra and 100 acres family
    lands.

-----------------------------------------------------------------------------------------
Sixth Generation

--------------------------------------------------------------------------------------

Children:
582 F      i Anna Magdalena BRADT, born on 28 Jan 1785 at Niagara, Ont. Canada; christened on 28 Sep
             1789 at Brunswick Gilead, Rensslaer Co.; died on 31 Aug 1854 at Ont. Canada; buried at
             Port Dalhousie, Ont. Canada.

             CHRISTENING PLACE Brunswick Gilead Ev.Luth.,Rensslaer Co.

             Anna Magdalena BRADT married (1) Peter MAY at Niagara, Ont. Canada. Peter, son of
             Wilhelm WILLIAM   and Lena JANSSEN, born on 25 May 1765 at Albany, NY, USA; died on 7
             Jun 1827 at St. Catherine's.

             OCCUPATION UEL Butler's Rangers

583 M     ii Albert BRADT, born at Niagara?; christened on 19 Apr 1791 at New Salem RC, NY, USA;
             died in Apr 1878 at Hamilton ON.
             He married (1) Nelly MARCLE. Nelly, born abt 1791.
584 M    iii Matthias BRADT, born at Niagara, Ont. Canada; christened on 3 Dec 1792 at Berne
             Lutheran, NY, USA; died in 1866.
             He married (1) ELizabeth UNKNOWN. ELizabeth, born abt 1795.

             This is very possibly Elizabeth YOUNG d/o Henry YOUNG of Grantham Twp. whose
             will dated 16 Feb. 1818 mentions a son George with wife Mary, dau. Elenor w/o
             Bernard SHULTES, dau. Mary w/o Elias FOX, dau. Charity w/o Christopher WINTE-
             MUTE, dau. Jemima w/o Silas OSTERHOUT, dau. Hannah w/o John MOORE, dau Marg't.
             w/o Jacob STULL, dau. Elizabeth w/o Mathias BRADT.

585 M     iv Isaac BRADT, born at Niagara, Ont. Canada; christened on 13 Sep 1794 at Niagara, Upper
             Canada.
586 M      v David BRADT, born in 1797 at Ont. Canada.
             He married (1) Catherine UNKNOWN.
587 M     vi John BRADT, born in 1806 at Niagara, Ont. Canada; died at Port Dalhousie, Ont.?.
             He married (1) Sarah HAINER at Port Dalhousie, Ont. Canada?. Sarah, dau. of Albert
             HAINER and Catharina (Catherine) VOLLICK, born abt 1812 at Ont. Canada; died at ?.

441 Catharina (Catherine) VOLLICK, born on 25 Jun 1769 at NY, USA; christened at Lutheran Church, Schoharie,
NY; died at ON.
She married (1) Albert HAINER aft 1784 at Niagara, Ont. Canada. Albert, born abt 1762 at NY, USA; died
at Ont. Canada.

Children:
588 F      i Dorothy HAINER, born abt 1785 at Niagara, Ont. Canada.
             She married (1) David PUTNAM on 24 May 1807. David, born abt 1780 at Niagara Falls?.
589 M     ii Isaac HAINER, born abt 1800 at Ont. Canada.
             He married (1) Anna Magdalena MAY. Anna, dau. of Peter MAY and Anna Magdalena BRADT,
             born on 16 Jun 1800.
590 M    iii Henry HAINER, born abt 1789 at Ont. Canada.
             He married (1) Nancy (Hannah) SCHRAM. Nancy, dau. of Valentine SCHRAM and Hannah
             BOWMAN, born at Niagara.

             There is confusion over Nancy/Hannah Schram. She might be Ann Darby also calle
             d Nancy or Hannah, who married John Schram. She may not be d/o Valentine & Han
             nah Bowman Schram.

591 F     iv Mary Anne HAINER, born abt 1812 at Ont. Canada.
592 F      v Deborah HAINER, born abt 1810 at Ont. Canada.
             She married (1) Mathias FISHER.
593 F     vi Catherine C. HAINER, born on 21 Mar 1812 at Ont. Canada; died on 17 Nov 1846 at Niagara
             Tp., Lincoln Co.; buried at Niagara Tp., Lincoln Co..


---------------------------------------------------------------------------------------

Sixth Generation

BURIAL  SOURCEL Virgil Cemetery as on  MS 451 Reel #7, OA

Catherine C. HAINER married (1) Jonas LARROWAY. Jonas, born on 25 Sep 1804; died on 14
Apr 1876 at Niagara Tp., Lincoln Co.; buried at Niagara Tp., Lincoln Co..

Line 6900 from GEDCOM File not recognizable or too long:
  BURI DATE VIRGIL CEM.

594 M      vii James HAINER, born abt 1810 at Ont. Canada.
               He married (1) Catherine --.
595 F     viii Hannah HAINER, born abt 1810 at Ont. Canada.
               She married (1) John SWACKHAMMER. John, born abt 1814.
596 F       ix Sarah HAINER.
               ***** This individual's information has already been printed. *****
               She married (1) John BRADT at Port Dalhousie, Ont. Canada?.
               ***** This individual's information has already been printed. *****
597 F        x ELizabeth HAINER, born abt 1812 at Ont. Canada.

442 Sarah VOLLOCK, born in 1770 at NY, USA.
She married (1) Benoni (Benjamin) CRUMB in 1785/1787 at Niagara, Ont. Canada. Benoni, born abt 1770 at
?.

Children:
598 F        i Margaret CRUMB, born abt 1789 at Niagara, Ont. Canada.
               She married (1) Jacob WEAVER.
599 F       ii Mary CRUMB.
600 M      iii Cornelius CRUMB.
601 F       iv Jane CRUMB married (1) John LAKE.
602 M        v Albert CRUMB.
603 M       vi Isaac CRUMB, christened on 13 Jul 1792.
604 M      vii Benjamin CRUMB.

443 Jan (John) VOLLICK, born on 25 Jul 1772 at Beaverdam, NY, USA; christened at Lutheran Church, Schoharie,
NY; died at ON.

    NOTES:
    Is this the John VOLLOCK, private, in Lt. John Williams' Co. of Militia in
    Brant Co. in War of 1812? He is with Abraham DeCOU, who is likely Sarah's bro.

    NAME:
    It appears that this John VOLLICK went by the surname VAN VALKENBURG later in
    life, and that his children adopted the original family name.

Jan (John) VOLLICK married (1) Sarah DECOW on 20 Oct 1798 at Niagara, ONt.. Sarah, dau. of Jacob DECOU,
UEL and ELizabeth BLOOME, born abt 1775.

Children:
605 M        i Cornelius VAN VALKENBURG.

               I believe this is Cornelius VOLLICK aka VAN VALKENBURG b. ca 1804 md. Rebecca
               POTTS and resided Townsend Tp. Norfolk Co. with children William? b ca 1825
               m. Elizabeth; Rebecca VV b ca 1832 m. Alexander DONALD; Isaac [Cornelius?] b
               1835 m Helen BOWER; Cornelius? b ca 1835; Almira VV b ca 1837 m. Stephen CARR;
               Sarah b ca 1841; Adam b ca 1842 m. Margaret BUSH; Bera b ca 1843.

606 M       ii Matthew VAN VALKENBURG.
607 F      iii female (____).

--------------------------------------------------------------------------------

      608 F    iv female {___}.
      609 F     v female {___}.

451 Lidia LARROWAY, christened on 12 Jun 1770 at Catskill NY.
    She married (1) John KELLER, UEL abt 1784. John, born on 7 Jul 1758 at Germantown, NY; died abt 1828 at Fredericksburg, ON?.

      John Keller served as a Loyalist in King's Royal Rangers of New York.

      SOURCES: _Loyalist Lineages of Canada_

Children:
      610 M     i Isaac KELLER.
      611 F    ii ELizabeth KELLER.
      612 F   iii Hannah KELLER.
      613 F    iv Marie KELLER.
      614 M     v John KELLER, born in 1793 at Fredericksburg, ON.
      615 F    vi Katreen KELLER.
      616 F   vii Jane KELLER.
      617 M  viii William KELLER.
      618 F    ix Lydia KELLER.
      619 F     x Peggy KELLER.
      620 F    xi Layana KELLER.
      621 F   xii Maryann KELLER.
      622 M  xiii Peter KELLER.

--------------------------------------------------------------------------------

--------------------------------------------------------------------------------

--------------------------------------------------------------------------------

| | | | | | | |
|---|---|---|---|---|---|---|
| 56 | VAN SLYKE, Adam | 7,17 | | 190 | VAN SLYKE, Engeltie | 18 |
| 306 | VAN SLYKE, Adam | 30 | | 55 | VAN SLYKE, Geertruy | 7 |
| 307 | VAN SLYKE, Adam | 30 | | 224 | VAN SLYKE, Geertruy | 24 |
| 370 | VAN SLYKE, Adriaan | 35 | | 227 | VAN SLYKE, Geertruy | 24 |
| 65 | VAN SLYKE, Adriaen | 7,19,30 | | 235 | VAN SLYKE, Geertruy | 24 |
| 237 | VAN SLYKE, Adrian | 24,35 | | 236 | VAN SLYKE, Geertruy | 24 |
| 217 | VAN SLYKE, Agnes | 23 | | 366 | VAN SLYKE, Geertruy | 35 |
| 331 | VAN SLYKE, Ahasuerus | 32 | | 378 | VAN SLYKE, Geertruy | 36 |
| 383 | VAN SLYKE, Ahasuerus | 36 | | 10 | VAN SLYKE, Geertruyt | 2,8 |
| 70 | VAN SLYKE, Albert | 8,21 | | 59 | VAN SLYKE, Gerrit | 7 |
| 382 | VAN SLYKE, Albert | 36 | | 79 | VAN SLYKE, Gerrit | 8 |
| 158 | VAN SLYKE, Annatje | 15,29 | | 209S | VAN SLYKE, Gerrit | 20 |
| 210 | VAN SLYKE, Annatje | 20 | | 57 | VAN SLYKE, Harmanus | 7,17 |
| 218 | VAN SLYKE, Annatje | 23 | | 156 | VAN SLYKE, Harmanus | 14 |
| 219 | VAN SLYKE, Annatje | 23 | | 182 | VAN SLYKE, Harmanus | 17,30 |
| 233 | VAN SLYKE, Annatje | 24 | | 303 | VAN SLYKE, Harmanus | 30 |
| 365 | VAN SLYKE, Annatje | 35 | | 304 | VAN SLYKE, Harmanus | 30 |
| 177 | VAN SLYKE, Anthony | 16,30,32 | | 305 | VAN SLYKE, Harmanus | 30 |
| 314 | VAN SLYKE, Anthony | 31 | | 318 | VAN SLYKE, Harmanus | 31,43 |
| 337 | VAN SLYKE, Anthony | 32 | | 329 | VAN SLYKE, Harmanus | 32 |
| 82 | VAN SLYKE, Ariantie | 8 | | 185 | VAN SLYKE, Harme | 18 |
| 330 | VAN SLYKE, Asehuerus | 32 | | 8 | VAN SLYKE, Harmen | 2,5,14 |
| 205 | VAN SLYKE, Carel Hansen | 20 | | 188 | VAN SLYKE, Harmen | 18 |
| 310 | VAN SLYKE, Caterina | 31 | | 213 | VAN SLYKE, Harmen | 20,32 |
| 72 | VAN SLYKE, Catharina | 8 | | 12 | VAN SLYKE, Helena | 2 |
| 312 | VAN SLYKE, Catharina | 31 | | 183 | VAN SLYKE, Helena | 17 |
| 223 | VAN SLYKE, Christina | 24,33 | | 184 | VAN SLYKE, Helena | 17 |
| 313 | VAN SLYKE, Christina Vrooman | 31 | | 333 | VAN SLYKE, Hendrick | 32 |
| 203 | VAN SLYKE, Claartje | 19,30,32 | | 544 | VAN SLYKE, Henry M. | 50 |
| 232 | VAN SLYKE, Claartje | 24 | | 191 | VAN SLYKE, Hermanus | 18 |
| 178 | VAN SLYKE, Clara | 16 | | 4 | VAN SLYKE, Hilletie Cornelise | 1,2 |
| 216 | VAN SLYKE, Clara | 23 | | 78 | VAN SLYKE, Jacob | 8 |
| 222 | VAN SLYKE, Clara | 24 | | 192 | VAN SLYKE, Jacob | 18 |
| 226 | VAN SLYKE, Clara | 24 | | 180 | VAN SLYKE, Jacobus | 17 |
| 230 | VAN SLYKE, Clara | 24 | | 308 | VAN SLYKE, Jacobus | 31 |
| 364 | VAN SLYKE, Clara | 35,48 | | 47 | VAN SLYKE, Jacobus (James) | 6,14,16 |
| 228 | VAN SLYKE, Clara Jean Clarissa | 24,33 | | 206 | VAN SLYKE, Jacobus Visscher (Cobus) | 20 |
| 316 | VAN SLYKE, Clarissa | 31 | | 538 | VAN SLYKE, Jacomyntje | 50 |
| 9 | VAN SLYKE, Cornelis | 2,7,16 | | 62 | VAN SLYKE, Jacques | 7 |
| 181 | VAN SLYKE, Cornelis | 17 | | 58 | VAN SLYKE, Jacques (Akers) | 7,18 |
| 204 | VAN SLYKE, Cornelis | 19 | | 63 | VAN SLYKE, Jacques (Akes) | 7 |
| 236S | VAN SLYKE, Cornelis | 24 | | 3 | VAN SLYKE, Jacques Cornelise | 1 |
| 1 | VAN SLYKE, Cornelis Antonissen | 1 | | 53 | VAN SLYKE, Jannetje | 7 |
| 73 | VAN SLYKE, Cornelius | 8,23 | | 187 | VAN SLYKE, Jannetje | 18 |
| 335 | VAN SLYKE, Cornelius | 32 | | 202 | VAN SLYKE, Jannetje | 19 |
| 379 | VAN SLYKE, Cornelius | 36 | | 317 | VAN SLYKE, Jannetje | 31 |
| 399 | VAN SLYKE, Cornelius | 37,50 | | 539 | VAN SLYKE, Jannetje | 50 |
| 231 | VAN SLYKE, Cornelius Petrus | 24,34 | | 541 | VAN SLYKE, Jemima | 50 |
| 309 | VAN SLYKE, Dorothea | 31 | | 545 | VAN SLYKE, Jemima | 50 |
| 374 | VAN SLYKE, Elisabeth | 35 | | 243 | VAN SLYKE, Jesse | 25,37 |
| 377 | VAN SLYKE, Elisabeth | 36 | | 535 | VAN SLYKE, Jesse | 50 |
| 380 | VAN SLYKE, Elisabeth | 36 | | 540 | VAN SLYKE, Jesse | 50 |
| 401 | VAN SLYKE, Elisabeth | 37 | | 208 | VAN SLYKE, Johannes | 20 |
| 209 | VAN SLYKE, ELizabeth | 20 | | 211 | VAN SLYKE, Johannes | 20 |
| 371 | VAN SLYKE, Engelina | 35 | | 332 | VAN SLYKE, Johannes | 32 |
| 372 | VAN SLYKE, Engelina | 35 | | 315 | VAN SLYKE, John Haverly | 31 |
| 361 | VAN SLYKE, Engelina (Angelica) | 34 | | 5 | VAN SLYKE, Lea | 1,2 |
| 48 | VAN SLYKE, Engeltie | 6 | | 220 | VAN SLYKE, Lena | 23 |

--------------------------------------------------------------------------------

--------------------------------------------------------------------------------

# PART TWO: CHARTS

## SECTION C

## DESCENDANTS OF PIETER TEUNIS VAN SLYCK

----------------------------------------------------------------------------------------------

First Generation


1 Pieter Teunis VAN SLYCK, born at Netherlands.
  He married (1) -- (___).

  Children:
+    2 M      i Willem Pieterse VAN SLYCK.
+    3 F     ii ELizabeth VAN SLYKE.



Second Generation



2 Willem Pieterse VAN SLYCK, born in 1635 at Beverwijck, Netherlands.

     NOTES: Willem Pieterse from Amersfoort arrived at NY April 1660 on DE TROUW.
     De Trouw (The Faith) sailed Dec 23, 1660 with Captian Jan Jansz Bestevaer.
     Willem is shown on the passenger list as Willem Petersen from Amsersfoort.
     Willem was known as Willen NEEf meaning "nephew" due to his status as the nephew
     of Cornelis Antonissen Van Slyke.

     RESIDENCES: His descendants settled in Albany NY

  Willem Pieterse VAN SLYCK married (1) Baertie (___) in 1658 at Kinderhook, NY. Baertie, born in 1636 at
  Kinderhook, NY; died in Dec 1699 at Albany NY.

  Children:
+    4 M      i Pieter Willemse VAN SLYCK.
     5 M     ii Jacob Willemse VAN SLYCK, born in 1661 at Kinderhook, Columbia Co., NY.
+    6 M    iii Dirk Willemse VAN SLYCK.
+    7 M     iv Teunis Willemse VAN SLYCK.
     8 F      v Janneke Willemse VAN SLYCK, born abt 1666 at Albany NY.

                MARRIAGE:
                At her marr. to Pieter in 1703, Janneke was listed as "Annetje Van Slyk, widow
                of Leendert de Grauw, from N.Y'm 3 Nov 1703 Pieter Gerritsz, from Esopus.

                Janneke Willemse VAN SLYCK married (1) Leendert Arentse DE GRAW on 26 Aug 1688.
                Leendert, died bef 1704.
                She married (2) Pieter GERRITS on 25 Nov 1704 at Dutch Reformed C, NY.

                MARRIAGE: Dutch Reformed Church, NY

     9 F     vi Tryntje Willemse VAN SLYCK, born abt 1667 at Albany NY.
                She married (1) Coenrad Mathys HOOGTEELING on 26 Aug 1688.
+   10 F    vii Metje Willemse VAN SLYKE.

3 ELizabeth VAN SLYKE, born abt 1640.

     BIRTH: Birth date estimate based on date of birth of her husband in 1637.



----------------------------------------------------------------------------------------------

------------------------------------------------------------------------------

ELizabeth VAN SLYKE married (1) Hendrick Cornelissen VAN BUREN. Hendrick, son of Cornelis Maessen VAN BUREN and Catalyntje aka Van Alstyne MARTENSE, born on 30 Jun 1637 at Atlantic Ocean.

BIRTH: Hendrick was born on board the ship "Rensellaerswyck" on 30 June 1637 as it crossed from the Netherlands to the New World.

RESEARCHER: Much of the data on the children of this family comes from Brenda S. Whelpy in Texas and Mike Wolfe in CA

SOURCE: LINEAL ANCESTORS OF RUFUS RENNINGTON YOUNG AND JANE VOSBURGH AND THEIR DESCENDANTS by Charles Henry Cory

Children:
11 M      i Maas Hendrickse VAN BUREN, died on 12 Apr 1734.

          DEATH: Death date comes from Frank Wolfe (wolfe@host.warwick.net) Nov. 1995

          Maas Hendrickse VAN BUREN married (1) Ariantje VAN WIE.

          SPOUSE: Frank Wolfe sends the info that she was the first wife of Maas Van Buren

          Maas Hendrickse VAN BUREN married (2) Magdalena BOGARD.

          SPOUSE: Frank Wolfe sends the info that she was the second wife of Maas Van Buren

12 M     ii Cornelis Hendrickse VAN BUREN.
          He married (1) Hendrickje VAN NESS on 27 Jan 1703.

          SPOUSE: Name of spouse comes from Frank Wolfe Nov. 1995

13 M    iii Hendrick Hendrickse VAN BUREN.

          COMMENT: The name of Hendrick as a son of Hendrick Van Buren and Elizabeth Van Slyke, comes from Brenda Whelpy in Texas, Nov. 1995. Frank Wolfe does not list Hendrick as a son, but does list Pieter Van Buren as a son, and states Pieter married on 2 May 1708, Geertruy Vosburgh. ACTION: Request source documentation from Brenda and Frank to resolve the discrepancy.

14 F     iv Gerritje Hendrickse VAN BUREN, born abt 1662 at NY; died in 1730.
          She married (1) Jacob Jacobse SCHERMERHORN. Jacob, born abt 1661 at NY; died in 1743.
15 F      v Marritie Hendrickse VAN BUREN, died in 1730 at Albany, NY; buried on 1 Feb 1730 at Albany, NY.
          She married (1) Cornelius Jacobse SCHERMERHORN on 21 Mar 1695. Cornelius, born abt 1668; died in 1722.


                              Third Generation



4 Pieter Willemse VAN SLYCK, born in 1659 at Kinderhook NY; died on 16 Jan 1741 at NY.

    NOTES: This is probably the Peter Van Slyck who along with Derick van der Carr,


------------------------------------------------------------------------------
                              Third Generation

--------------------------------------------------------------------------------

was elected trustee "by and for the inhabitants of the township of Kinderhook"
on 12 June 1703 [VAFA:7]

WILL: Pieter Van Slyck of Kinderhook, farmer. Wife not named. Children Thunes,
Dirck, Pieter, Elizabeth wife of Arie Gardenier, Catharyna, wife of Moses
Ingersole, Anna wife of Johann Jacob Eal, Barentje. Left real and personal
estate. Executors sons Thunes, Pieter and Dirck. Witnesses: Aarent Van Dyck,
Lambert Huyck and Johannis Juick. written March 25 1735 and proved 1740.
SOURCE: Calendar of Wills Albany County...

Pieter Willemse VAN SLYCK married (1) Johanna Hansen BARHEIT on 9 Apr 1683. Johanna, born in 1660 at
Kinderhook NY; died on 16 Jan 1741/1742.

  NAME: She was listed at some baptisms of her children as Barrentie Barheit and
  as Joanna Janse.

Children:
    16 M      i Willem Pieterse VAN SLYCK, christened on 20 Sep 1685 at Albany NY.

              He is not listed in his father's will of March 1735

    17 M     ii Hans Pieterse VAN SLYCK, christened on 25 Sep 1687 at Albany NY.

              He is not listed in his father's will of March 1735.

    18 F    iii ELizabeth (Lysbeth) VAN SLYCK, christened on 2 Feb 1690 at Albany NY.
              She married (1) Arie GARDINER.
  +  19 M     iv Teunis Pieterse VAN SLYCK.
    20 F      v Johanna (Anna) VAN SLYCK, christened on 26 May 1695 at Albany NY.

              In her father's will her husband's surname is given as EAL

              Johanna (Anna) VAN SLYCK married (1) John Jacob RAL.

              Is his surname EAL?

  +  21 F     vi Catherine (Tryntie) VAN SLYKE.
  +  22 M    vii Pieter Pieterse VAN SLYCK.
    23 F   viii Barentjie VAN SLYCK, christened on 3 Jan 1703 at Albany NY.

              At her bptsm her mother was listed as Anna HANSSE

              Did she marry a SNUR and die in 1775? A will of Barentie SNUR of Kinderhook
              dated May 28, 1770 and proved on Aug. 17 1775 lists bequests to the children of
              Pieter Pieterse Van Slyke, who would be this Barentie's brother. As well there
              are bequests to several other Van Slykes, leaving me to suspect that this is
              the Barentie SNUR in question.

    24 M     ix Dirk Pieterse VAN SLYCK, christened on 28 Oct 1705 at Albany NY.

6 Dirk Willemse VAN SLYCK, born in 1663 at Kinderhook, Columbia NY.
He married (1) Anneke JANSE in 1686. Anneke, died bef 1691.

Children:
    25 M      i Willem VAN SLYCK, christened on 8 Jan 1688.
    26 F     ii Marritje VAN SLYCK, born in 1690; christened on 27 Apr 1690 at Albany NY.

He married (2) Hendrickje HENDRICKSE on 9 Dec 1691. Hendrickje, died bef 1705.

--------------------------------------------------------------------------------

NAME: It is very possible that she is a VAN WIE. Descendants should check on this.

Children:
```
    27 F   iii Jannetje VAN SLYKE, christened on 21 May 1693.
    28 F    iv Baertje VAN SLYCK, christened on 12 Mar 1696.
    29 M     v Hendrick VAN SLYCK, christened on 4 Mar 1698 at New York.
    30 F    vi Marritie VAN SLYCK, christened on 20 Mar 1700 at New York.
    31 F   vii Marritie VAN SLYCK, christened on 10 Aug 1701 at New York.
```

He married (3) Annetje VAN NORDEN on 1 Mar 1705.

Children:
```
    32 M  viii Pieter VAN SLYCK, born in 1706; christened on 21 Oct 1706 at New York.
```

7 Teunis Willemse VAN SLYCK, born in 1665 at Kinderhook, NY; died in Nov 1748 at Coxsackie, Albany Co. NY.

Will written Nov. 4 1746. Names his wife Jannetie, children William, Hendrick, Andries, Gerrit, Peter, Eybie, Alida, Chatrina

Teunis Willemse VAN SLYCK married (1) Jannetie Hendrickse VAN WIE on 5 Feb 1696 at Albany NY. Jannetie, died on 4 Nov 1746 at Coxsackie, Greene Co. NY.

Children:
```
    33 F     i Baertje VAN SLYKE, christened on 15 Nov 1696; died bef 1746.
```

Did she m. 1727 Albany Reformed Church, Storm BECKER g-s/o Storm VANDERZEE & Hilletje LANSING? See Bradt Book p. 19. Storm BECKER m2 1735 so Baertje VS was dead by then. Baertie is not listed in her father's will of Nov. 4 1746 so it is likely she was deceased.

```
    34 M    ii Willem Teunise VAN SLYCK, christened on 23 Oct 1698 at Albany NY.
               He married (1) Catharina VAN SCHAIK.
    35 F   iii Cathrina VAN SLYKE, born abt 1716 at Coxsackie, Greene Co. NY.
  + 36 M    iv Hendrick Teunise VAN SLYCK.
    37 F     v Ida (Eybie) VAN SLYCK, christened on 28 Jun 1702 at Albany NY.
  + 38 M    vi Andries Teunise VAN SLYCK.
  + 39 M   vii Gerritt Teunise VAN SLYCK.
  + 40 M  viii Pieter Teunise VAN SLYCK.
    41 F    ix Alida VAN SLYCK, christened on 5 Nov 1710 at Albany NY.
    42 M     x Dirk Teunise VAN SLYCK, christened on 1 Mar 1713 at Albany NY.
```

He is not listed in his father's will of 1746

```
    43 F    xi Agnietje VAN SLYCK, christened on 19 Jun 1720 at Albany NY.
```

She is not listed in her father's will of 1746

10 Metje Willemse VAN SLYKE, born abt 1669 at Albany NY.
She married (1) Adam Anthonisze SWART on 15 Jan 1690 at Schenectady, NY. Adam, son of Teunise Cornelise SWART and Elisabeth LENDT.

MARRIAGE: Genealogies of First Settlers of Schenectday by Pearson

Children:
```
    44 M     i Teunis Adam SWART, born abt 1690 at Rensellaerswyck, NY.
```

---

Third Generation

-------------------------------------------------------------------------------------

He married (1) Aagjen (Agatha) VAN VLIET on 26 Nov 1715 at Kingston, NY.
45 M      ii Adam SWART, born in 1716; christened on 23 Sep 1716 at Kingston, NY.
He married (1) Helena BURHANS on 30 Nov 1745. Helena, christened on 15 Sep 1723; died
on 13 Sep 1789.
46 F     iii Johanna SWART, born in 1706 at Albany, NY; christened on 13 Jan 1706 at Albany, NY.

BAPTISM: Genealogies of First Settlers of Schenectday by Pearson



Fourth Generation



19 Teunis Pieterse VAN SLYCK, christened on 20 Nov 1692 at Albany NY.

Did he witness the will of Adam Van Alen made 20 jan. 1749?

Teunis Pieterse VAN SLYCK married (1) -- (___).

Is this wife Antje Vosburg b 4 Jan 1702 Kinderhook married 15 Feb. 1725 Albany
and died pre 1739? Antje was d/o Isaac Vosburgh & Annetje Janse Goes.

Teunis Pieterse VAN SLYCK married (2) Cathalyna GOEWAY on 7 Jun 1739 at Albany NY.

Children:
47 M       i Johannes VAN SLYCK, christened on 29 Jun 1740 at Albany NY.

21 Catherine (Tryntie) VAN SLYKE, born in 1697 at Kinderhook NY; christened on 14 Nov 1697 at Kinderhook,
NY; died on 9 Mar 1772 at Great Barrington, MA.
She married (1) Moses INGERSOLL abt 1725. Moses, son of Thomas INGERSOLL and Sarah ASHLEY, born on 10
Feb 1694 at Westfield, CT; died on 23 May 1751 at Great Barrington, MA.

Children:
48 M       i Thomas INGERSOLL, born on 7 Jun 1720 at Westfield; died on 6 Nov 1742 at Great
Barrington, MA.
49 F      ii Eleanor INGERSOLL, born on 11 Nov 1722 at Springfield, MA; died on 25 Feb 1772 at Great
Barrington, MA.
50 F     iii Joanna INGERSOLL, born on 1 Feb 1726 at Springfield, MA; died on 31 Aug 1793 at Great
Barrington, MA.
+    51 F      iv Lydia INGERSOLL.
52 F       v Elizabeth INGERSOLL, born on 9 Oct 1729 at Great Barrington, MA; died on 11 Feb 1793.
53 M      vi Captain Peter INGERSOLL, born on 11 May 1733 at Great Barrington, MA; died in 1785 at
Great Barrington, MA.
54 M     vii David INGERSOLL, born on 1 Mar 1736 at Great Barrington, Berkshire, MA.
55 F    viii Bathsheba INGERSOLL, born on 5 Jun 1738 at Great Barrington, MA; died on 12 Nov 1800 at
W. Medway, MA.

22 Pieter Pieterse VAN SLYCK, born on 22 Apr 1700; christened on 28 Apr 1700 at Albany NY.
He married (1) Engeltie VAN VALKENBURG. Engeltie, dau. of Jochem Lambertse VAN VALKENBURG and Eva
Hendrickse VROOMAN, christened in 1695 at Albany NY USA.

BAPTISM: either 5 June or 24 Nov 1695


-------------------------------------------------------------------------------------
Fourth Generation

--------------------------------------------------------------------------------------------

Children:
    56 M     i Petrus VAN SLYCK, born on 4 Dec 1724; christened on 14 Feb 1725 at Claverack NY.
                He married (1) Jesyntje GARDINIER on 30 Jun 1763 at Claverack, NY.
+   57 M    ii Jochum VAN SLYCK.
    58 M   iii Willem VAN SLYCK, christened on 8 Sep 1729 at Kinderhook NY.
                He married (1) Dorothe VOSBURGH on 20 May 1759.
    59 M    iv Johannes VAN SLYCK, christened on 16 Apr 1732 at Kinderhook NY.
                He married (1) Helena (Lena) GARDINIER on 30 Jun 1763 at Claverack, NY.
    60 F     v Eva VAN SLYCK, christened on 29 Sep 1734 at Kinderhook NY.

                twin to Johanna bp 29 June 1734 who must have died young

                Eva VAN SLYCK married (1) Harmen VAN BUREN on 10 Jun 1763 at Claverack NY.
    61 F    vi Johanna VAN SLYCK, christened on 29 Sep 1734 at Kinderhook NY; died bef 1737.
+   62 F   vii Johanna (Hannah) VAN SLYCK.

36 Hendrick Teunise VAN SLYCK, christened on 3 Nov 1700 at Albany NY.
He married (1) ELizabeth VISSCHER on 21 Oct 1737.

He married (2) ELizabeth VAN BENTHUYSEN on 21 Jun 1740.

Children:
    63 M     i Teunis Hendrickse VAN SLYCK, christened on 4 Apr 1742 at Albany NY.
    64 F    ii Jannetie VAN SLYCK, christened on 8 Jan 1744 at Albany NY.
    65 F   iii Agnietje VAN SLYCK, christened on 8 Jan 1748 at Albany NY.
    66 M    iv Baltus VAN SLYCK, born in 1749; christened on 31 Dec 1749 at Albany NY.
    67 F     v Catalyntje VAN SLYCK, christened on 10 Nov 1751 at Albany NY.
    68 M    vi Baltus VAN SLYKE, born in 1753 at NY; christened on 10 Dec 1753 at Coxsackie, NY.
    69 M   vii Baltus VAN SLYKE, born in 1762 at NY; christened on 18 Apr 1762 at Coxsackie, NY.

38 Andries Teunise VAN SLYCK, christened on 17 Sep 1704 at Albany NY; died in 1769 at Coxsackie, Albany
Co., NY.

    Will written Feb. 11, 1769. Names his wife Mary and children Baltus, Teunis,
    Jannitie, Lyedia, Mary, Catrina, Geertruy, Alida

Andries Teunise VAN SLYCK married (1) Maria VAN BENTHUYSEN.

Children:
    70 F     i Jannetie VAN SLYCK, born in 1747; christened on 1 Mar 1747 at Albany NY.
+   71 M    ii Baltus VAN SLYCK.
    72 F   iii Lydia VAN SLYCK, born in 1751; christened on 9 Jun 1751 at Albany NY.
    73 M    iv Teunis VAN SLYKE, born in 1754; christened on 3 Feb 1754.
    74 F     v Marytje VAN SLYKE, born in 1756; christened on 28 Mar 1756.

                Did she m. Peter Van Pelt pre 1785?

    75 F    vi Cathrina VAN SLYKE, born in 1757; christened on 3 Jul 1757.

                NOTES: It is possible that this is the Catharine Van Slyke who married Albert
                S. Vanderzee, son of Storm VanderZee and Elizabeth Slingerland. Albert was bapt
                10 April 1743 Albany. He and Catherine had two children known:
                Andrew Van Der Zee b. 10 April 1781 died 8 March 1828, and Storm Van Der Zee.
                I believe that Catherine followed Dutch naming traditions and named their first
                child after her father (Andries=Andrew) and their second after Albert's father
                (Storm). For more information on this family, refer to p174 of DESCENDANTS OF
                ALBERT AND ANDRIESSEN BRADT by Cynthia Brott Biasca.

--------------------------------------------------------------------------------------------

76 F    vii Geertruy VAN SLYKE, born in 1761; christened on 1 Mar 1761.
77 F   viii Alida VAN SLYCK, born on 5 May 1765 at Albany NY.

          Did she m. Pieter ADAIR in Albany 25 Sept. 1780? Child Hendrik bp 5 Aug. 1781
          Schenectady?

78 M     ix Andries VAN SLYKE, born abt 1767.

39 Gerritt Teunise VAN SLYCK, christened on 19 May 1706 at Albany NY.

   MARRIAGE: New York Marriages Previous to 1784 with Index by Kenneth Scott,
   Genealog. CONT Publ. Co. Inc. Baltimore 1984

Gerritt Teunise VAN SLYCK married (1) Annatje TURK on 1 Sep 1736 at NY.

Children:
   79 F     i Catharyna VAN SLYCK, christened on 3 Sep 1738 at Albany NY.
   80 M    ii Gerrit VAN SLYKE, born abt 1740.
   81 F   iii Sara VAN SLYCK, christened on 15 Aug 1742 at Albany NY.
   82 M    iv Johannes VAN SLYCK, christened on 7 Jul 1745 at Albany NY.
   83 F    v Sara VAN SLYCK, christened on 23 Jul 1749 at Albany NY.
   84 M    vi Teunis VAN SLYCK, christened on 26 Dec 1751 at Albany NY.
   85 M   vii Jacobus VAN SLYKE, born in 1753; christened on 10 Dec 1753.

          RESIDENCES: 1790 census Palatine NY in Sneidersbush area near the Windecker
          family.

          Jacobus VAN SLYKE married (1) Gertraud WINDECKER bef 1783. Gertraud, dau. of Frederick
          WINDECKER and Barbara (___), born in 1756; died in 1795.

          d/o Frederick Windecker & Anna Barbara Keller

40 Pieter Teunise VAN SLYCK, christened on 26 Sep 1708 at Albany NY.
   He married (1) Anna Ryckse VAN VRANKEN.

Children:
   86 M     i Teunis VAN SLYCK, christened on 17 Feb 1751 at Albany NY.
   87 F    ii Marritie VAN SLYCK, christened on 12 Nov 1752 at Albany NY.
   88 M   iii Evert VAN SLYCK, christened on 19 May 1754 at Coxsackie, Greene Co., NY.
   89 F    iv Jannetjie VAN SLYCK, christened on 17 Apr 1757 at Coxsackie, Greene Co., NY.
   90 F    v Jannetjie VAN SLYCK, christened on 6 Jan 1760 at Coxsackie, Greene Co., NY.
   91 M    vi unknown VAN SLYCK, born abt 1761 at NY.
   92 F   vii Marritie VAN SLYCK, born abt 1763 at NY.

Fifth Generation

51 Lydia INGERSOLL, born on 1 Oct 1727 at Great Barrington, MA; died on 2 Jun 1804 at Great Barrington, MA.

   NOTES:
   Lydia married her first cousin, William Ingersoll, who I believe was the s/o
   Cptn Peter Ingersoll

Lydia INGERSOLL married (1) William INGERSOLL on 11 Dec 1746 at Great Barrington, MA. William, son of
David INGERSOLL and Lydia CHILD, born on 1 Apr 1724 at Springfield MA; died on 10 Aug 1815 at Lee, MA.

Children:
    93 M     i William INGERSOLL, born in 1761; died in 1837.

                Paul Ingersoll of Chicago Illinois is a descendant, and the info on this lines
                come from him, as of 1995.

                William INGERSOLL married (1) Mercy Hamelin CROCKER.
+   94 M   ii Elijah INGERSOLL.
    95 M  iii David INGERSOLL.

                This child's name is from Nancy Rinsma.

57 Jochum VAN SLYCK, christened on 14 May 1727 at Kinderhook NY.
   He married (1) Cornelia VAN VALKENBURG on 19 Oct 1753 at Albany NY. Cornelia, dau. of Johannes VAN
VALKENBURG and Margriet BARHEIT, christened on 1 Aug 1731.

     Cornelia was the d/o Johannes Van Valkenburg and his second wife Antie Van
     Sardam.

Children:
+   96 F    i Engeltie VAN SLYCK.
    97 F   ii Antje VAN SLYCK, born in 1757; christened on 23 Apr 1757 at Kinderhook NY.

                Was Antje also md. to Thomas Van Valkenburg? He md an Antje VAN SLYKE who was
                sp with him at bpts of Rachel d/p Engeltie VAN SLYKE & Bartholomeus Van Valk
                enburg, in 1775.

                Antje VAN SLYCK married (1) Cornelis GARDENIER on 29 Jun 1777. Cornelis, born in 1752
                at Albany NY; christened on 15 Mar 1752 at Albany NY.
    98 M  iii Pieter VAN SLYCK, christened on 1 Jun 1760 at Kinderhook NY.
    99 M   iv Pieter VAN SLYCK, christened on 27 Sep 1761 at Kinderhook NY.

                Pieter may have md. Christina Schermerhorn [Ref: VV Fam. in America Vol. 1]

   100 F    v Margrietje VAN SLYCK, christened on 12 Aug 1764 at Kinderhook NY.

62 Johanna (Hannah) VAN SLYCK, born on 23 Oct 1736; christened on 15 Jan 1737 at Kinderhook NY.
   She married (1) Frances VAN BUREN on 30 Sep 1761 at Claverack NY.

Children:
+  101 M    i Barent VAN BUREN.
+  102 M   ii Peter H. VAN BUREN.

71 Baltus VAN SLYCK, christened on 26 Feb 1749 at Albany NY.
   He married (1) Anna CONYN.

Children:
   103 F    i Elizabeth VAN SLYCK, born on 11 Sep 1796 at Albany NY.
   104 F   ii Jane VAN SLYCK, christened on 27 Jul 1803 at Coxsackie, Greene Co., NY.

-----------------------------------------------------------------------------------------------


                                        Sixth Generation



   94 Elijah INGERSOLL married (1) (___).

      Children:
          105 M       i Isaac INGERSOLL married (1) (___).

   96 Engeltie VAN SLYCK, born abt 1750; died on 4 Aug 1831.
         She married (1) Bartholomeus VAN VALKENBURG. Bartholomeus, born in 1753; died in 1831.

           Branch 4: Bartholomeus>Thomas & Rachel Van den Berg>Bartholomeus VV & Catherin
           Van Alsteyn

      Children:
          106 F       i Rachel VAN VALKENBURG, christened on 3 Jun 1775 at Kinderhook, NY.
          107 F      ii Cornelia VAN VALKENBURG, born on 9 Feb 1778; christened on 1 Mar 1778 at Claverack, NY.

                         BAPTISM:Sponsors were Jochem Van Sluyck [sic], Cornelia Van Valkenburg

          108 F     iii Geertruy VAN VALKENBURG, christened on 4 Sep 1780 at Kinderhook, NY.
          109 F      iv Antje VAN VALKENBURG, christened on 1 Dec 1782 at Claverack, NY.

                         BAPTISM: Sponsors were William Vosburg, Margretha Van Slyck

          110 M       v Thomas VAN VALKENBURG, born on 15 Apr 1785; christened on 29 May 1785 at Ghent, NY.
          111 M      vi Joachim VAN VALKENBURG, christened on 25 Nov 1787 at Claverack, NY; died on 28 Dec 1859
                        at Hudson, NY.
                        He married (1) Orinda Maranda HODGE on 26 Jan 1812 at Claverack, NY. Orinda, born in
                        1792; died on 20 Mar 1871 at Hudson, NY.
          112 M     vii Barent VAN VALKENBURG, born on 14 Feb 1743; christened on 31 Mar 1793 at Claverack, NY.
          113 M    viii Isaac VAN VALKENBURG, born on 18 Oct 1795.

  101 Barent VAN BUREN, born on 26 Nov 1769; died on 7 Jan 1862 at Mayfield NY.

          Info this family from _The Brodhead Family: The Story of Captain Daniel Brod-
          head, his wife Ann Tye and their descendants_ by Anne Goodwill & Jean M. Smith

       Barent VAN BUREN married (1) Mary UPHAM on 15 Jan 1792. Mary, christened on 28 Aug 1768 at Claverack NY;
       died on 19 Apr 1833 at Mayfield NY.

      Children:
          114 F       i Hannah VAN BUREN, born in 1794.
          115 F      ii Magdalena VAN BUREN, born in 1796.
          116 M     iii Francis B. VAN BUREN, born in 1799.
          117 F      iv Susannah Upham VAN BUREN, born in 1802.
          118 F       v Ann Eliza VAN BUREN, born in 1805.
          119 F      vi Margaret VAN BUREN.


                        BIRT DATE ca 1810

          120 M     vii Marcus John VAN BUREN, born in 1812.

  102 Peter H. VAN BUREN, born on 2 Aug 1772.



-----------------------------------------------------------------------------------------------

--------------------------------------------------------------------------------

Info this family from The Brodhead Family book

Peter H. VAN BUREN married (1) ELizabeth UPHAM on 15 Feb 1789. ELizabeth, christened on 28 Aug 1772 at Claverack NY; died on 7 Jan 1862 at Mayfield NY.

Children:
```
121 F      i Evelyn VAN BUREN, born in 1790.
122 M     ii John Philip VAN BUREN, born in 1794.
123 M    iii Harmon Winne VAN BUREN, born in 1799.
124 M     iv James VAN BUREN, born in 1801.
125 M      v Henry Brodhead VAN BUREN, born in 1804.
126 F     vi Lucretia VAN BUREN, born in 1809.
```

--------------------------------------------------------------------------------

# PART THREE

# MAPS

Pages 183 to 189

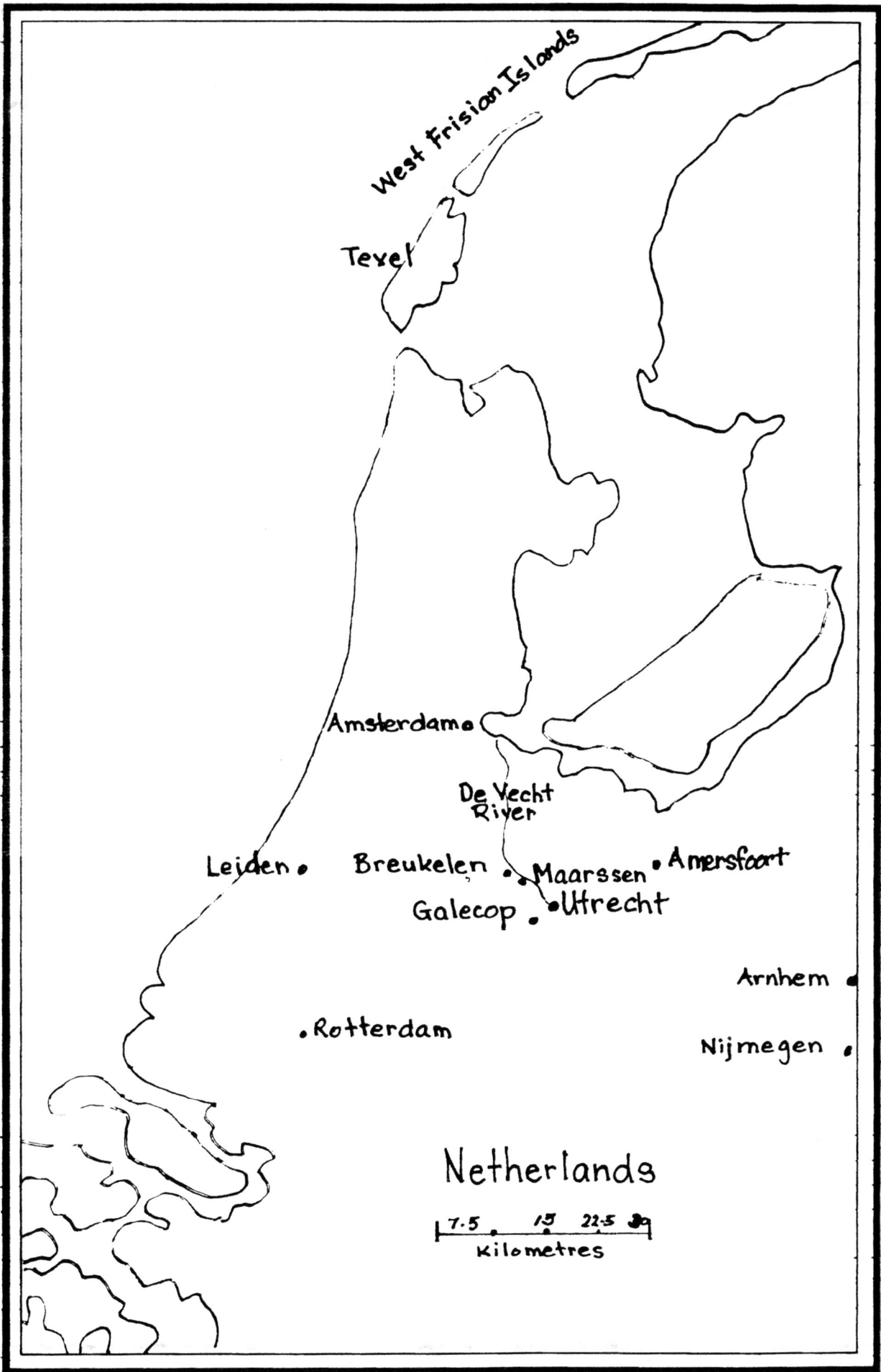

West Frisian Islands

Texel

Amsterdam

De Vecht
River

Leiden    Breukelen    Maarssen    Amersfoort

Galecop    Utrecht

Arnhem

Rotterdam

Nijmegen

Netherlands

7.5    15    22.5    30
Kilometres

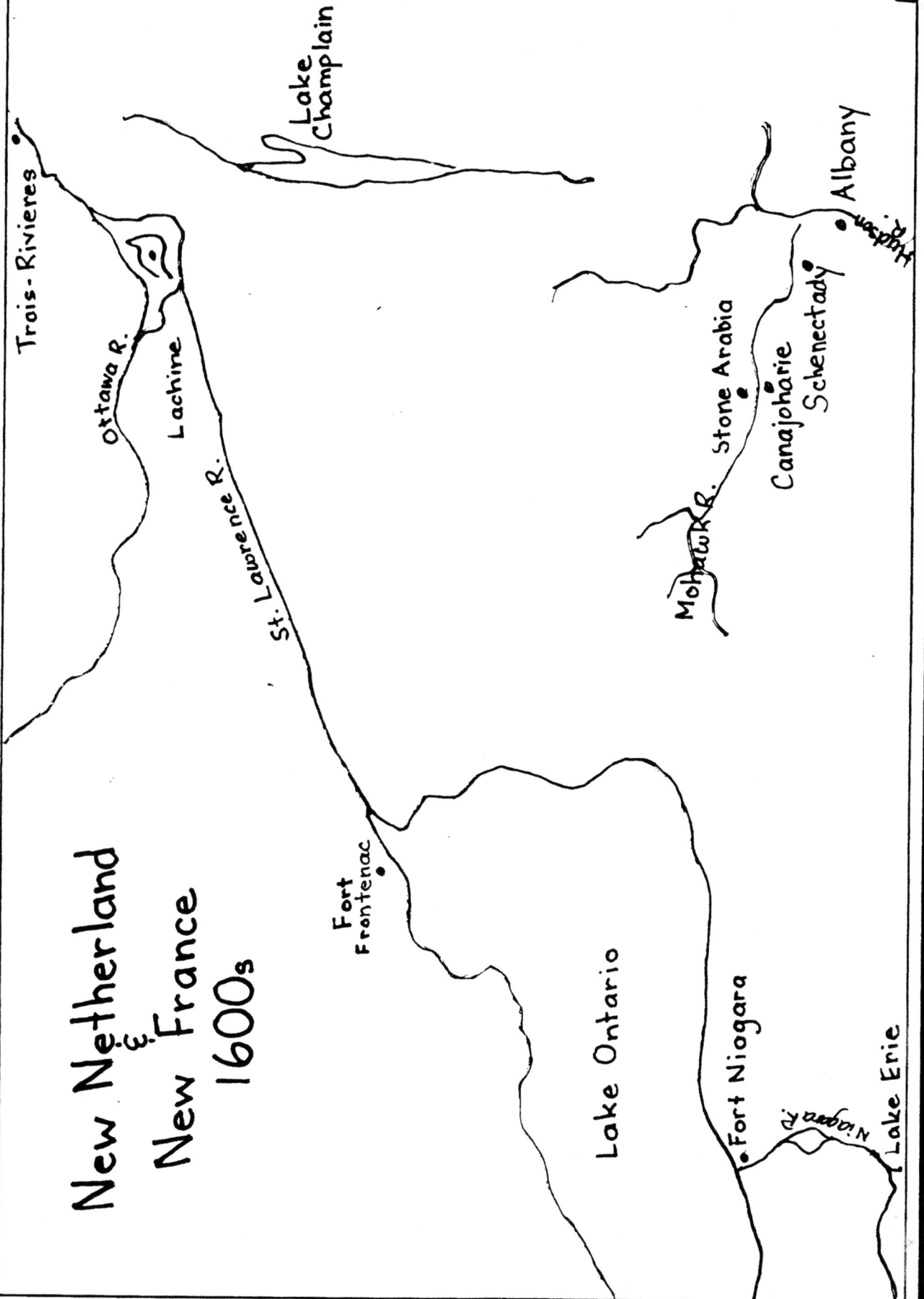

New Netherland
&
New France
1600s

Lake Erie
N. Niagara
Fort Niagara
Lake Ontario
Fort Frontenac
St. Lawrence R.
Ottawa R.
Lachine
Trois-Rivieres
Lake Champlain
Mohawk R.
Stone Arabia
Canajoharie
Schenectady
Albany
Hudson R.

lms

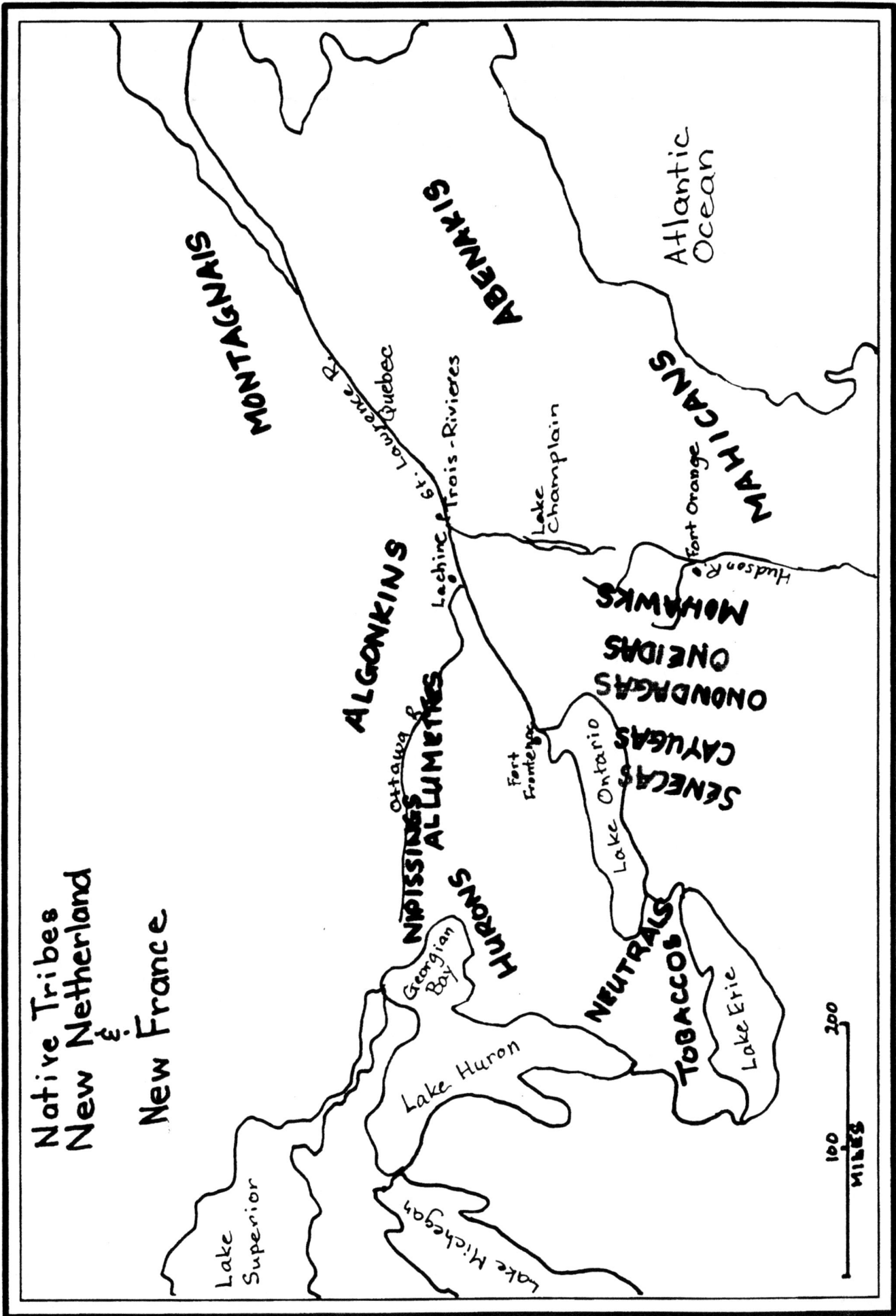

Native Tribes
New Netherland
&
New France

MONTAGNAIS

ABENAKIS

Atlantic Ocean

St. Lawrence R.

Quebec

Trois-Rivieres

Lachine

Lake Champlain

MAHICANS

Fort Orange

Hudson R.

ALGONKINS

MOHAWKS

ONEIDAS

ONONDAGAS

CAYUGAS

SENECAS

Ottawa R.

NIPISSINES

ALUMETTES

Fort Frontenac

Lake Ontario

HURONS

Georgian Bay

NEUTRALS

Lake Huron

TOBACCOS

Lake Erie

Lake Superior

Lake Michegan

100    200
MILES

Original Land Grants

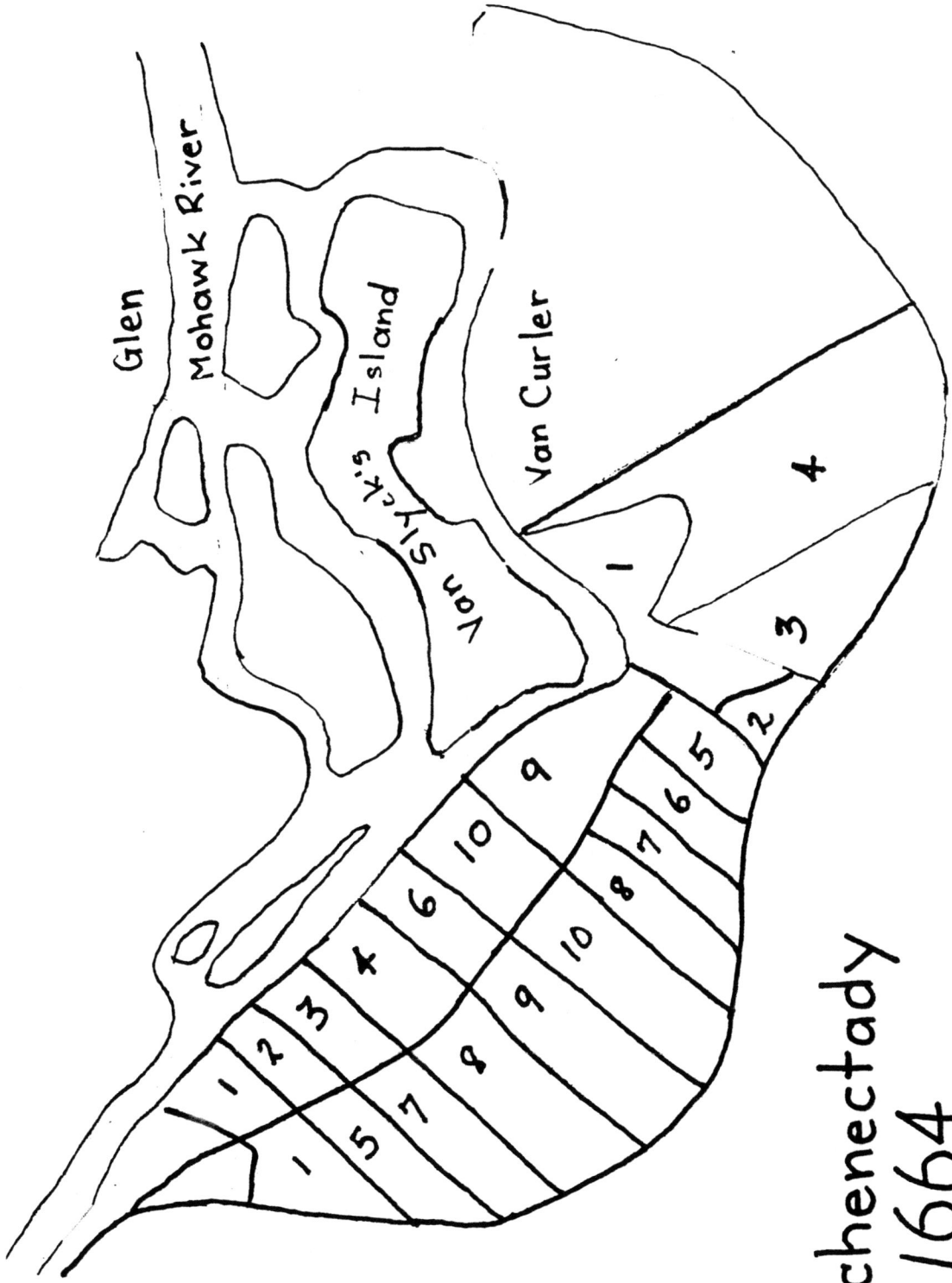

Glen

Mohawk River

Van Slyck's Island

Van Curler

1
3
2
4
5
9
10
6
4
3
2
8
7
6
8
10
9
1
5
7

Schenectady
1664

189

ims

Appendix A: Corrections:

1) page 24. #78 Peter Van Slyke married (1) Angelica Erickson on 30 Aug 1734. Angelica, born on 30 Aug 1734 at Europe. The marriage date is Aug. 1734 so I suspect my source simply gave the date of marriage as the date of birth. I would suspect she was born ca 1714.

2) page 2-3. Lea Van Slyke #5 died in 1692 at Port Jackson but married second Johathon Stevens on 24 Jul 1693 at Schenectady. This is a puzzle - Lea was born ca 1646, Jonathon was born 1675 --older women do marry younger men, but considering that her children were born 1695, 1700, 1702 this puts her age at childbirth as 49, 54 and 56 - she could of course have been having kids at age 50+ but not likely!

3) page 8. Geertruyt Van Slyke, born abt 1760. Children #76 Margarita Van Every and #77 Jacobus Van Every born 1707 and 1709. Correction: Geertruyt was born 1660 not 1760.

4) page 97 INDEX PART ONE. For "Maurtis" read "Maurits"

5) Documents from "Van Rensselaer Bowier Manuscripts", A.J.F. van Laer, 1908, p 495-496, appear to indicate that Cornelis Antonissen's brother, Pieter Antonissen, certainly planned to come to the New World. Whether he actually arrived is therefore open to further research and descendants of Pieter may wish to research this further.

Kiliaen van Rensselaer to Cornelis Teunisz van Breuckelen June 25, 1640
"Cornelis Teunissen Van Breuckelen, farmer in the colony of Rensselaerswyck
This 25th of June 1640, in Amsterdam

> What became in 1636 of your 25 or 30 morgens of summer and winter grain which you promised me and what has become of the servant whom your brother would bring with him? "

6) Documents have also been found that show that Jacques Cornelise Van Slyke was absent from Schenectady on the night of the massacre - shipping records have been found showing he was in the Netherlands at the time.

7) Part 2,, Sect A, p. 33: Barbara Perricelli corrects the statement that Clara Van Slyck's sister was the grandmother of Pres Van Buren. According to Barbara, President Van Buren was the son of Abraham Van Buren & Maria Hoes. Abraham was the son of Martin Van Buren & Dirkje Van Alstyne. Maria was bp 1747, the dau of Johannes D. Hoes/Goes & Jannetje Van Schaick. [Maria Hoes married 1st John Van Alen & 2d Abraham Van Buren.] Ref: History Of Cornelius Maessen Van Buren by Harriet Waite Van Buren Peckham, pub. 1913, pp 68, 88ff, & 274.

8) Part 2, p.2, #13: Barbara Perricelli also sends this correction: "It is easily provable that the Hendrick Hendricks cited by Peckham, was a Hendrick Bries, not a Hendrick Hendricks Van Buren, so he can be eliminated from the list of VB children. As best anyone can tell without absolute proof, Peter VB who married Gertrude Vosburgh, was indeed a son of Hendrick Cornelise Van Buren & Elizabeth Van Slyke. Childrens' names, baptismal sponsors, et al, fit perfectly. The one counter-indication is that Hendrick was b. 30 Jan [not June. Note he couldn't have been "born at sea" in June, when the family was already at Ft Orange by May] 1637 but this "son" did not marry until 1708.

9) Part Two, Section C Descendants of Pieter Tunis Van Slyck, page 1: Please note that there is a rather obvious time discrepancy regarding Willem Pieterse Van Slyck, who was on the passenger list of De Trouw in December 1660. I have listed him as marrying Baertie in 1658 in Kinderhook NY. Unless he arrived twice, and the 1660 trip was his second (as could very well be) his marriage date is in error. The birth of his first son Pieter in 1659 Kinderhook is likewise in question.